EVALUATION AND LIBRARY
DECISION MAKING

INFORMATION MANAGEMENT, POLICY, AND SERVICES
Charles R. McClure and Peter Hernon, Editors

Evaluation and Library Decision Making

Peter Hernon
Simmons College

Charles R. McClure
Syracuse University

ABLEX PUBLISHING CORPORATION
NORWOOD, NEW JERSEY

Second Printing 1994

Printed in the United States of America.

Library of Congress Cataloging-in-Publication Data

Hernon, Peter.
    Evaluation and library decision making / Peter Hernon, Charles R. McClure.
        p.   cm. — (Information management, policy, and services)
    Includes bibliographical references and index.
    ISBN 0-89391-640-4; 0-89391-686-2 (ppk)
    1. Libraries—Evaluation.   2. Library administration—Decision making.   I. McClure, Charles R.   II. Title.   III. Series.
Z678.85.H47   1990
025.1—dc20   90-40478
                                                                   CIP

Ablex Publishing Corporation
355 Chestnut St.
Norwood, NJ 07648

Contents

List of Figures

List of Tables

Copyright Permissions

The authors wish to thank the following publishers for permission to reprint parts of their works in this book:

Preface

As we move into the 1990s, there is likely to be increased pressure on librarians to maintain or cut costs, while, at the same time, increasing both the range and quality of services and programs. To accomplish this seemingly paradoxical set of objectives, librarians must be better able to evaluate library services, identify those factors that hinder or promote high quality services, and be able to demonstrate to various governing bodies why a certain decision was made. Ongoing and regular evaluation of library services will be a key and critical component for effective planning and decision making.

Planning, a topic that has received much attention in recent years, is the process of setting goals and objectives, developing programs and activities to accomplish those objectives, and evaluating the effectiveness and efficiency of those programs and activities in comparison to the original goals and objectives. The purpose of evaluation "is to allow us to make better decisions about the library—to identify aspects that might be improved and functions that need to be speeded up or made less expensive" (Robbins and Zweizig, 1988, p. 1).

Evaluation, which is the accountability aspect of planning, represents a measurement of effectiveness or efficiency in reaching some predetermined goal. Evaluation is an essential component for any organization wanting to modify its goals and objectives, establish priorities, and allocate resources in such a manner that the various programs and activities can be accomplished effectively and efficiently.

An increasing number of works present the results of an evaluation study, provide a general overview of the application of the process in libraries, or suggest the types of data that libraries might collect. Librarians are encouraged to collect standardized datasets over time so that they can identify, monitor, and respond to shifting patterns. Yet, no textbook focuses on the entire evaluation process from the perspective of library and information centers (see Chapter 3). In addition, the research methods textbooks rarely address evaluation and its uniqueness as part of the research process.

Evaluation and Library Decision Making views evaluation as a research activity essential for appraising the utility of library programs and services and for providing feedback to organizational planning and change. The book presents evaluation from two different perspectives: the collection of *research* and *management* data. Evaluation can, but need not, comprise a complex, time-consuming, and precise process of data collection, interpretation, and presentation. Herein is the basic difference between a research and management study. One provides a truer image of some phenomenon than the other does. However, obtaining that image may have a high cost.

The purpose of this book is to assist librarians, library school students, and public officials in understanding evaluation as a research activity and the relationship between evaluation and planning. It is our hope that *Evaluation and Library Decision Making* fills a void in the literature and accomplishes the following objectives:

- To introduce readers to the relationship between planning and evaluation
- To discuss the components of an evaluation study in clear prose so that readers can easily understand the different steps
- To foster an attitude that recognizes the importance of evaluation for the development of library programs and services
- To offer examples of the evaluation process that can serve as models for those conducting similar studies
- To identify writings on evaluation in libraries and information centers
- To encourage organizational change and underscore the importance of evaluation to library decision making.

The 14 chapters provide an overview of the evaluation process and the relationship between evaluation and planning; the literature on evaluation; steps in conducting an evaluation study; performance measures; reference services; communication of study findings; political barriers to the conduct of evaluation research; and organizational change. Two chapters (10 and 11) offer examples of simple evaluation studies conducted in an academic library setting. In addition, the bibliography and chapter figures identify a wealth of writing on evaluation.

This book does not discuss the statistical analysis component of data collection because *Statistics for Library Decision Making* (Hernon et al., 1989) discusses the application of descriptive and inferential statistics. That handbook also notes examples of studies employing such statistics on topics of interest to library managers. In addition, *Microcomputer Software for Performing Statistical Analyses* (Hernon and Richardson, 1988) describes how evaluators can perform statistical analyses on microcomputers. Together, *Evaluation and Library Decision Making* and these two books in the Ablex series on "Information Management, Policy, and Services" complement each other and provide a three-volume set useful to both the evaluation novice and specialist.

We have tried to present evaluation within a conceptual framework and to suggest political constraints and internal library dynamics that evaluators must address in order for their study to be successful—that is, provide the library with information useful for planning purposes. It is our hope that this book will stimulate and challenge librarians to conduct more and higher quality evaluation studies.

Peter Hernon
Charles R. McClure

December 15, 1989

Chapter One
Evaluating Library and Information Services

Many library decision makers need to know about the quality of existing services and whether to add, discontinue, or modify these services. They also want to know how well the library meets stated goals and objectives and the information needs of its clientele. Evaluation provides decision makers with insights into services, collections, and staff (their satisfaction, motivation, sense of achievement, effectiveness, and efficiency). These insights can then be used to produce changes and improve planning. Clearly, the prevailing belief is that libraries should operate effectively and efficiently, provide a certain quality of service, and meet existing demands while adapting to new ones (DuMont and DuMont, 1979).

Simply stated, evaluation is the process of identifying and collecting data about specific services or activities, establishing criteria by which their success can be assessed, and determining both the quality of the service or activity and the degree to which the service or activity accomplishes stated goals and objectives. As such, evaluation is a decision-making tool that is intended, primarily, to assist library staff in allocating necessary resources to those activities and services that *best* facilitate the accomplishment of organizational goals and objectives.

In one sense, evaluation is primarily an information gathering, analysis, and reporting process. Librarians identify specific activities, questions, or areas as appropriate for evaluation, and they develop research designs and methodologies to guide the evaluation. In addition, library decision makers collect data that specifically assess the service or activity to be evaluated, and analyze the data in such a way that they can describe and compare the quality and performance of the service or activity against appropriate criteria. Then they report and implement the results to change or improve the service or activity.

As Figure 1-1 suggests, libraries *could* provide a broad range of possible services and activities. Numerous constraints, however, limit the number and diversity of services and activities that the organization can actually provide. Decision makers must rely on information gained from the evaluation process and must constantly ask themselves about which services and activities the library should support, what levels of resource support are necessary, and whether the offering of these services and activities successfully contributes to the overall effectiveness of the library.

1

Figure 1-1. Potential Opportunities and Constraints

Opportunities	Constraints

Cable TV

More Books, Journals, and Other Resources, regardless of Format

Outreach Programs

Automation

Information and Referral Services

Delivery System

Marketing

Increase Constituency User Group

Educational Programs

Increase Quality of Collection

Library

Lack of Staff

Space

Budget

Conflicting Perceptions of Library

Limited Staff Skills

Physical Location

Limited Bibliographic Control

Apathy of Clientele about Library

Poor Organizational Structure, Planning, and Decision Making

.... And More ....

The evaluation process provides a method by which basic assumptions about the organization's activities and services can be assessed. The process identifies alternative strategies to improve those activities and services, and assists the organization in better meeting the information needs of its clientele. For example, evaluation addresses the following types of questions (Rossi and Freeman, 1989, p. 18):

- "What feasible interventions are likely to ameliorate the problem significantly?
- What are the appropriate target populations for a particular intervention?
- Is the intervention reaching its target population?
- Is the intervention being implemented in the ways envisioned?
- Is it effective?
- How much does it cost?
- What are its costs relative to its effectiveness and benefits?"

Many fundamental decisions have rested on untested assumptions about why people use libraries, how their information needs can be identified and resolved, and the process by which they acquire information. As Metz (1983, p. 3) notes,

Figure 1-2.   Questions Relating to Information Needs*

A. Who are library users, non-users, and potential users?
- What brings users to libraries?
- What information needs do they expect to satisfy at libraries?
- Are their needs met? How can measurements be devised to test this?

B. What information do they need/want?
- What information or assistance are they looking for?
- What will the needs of users be in 10 to 15 years?
- What shapes users' perceptions of their own needs? Can these perceptions be influenced?
- How can we learn more about potential users to satisfy their information needs better?
- How do needs of various groups within a community get served?

C. How do they get information?
- Can information models be constructed?
- How do people find out that some piece of information exists and is available?
- What sources of information are available? Can an inventory of information available to a community be constructed?
- How can information seeking, information use, and information analysis skills be developed from the elementary school level on?
- What effect does the physical format of materials have on access to information?
- What effect does technology have on users' access to information?
- Is technology changing the way people use information?
- How does access to distant terminals and work stations affect library use?

D. Where does the library fit in as an information source?
- Does a library understand user needs?
- Should assumptions about these be examined to identify what information requirement needs people have, who uses the library, and why?
- How can libraries best be organized to meet user needs and the needs of others in the community who are currently not being served?
- What are the frequencies of library use and why?
- How successful are libraries in effecting an appropriate cultural match with institutions and groups?

* Source: *Rethinking the Library in the Information Age*, 3 vols. (Washington, D.C.: U.S. Department of Education, Office of Library Programs, Office of Educational Research and Improvement, 1988).

"only when these assumptions have been tested can libraries . . . evaluate the policies which depend on them."

Because evaluation is part of decision making and encourages organizational change, library staff that embark on an ongoing evaluation process should recognize that:

- Evaluation reflects value judgments about what the library *should* be doing, *adequate* levels of performance, and criteria that describe *success* or organizational *effectiveness*
- Evaluation requires a clearly stated and carefully thought-out statement of organizational goals and objectives
- Evaluation is tantamount to saying that change is both possible and desirable for the organization
- The availability of adequate staff time and organizational resources is essential for evaluation research to be done successfully.

Figure 1-3.   Environmental Impacts on the Library

Thus, to engage in an ongoing evaluation process is to question what the library *should* be doing, develop methods to accomplish those objectives, and encourage constant change to occur. Figure 1-2 offers examples of the types of questions that library decision makers might ask in one area—user information needs.

Although change simply for the sake of change is of little value for any organization, all organizations must constantly respond to changing conditions internal and external to the library. Policies emanating from the Federal and state governments, technological developments, institutional mandates for library actions, changing demographics of the library's constituencies, and new or different competitors providing information services are only some of the external environmental factors that could affect library services and activities (see Figure 1-3).

Internal conditions include budgetary increases or decreases, the addition of new personnel, changing or revised organizational or institutional missions, and new methods to access information resources and services. Thus, a library may have to change its services and activities *just to maintain* its current level of effectiveness! Determining what to change, and how to change it, is an important component of evaluation.

USE OF EVALUATION

Decision makers might engage in evaluation to gain information useful in deciding whether or not to continue or discontinue a program or activity, in improving practices or procedures, in adding or dropping program strategies and techniques, in instituting similar programs elsewhere, or in allocating resources among competing programs. Evaluation incorporates planning, research, and change, and ongoing evaluation is integral to a dynamic, effective, and efficient organization. Evaluation involves five, key measurement concepts:

- *Extensiveness*, or the amount of a service provided in relation to the population served. This criterion is generally a measure of quantity rather than quality
- *Effectiveness*, or the extent to which a service or activity accomplishes stated objectives. This criterion might also examine the extent to which a service satisfies the demands that users place on it
- *Efficiency*, or the appropriateness of resource allocations. This criterion might be judged in the context of stated objectives
- *Cost-effectiveness*, or the accomplishment of objectives expressed in terms of costs
- *Cost-benefit*, or the justification for the expense of providing a service or program in terms of the benefits derived from it.

To conduct a cost-effectiveness or cost-benefit study, librarians determine all costs—direct, indirect, immediate, and long-term related to a specific activity or service.[1] The difference between a cost-effectiveness and cost-benefit study is that the former compares costs to the actual impact of a service or activity, and the latter requires the assignment of a monetary value to that service or activity.

One or more of these concepts would likely be incorporated in any evaluation effort. But a number of different objectives can be accomplished by the evaluation (see Rossi and Freeman, 1982, 1985, 1989):

- *Appropriateness of Organizational Goals or Program Objectives.* A key reason for evaluation is to assist library staff in determining if their activities are appropriate for their particular clientele, the impact of the larger environment on the organization, and the availability of resources. This application addresses the mission of the organization and attempts to justify why the organization does what it does
- *Objective Accomplishment.* This use of evaluation simply seeks to determine the degree to which library services and activities accomplish the stated objectives for which either the activity or the service was established. As such, this type of evaluation is effectiveness-oriented
- *Appropriateness of Resources Allocation.* Typical resource categories include personnel, equipment, information resources and materials, supplies, space, and time. This use of evaluation asks if resources were necessary to accomplish specific objectives, and if the library might have used such resources elsewhere and thereby have generated a larger impact. Such evaluations tend to be efficiency-oriented
- *Monitoring and Accountability.* This application of evaluation provides ongoing information about a specific library program or service and can include both effectiveness and efficiency criteria. Further, such evaluation determines the degree to which the activity or service can be justified to external funding bodies, and demonstrates how and why the evaluator used resources to accomplish specific objectives
- *Impact Assessment.* This type of evaluation reflects the extent to which a specific service or activity "made a difference" in terms of a predetermined set of criteria. For instance, did the bibliographic instruction program actually increase library use, student ability to locate needed items, or student grades on a term paper or other classroom assignment? Impact assessment stresses the *benefits* resulting from an activity or service rather than looking only at whether that activity or service accomplished objectives (effectiveness) and resources were used appropriately (efficiency)
- *Assess Innovative Programs.* This type of evaluation assesses a unique or new

---

[1] For examples of cost analyses, see Cummings (1989); Gherman and Cochrane (1989); Mitchell, Tanis, and Jaffee (1978); and Schauer (1986).

service or activity that either has not been done before or is being done in an entirely new way. Such assessments begin without an historical perspective and are considered in terms of their method and procedures as well as standard criteria of efficiency and effectiveness. Such assessments are an essential part of "new" library programs, otherwise decision makers would not know if innovative programs were beneficial

- *Fine-tuning of Library Services and Activities.* Many ongoing activities and services that are both effective and efficient may, from time to time, require fine-tuning of the way in which they are administered, planned, and implemented. Fine-tuning is necessary to maintain levels of performance and to make certain that the staff do all that they can do to improve those performance levels

- *Program Continuance or Discontinuance.* This type of evaluation is typically summative, that is, done at the end of the program with the expressed objective of collecting data that demonstrate whether or not that program should be either continued or discontinued. Either way, data lend support to the resulting decision. Such evaluations are essential for activities and services that require significant resources and do not contribute to the accomplishment of organizational goals.

These reasons for conducting an evaluation and the measurement concepts that can be used in the evaluation are important factors to consider in the design and implementation of an evaluation effort.

EFFECTIVENESS AND EFFICIENCY

Traditionally, libraries have tended to concentrate on efficiency criteria, e.g., the number of items cataloged per day, or the number of reference transactions completed per day. However, libraries must also consider effectiveness-related questions, such as:

- Is this library performing activities and offering services that *should* be provided?
- Are library staff accomplishing organizational goals and objectives?
- How can staff ensure that the library offers *high-quality* services and activities?

Confusion between effectiveness and efficiency has resulted in the following:

- Doing things well (efficiency) that need not be done (ineffectiveness)
- Constantly striving to obtain more resources (staff, books, equipment, etc.) as an end unto themselves—with limited consideration of the degree to which the resources are accessible and meet user information needs

- Inability to describe how *well* services are performed or the overall *quality* of library services and activities
- Failure to identify specific priorities for library activities and services. As a result, librarians might believe that the library can provide all information services to all constituencies all the time
- Believing that bigger collections automatically mean better service to users.

Limited attention given to evaluation of library activities and services has resulted in:

- Continuation of many library services and activities that are ineffective and/or inefficient
- A blind faith that governing bodies accept the overall "goodness" of libraries and fund them at least at current levels
- Failure to set priorities and improve mediocre services
- An inability to demonstrate to outside agencies the excellence of those services and activities that are of high quality
- Limited understanding on the part of a number of librarians about what evaluation is, why it is important, and how it can be accomplished.

Library staff members often make decisions based on untested assumptions about existing services or activities.

Attention to efficiency rather than effectiveness fails to consider the likely tradeoff relationships between the two types of measures. Efficiency of an activity or service cannot be improved past a certain "critical point" without injuring the effectiveness of that activity or service, and vice-versa. Thus, continued attention to increasing the efficiency of various activities and services may become dysfunctional or counterproductive to effectiveness criteria (see Figure 8-3). For example, having reference staff drastically increase the number of transactions completed (efficiency) will reach a point at which additional transactions will not be answered correctly (ineffectiveness), if for no other reason, due to the overload of questions asked and answered.

LEVELS OF EVALUATION

Evaluation research takes place at four primary levels of analysis: societal, organizational, programs, and individuals. At a societal level, evaluation is concerned with changes that have occurred in a society or community of individuals as a result of regulations, legislation, cultural values, or economic, political, or sociological factors. At this level, the evaluator exercises limited control over the research design, and findings from such studies tend to be quite general.

At an organizational level, the evaluator has greater control over the variables to assess. Further, organizational goals and objectives are likely to be more concrete than those at a societal level, and specific measures of organizational effectiveness can be established. The time frame for such evaluation to occur can be shorter, say three to five years, and intervention strategies to change organizational behavior can be more easily established at an organizational level than at a societal level.

At a program level, the evaluator is concerned about specific services and activities. An *activity* comprises routines or procedures undertaken by staff members in support of services (such as cataloging). *Services* provide the clientele of the organization with specific products or outputs. *Programs* are the combination of activities and services that accomplish specific objectives. Evaluation at this level is more straightforward than evaluation at an organizational level because activities and services can be closely defined, variables better controlled, and the time frame for evaluation of programs can be limited to one to two years.

Evaluation of individual performance is better known as personnel evaluation. The purpose of such evaluation is to determine the quality and quantity of work performed, offer guidance and strategies for how the individual can be more creative, productive, and effective, and assist the organization to better accomplish stated objectives in the future.

Each level of evaluation is interdependent, and clearly an individual's performance affects program and organizational quality. For most libraries, assessment of *organizational* and *program* performance provides a mechanism by which individual performance can be improved. Focusing on organizational and program evaluation can enhance the quality of library services as well as the competitive edge of libraries against other information providers.

BASIC EVALUATION APPROACHES

Formative evaluation is an ongoing assessment that provides information to monitor and improve an in-progress activity or service. *Summative* evaluation determines the level of program success or failure. The purpose of formative evaluation is to *improve*, while that of summative evaluation is to *prove*.

One purpose for engaging in evaluation is to monitor the degree to which the organization or program meets stated goals and objectives, and to readjust the program to better accomplish such objectives. As such, the approach is effectiveness-oriented and done on a formative basis. An example of such evaluation is the regular monitoring of the degree to which clientele obtain a specific title or resource (that they already have in mind) when they visit the library. If their "success rate" suddenly drops, the formative nature of the evaluation process provides a signal, warning the staff to take corrective action.

Another purpose of evaluation is to provide a "once only" assessment of how well the organization or individual programs meet stated goals and objectives. In this instance, the evaluation, although effectiveness-oriented, is concerned with whether the program or activity should be continued or discontinued. For example, where a bibliographic instruction program based on the use of videotapes is evaluated by a student questionnaire administered at the end of the semester, it is too late to change the nature of the program as a result of the responses. However, the information collected about the program indicates whether that program should be continued in the future.

A third purpose of evaluation is to monitor the manner in which organizational resources are allocated. This approach is efficiency-oriented because it assesses how the organization uses standard resource categories (personnel, equipment, books and other information resources, supplies, and other forms of budgeted items). Another type of efficiency criterion includes time. For instance, the number of books cataloged per day is an efficiency assessment, and if such an assessment is conducted on an ongoing basis, it can identify and monitor delays in the cataloging process.

In terms of the ease of effort required for each of these evaluation purposes, summative evaluation of resource allocation takes less effort than formative evaluation of resource allocation, which in turn takes less effort that summative evaluation of organizational/program effectiveness. Formative evaluation of organizational/program effectiveness may require the greatest effort. This is because:

- Evaluation of effectiveness criteria requires the existence of clearly stated library goals and objectives
- Formative evaluation involves *ongoing* monitoring of an activity and requires the establishment of regular data collection and analysis procedures. In contrast, summative evaluation is a "one shot" activity.

Thus, the greater the use of effectiveness-oriented evaluation that relies on formative assessment procedures, the greater is the evaluation effort in terms of planning, staff time, commitment, and resource support. The greatest payoffs, in terms of meeting the information needs of the library's clientele, competing successfully against other information providers, and offering improved access to information sources and services, come from the use of evaluation that is formative and effectiveness-oriented.

PLANNING, ACTION RESEARCH, AND EVALUATION

Evaluation supports a number of organizational and administrative activities. Many of these activities (e.g., decision making, needs assessment, development of goals and objectives, and communication) are essential ingredients for planning. Effective planning cannot be accomplished without an evaluation compo-

Figure 1-4. Planning and Evaluation

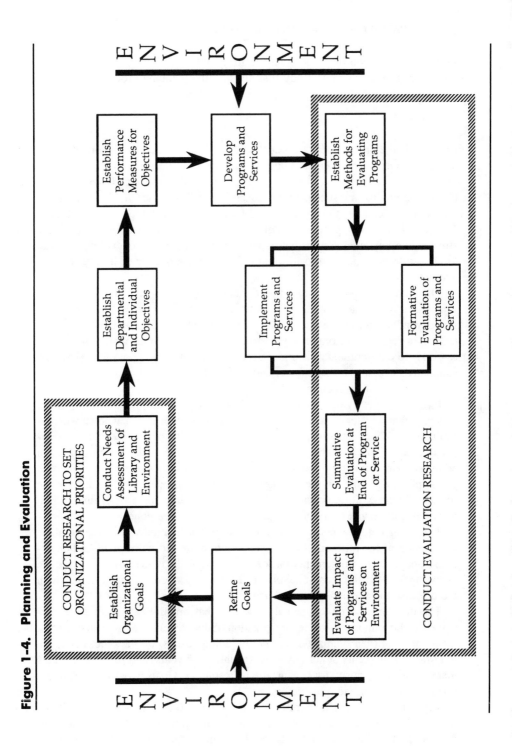

11

nent, and evaluation has little practical utility unless staff members initiate specific strategies to integrate study findings into the planning process.

Planning

Planning is the process of (1) conducting a needs assessment of the organization and the environment, (2) developing written goals and objectives, (3) implementing services and activities to accomplish those objectives, and (4) evaluating the overall quality and success of those services and activities vis-á-vis the stated objectives (McClure, Owen, Zweizig, Lynch, and Van House, 1987). Figure 1-4, which offers a general model of the planning and evaluation process, stresses two key areas for evaluation research to take place: conducting research to (1) set organizational priorities, and (2) assess the quality of library services and activities.

The planning model assumes that the environment has significant impact on library activities and services, that components and activities of the library are interdependent, that there is a rationale for why the organization exists, and that there is a regular and ongoing assessment of the manner in which the library responds to environmental factors. Successful planning uses both formative and summative evaluation techniques, and recognizes that evaluation research is a major component of planning.

Integrating the evaluation process with organizational planning is essential because planning tends to focus attention on the library as a whole, whereas evaluation focuses on specific aspects of an activity or service without considering the impact of that activity or service on the entire organization. In addition to relating the "parts" of library activities to overall organizational goals, planning assists in the setting of priorities for what should be done in the library. Because libraries cannot do *everything*, they must determine which activities and services are most important and *should be* done.

The main components of planning comprise a hierarchy ranging from the articulation of the mission of the organization to the setting of goals and objectives, and then to implementation of services and activities. A key aspect in assessing the effectiveness of the plan is the use of performance measures, which are discussed in greater detail in Chapter 8.

The mission is a philosophical statement that broadly sets forth areas perceived to be important to the organization. Such statements are value assessments of what the organization *should* be doing. Goals, on the other hand, are long-range statements of activity areas (usually 3–5 years) and suggest activities that will receive priority for organizational resources. Goals may focus on collections, services, and administration.

Typically, a goal has numerous objectives. Objectives typically begin with an action verb and must be measurable, challenging, time-limited, and clearly understood. They suggest what is to be done and not *how* it will be done. Each objective mentions programs, which in turn specify performance measures by

Figure 1-5.   Hierarchy of Planning Components*

Mission:

The Morningside Public Library provides materials and services to help community residents obtain information meeting their personal, educational, and professional needs. Special emphasis is placed on supporting students at all academic levels and on stimulating young children's interests and appreciation for reading and learning.

Goal:

High school students are able to obtain materials and services that support classwork requirements.

Objectives:

a) to assess the materials and services needs of high school students by June 19XX.

Activity: Curriculum survey of high school teachers.
Measure: Inspection (production of a Final Report).

b) to increase area high school students' attendance at classwork support programs by 30% by June 19XX.

Activity: Current awareness/publicity campaign.
Measure: High school program attendance per capita.

Goal 2:

Community children and young adults have access to a wide range of high quality services.

Objectives:

a) to increase young adult annual library visits per capita by 40% by June 30, 19XX.

Activity: Young adult "Great Books" discussion groups.
Measure: Young adult program attendance per capita.

b) to provide reading readiness programs to a minimum of 250 preschoolers during the current fiscal year.

Activity: Reading readiness programs.
Measure: Number of preschoolers attending programs.

---

* Same public libraries include service roles as part of the hierarchy of planning components (see McClure et al., 1987).

which the effectiveness of the program and the degree to which the objective is accomplished can be assessed. Figure 1-5 is an example of the hierarchy of planning components.

In times of austerity, the setting of goals and objectives and formalized planning take on increased importance. Indeed, there is an increased need to establish "realistic" goals and objectives, i.e., those that accurately represent the needs and intentions of the organization and have a likelihood for success (Johnson, 1984). Furthermore, as Pings (1980, p. 61) has pointed out, "the mark of a healthy organization does *not* rest on goal statements or on studies to set goal statements, but it does rest on the fervor with which it tests goals." This constant testing, or reassessment, comprises the evaluation component of planning.

ACTION RESEARCH

Understanding the relationship between planning and evaluation is essential for improving the effectiveness of the library. The research process, as typified by action research, links planning to evaluation. Action research is a process of collecting and analyzing data specifically for the purpose of making changes and improvements in library services and activities (Swisher and McClure, 1984, pp. 22–29).

Action research supports the planning process by supplying empirical evidence regarding the success with which goals and objectives are accomplished, resources allocated, and the quality of individual services and activities assessed. In short, action research is targeted at problem solving, improved decision making, and increased organizational effectiveness. In contrast, basic and applied research has a broader intent—the generation and testing of theory, leading perhaps to revision of that theory (see Hernon et al., 1989).

Library staff simply are too busy, have too many responsibilities, and have too few resources to waste on evaluation projects that are not likely to have immediate and significant payoffs for the library. Indeed, if the evaluation process does not have a high probability of having direct impact on decision making and planning, a library should allocate resources to other areas of activities rather than supporting action research and a superficial and nonproductive evaluation study. Thus, it is likely that library evaluation efforts will be designed in the context of action research.

OBSTACLES TO EVALUATION

Organizational and individual obstacles to evaluation may exist in any particular library. Perhaps the most deadly and insipid obstacle is the belief that "everything is fine in my library." In the vast majority of instances, librarians simply do not *know* how well library activities and services meet clientele information needs, if specific services and programs are effective and efficient, or if resources could be *better* spent on supporting different activities and services.

One set of obstacles related to evaluation efforts is that the library could apply evaluation inappropriately or merely serve organizational or administrative self-interests (Suchman, 1972, p. 81). For example, evaluation might be used to:

- Justify a weak or bad program by deliberately selecting for evaluation only those aspects that "look good" on the surface. Appearance replaces reality

- Cover up program failure or errors by avoiding objective appraisal. Vindication replaces verification
- "Torpedo" or destroy a program regardless of its effectiveness. Politics replaces research
- Treat evaluation as a "gesture" of objectivity or professionalism. Ritual replaces research
- Delay needed action by pretending to seek the "facts." Research replaces decision making.

Staff members could subvert the evaluation process by deciding to "fool" someone or a governing body. Evaluation under such circumstances is a waste of time, personnel, and other resources. Furthermore, it damages the credibility of the organization and the morale of the organizational staff.

In some instances, there is a real fear of evaluating library services and activities. Such fears can result from recognition that evaluation will, in fact, show that the library is ineffective or inefficient; that existing resources are poorly allocated to activities that do not fulfill clientele information needs; or that individuals in the library may be identified as incompetent, inadequately trained, or lacking specific knowledge and skills necessary to perform their responsibilities effectively.

The attitude that evaluation is not really necessary, that the librarians *really* know what is happening in their library, and that the librarians have a good "feel" for knowing when a service or activity is effective or ineffective is an obstacle to successful library evaluation. Faith in "common sense" approaches to organizational effectiveness is simplistic and unrealistic in these times of complex organizations, innovative technologies, and limited available resources.

Another area of obstacles to successful evaluation comes from inadequate training of librarians to conduct evaluation research. In most schools of library and information science, for various reasons, many students simply do not take courses on research methods, planning and evaluation, and systems analysis. Once in the field, librarians then find it difficult to conduct evaluations because they are unfamiliar with data collection and analysis techniques, evaluation research designs, and methods for the implementation of evaluation results.

Other obstacles to successful evaluation include the perceived lack of resources to support the evaluation process, and, upon completion of the study, an unwillingness on the part of decision makers to implement study recommendations. Implementation requires a knowledge of basic planning techniques and an ability to develop practical strategies and recommendations. Evaluation without implementation is like taking a college test that shows a need for a remedial English writing course but never taking that course.

The comment that there is a "lack of time" to do evaluation simply means that the library does not regard evaluation as important. The comment that "we don't know how to do evaluations" means that decision makers do not encourage staff to develop evaluation skills, do not perceive a need for them to do so, and so forth. Library staff who want to establish a meaningful program of evaluation can do it. All that is necessary is: (1) a commitment to evaluation, (2) a learning of basic planning and evaluation skills and competencies, and (3) a recognition that evaluation of library activities and services must be accomplished if the library is to compete successfully against other information providers.

NEED FOR ONGOING EVALUATION

Librarians must not accept as a "given" that their services, collections, and administrative activities are effective; rather, they must test their assumptions about the quality of library services and collections through an ongoing process of evaluation. Second, there are numerous methods to assess the quality or performance of library activities; frequently, it is important to select intelligently which evaluation design and methodology to use. Adoption of an inappropriate design or methodology invalidates the entire evaluation process and provides librarians with a false sense of security that they understand a problem situation when, in fact, their understanding is based on erroneous evaluation.

Ongoing evaluation activities are also essential to support the library's planning process. Planning and evaluation are two sides of the same coin. Each will be much more successful when the other is part of the overall management approach. Knowledge of evaluation techniques will significantly improve the effectiveness of the library's planning efforts.

And, finally, individual library staff are responsible for implementing a program of evaluation. All staff members have as their professional duty a commitment to excellence, provision of quality services and collections, and a responsibility to make certain that they meet and resolve the information needs of their clientele. Unless evaluation is ongoing, such assessments cannot be made.

DISCUSSION ITEMS

1. Give an example of a library problem meriting the conduct of action research.
2. Differentiate between planning and evaluation.
3. Provide an example of a mission statement, goals, and objectives for a library setting of your choice.
4. Differentiate between effectiveness and efficiency, and provide an example of each.
5. Differentiate between formative and summative evaluation, and provide an example of each.
6. What are the most significant obstacles to the conduct of evaluation?

7. Find an example of a cost-benefit and cost-effectiveness study in the literature of library and information science.
8. Find an example of an effectiveness and an efficiency study in the literature of library and information science.
9. Assess your strengths and weaknesses as an evaluator of a library service or activity.

Chapter Two
Overview of the Evaluation Process

Evaluation is the process of identifying and collecting data about specific services or activities, establishing criteria by which the success of those services or activities can be measured, and determining both the quality of the service or activity and the degree to which it accomplishes stated goals and objectives. As a *process*, evaluation is a systematic means that offers insights into the appropriateness, quality, or benefit of a service or activity. Further, the evaluation process is a catalyst for change; it is a tool that assists librarians in assessing organizational effectiveness and efficiency and in developing strategies to improve that effectiveness and efficiency.

The concept of measurement, which is closely related to evaluation, is the process of assigning numbers to describe or represent some object or phenomenon in a standardized manner (Kaplan, 1964, pp. 171–213). While measurement may lead to evaluation and evaluation usually requires measurement, the two processes differ. Evaluation includes the measurement process and adds components of the research process, planning, and implementation strategies to change or improve the organization or a specific activity.

This chapter combines elements of the research process, the measurement process, and program planning and evaluation to suggest a generalized procedure of evaluation research appropriate for library and information centers. The evaluation process should:

- Rely on rigorous yet innovative evaluation research designs and methods
- Include broad staff, and if appropriate some library clientele, involvement
- Emphasize areas, activities, programs, and services that are actionable—that is, where it is likely that intervention strategies can produce change
- Be practical and feasible so that it can be applied straightforwardly and with relative ease.

Additional assumptions about specific evaluation component parts will be identified as they are introduced.

While there are a number of different methods by which evaluation research can be successfully accomplished, this chapter offers a general description of how the evaluation process can be developed and implemented as a strategy to improve overall organizational effectiveness. The actual components, procedures, and order of implementation may vary from situation to situation, but in general, the approach suggested in this chapter provides an introduction for those individuals wanting to develop formalized processes of evaluation. Chapters 3 through 7 provide detailed discussions and techniques about the basic steps outlined in this chapter.

OVERVIEW

Figure 2-1 offers an overview of the evaluation process. Evaluation is not done in a vacuum, but, rather, as part of the larger organizational activities of planning and decision making. Environmental factors and constraints, institutional missions and resource availability, and clientele information needs influence specific library evaluation activities and procedures. These factors provide a framework or a context in which the library determines the level of commitment and activity to be dedicated to a formalized, ongoing, evaluation process.

Within this context, there are three broad phases of the evaluation process:

Phase I: *Preparation.* In this phase, the library makes certain that organizational goals and quantifiable objectives are established; staff are adequately trained to perform evaluation research; potential areas for evaluation are identified; and evaluators gain a basic understanding of the issues, topics, and techniques related to that evaluation

Phase II: *Evaluation Research.* During this phase, evaluators develop and implement the specific research questions, evaluation designs, and methodologies in order to investigate the effectiveness and efficiency of library programs, collections, and administration

Phase III: *Organizational Development.* The final phase is one in which the library assesses the results of the evaluation process and makes value judgments concerning which services or activities should be modified and how these services and activities should be modified. The library then implements strategies to change those services or activities for improved organizational performance.

Successful evaluation depends on the ability of library staff to orchestrate the components of each phase with other phases to provide information useful for organizational planning and decision making.

PHASE I: PREPARATION

The preparation phase establishes an organizational setting that encourages successful evaluation and ensures that the staff understand the basic components of the evaluation process. Successful evaluations *do not* begin with data collection; rather, they rely on the establishment of organizational goals and objectives, staff

Figure 2-1. The Evaluation Process

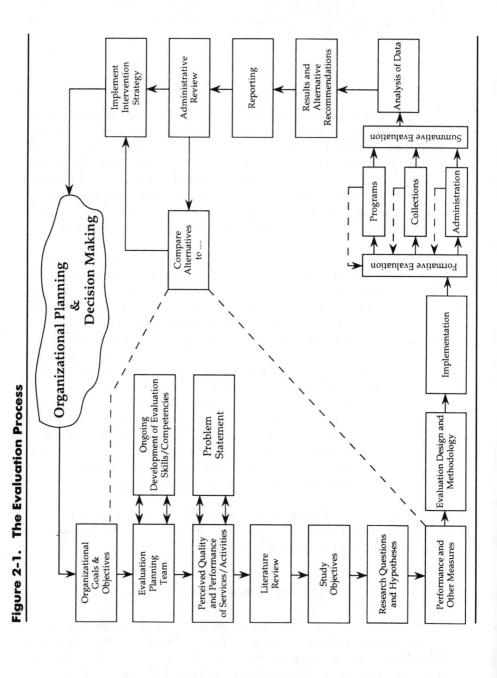

training, and identifying/reviewing topics for possible evaluation. Preparing for successful evaluation is critical for the success of the evaluation process and may, in fact, require a number of months before the library can move into Phase II.

Organizational Goals and Objectives

The effectiveness of the organization and its various activities cannot be determined without a statement of goals and objectives,because, by definition, effectiveness is the degree to which the library accomplishes objectives. Establishment of objectives depends on the setting of broader goals and, of course, stating the mission of the organization. Equally as important, establishment of goals and objectives forces the library to set *priorities* concerning what is *most* important (not unimportant). These priorities suggest which services and activities should be considered first for evaluation.

McClure et al. (1987) describe one straightforward approach for developing library goals and objectives. Although the presentation is cast in a public library context, the procedures and techniques can be adapted to other library settings as well. The key part here, however, is that the library has a statement of goals and objectives in place to provide a context for the evaluation process.

Evaluation Planning Team

A "planning team" might take the form of a formalized group, a committee with rotating membership, or an assignment of one individual with responsibility for organizational planning and evaluation who enlists assistance from other individuals in the library as needed. Another approach is to establish "evaluation liaisons" throughout the various library departments.

Inclusion of library clientele in the evaluation process can also be beneficial. First, such individuals provide a *user's* perspective on the service or activity. Second, they may be able to contribute external resources toward the evaluation that cannot be obtained within the organization. And, third, their inclusion may provide political benefits—especially if such individuals are associated with the governance of the library.

Decision makers should encourage group involvement in the evaluation process for a number of reasons:

- Greater involvement in the evaluation process will increase staff understanding and knowledge of organizational services and activities
- Staff can better see the relationships among various library services and activities and recognize the interdependency of these activities on overall organizational effectiveness
- Participation in the evaluation may reduce potential fear of such evaluation

and assist in the implementation of strategies to change the activity at a later date

- A team can accomplish evaluations that require too much time and effort for one staff member
- Staff inclusion in the evaluation process provides them with an opportunity to assume new responsibilities, develop or expand their skills, and broaden their professional horizons.

Of course, staff participation assumes that the librarians want to be involved and that they have the necessary skills or competencies. Library administrators need to provide appropriate mechanisms for that involvement to take place (Burckel, 1984).

There must also be a clear line of responsibility for who is in charge of the evaluation, who has authority to make decisions related to the evaluation, and who has day-to-day control over the evaluation itself. Upper administrative involvement in evaluation is important, and the person(s) responsible for conducting evaluations must have the confidence and direct support of the library administration.

Development of Staff Evaluation Skills

Another key aspect of the preparation phase is to develop a program of staff training related to the evaluation process. Implementation of ongoing evaluation without corresponding staff skills and competencies significantly increases the probability for failure of the evaluation process. Conducting a simple needs assessment of staff skills in this area can be easily accomplished. Based on that assessment, the library can develop appropriate training programs and education. Conroy (1978) offers an excellent overview of possible training techniques and approaches.

In general, for successful evaluation of library services and activities to occur, the staff need two types of competencies:

- *Technical Skills*, which refers to the ability of the staff to perform basic procedures related to evaluation (e.g., establish goals and objectives, collect and analyze data, write clear and concise reports, and demonstrate a host of interpersonal/group skills)
- *Knowledge and Understanding*, which refers to the ability of the staff to understand the conceptual basis of evaluation and how the evaluation process relates to overall library effectiveness, to relate the various evaluation components one to another, and to modify those components as needed.

Staff need *both* technical skills and knowledge/understanding if they are to participate successfully in the evaluation process. Anderson and Ball (1978, pp. 172–180) describe the content and skills for both areas.

Staff development should be an *ongoing* process and occur throughout the evaluation process. Indeed, engaging in ongoing evaluation provides a unique opportunity to not only improve the performance of the library, but also provides a mechanism whereby staff can increase their personal and professional competencies.

Perceived Quality and Performance of Services/Activities

The identification of priority topics for evaluation involves two components: reviewing the existing quality or performance of various library services and activities, and developing problem statements. These components are separated for purposes of discussion, but in practice, evaluators frequently accomplish them simultaneously.

The review of library services and activities occurs in the context of existing organizational goals and objectives. The review identifies *primary* areas where evaluation is necessary or appropriate. The process, which can be formal or informal, relies on objective or subjective evidence. Either way, the intent is to identify an area where evaluation is necessary, and to narrow that area to a manageable problem statement with clear study objectives and feasible research questions.

Broad questions to consider as a means of identifying areas for possible evaluation include:

- Do staff members suspect or "have a hunch" that a problem exists?
- Is there existing data or other evidence that suggest performance or service problems in this particular area?
- Is existing performance decreasing or inadequate compared to previous performance in this area?
- Has the cost or allocation of other resources to this service or activity increased substantially in recent months, but no straightforward explanation is available?
- Have the institution, clientele, or other external factors changed and thereby necessitated a reassessment of the "appropriateness" of a service or activity?
- Can alternative approaches be considered to improve performance in a given area, and is there a need for some method or measure to compare these alternatives?

If the area has not been formally evaluated before, decision makers might ask: "How well is this area performing, and to what degree are objectives being accomplished?"

At a more specific level, that of relating possible areas to library goals and objectives, questions such as the following might be asked:

- How do these services and activities contribute to the accomplishment of organizational goals and objectives?

- How well do these services and activities contribute to meeting the information needs of library clientele?
- Are the resources necessary for the support of these activities and services being spent appropriately, or could resources be better spent elsewhere?
- To what degree is this service or activity "actionable," i.e., does it have the potential for being changed?

Asking such questions can assist library staff in identifying potential areas for evaluation. Of course, a critical assumption is that library staff consider such evaluation important and *look* for services and activities that might require evaluation.

Based on this preliminary assessment, the staff investigate the scope of the service or activity to be evaluated, define key terms related to the service or activity, and determine the feasibility of conducting an evaluation in this particular area.

Literature Review

The last component of the preparation phase for evaluation is the traditional, yet essential, review of related literature on the topic. Although this component is introduced in the preparation phase, it is necessary to return to the literature throughout the evaluation process. Chapter 3 provides additional discussion about the evaluation literature and its importance when conducting an evaluation study.

During the literature review, it is essential to discover what others have done with similar problems, what types of evaluation methodologies have been employed to address the problems, and how one might *best* approach an evaluation of this particular service or activity. Use and review of the literature at this stage can save the evaluators time and help them to avoid "re-inventing the wheel."

PHASE II: EVALUATION RESEARCH

The second phase of the evaluation process includes data collection. However, the staff must carefully consider *what* data will be collected, as well as *why* and *how* the data will be collected. Indeed, this phase of the evaluation process requires a number of staff skills and competencies in the area of evaluation research for the assessment to be successful and impact organizational effectiveness.

The specific nature of the evaluation research to be conducted depends, in part, on the problem, and its significance to decision making; what type of data the evaluation team needs to gather; and why they selected the problem area. There may be numerous reasons for initiating an evaluation study—including political justifications, budgetary cutbacks, etc. The evaluation team should have a sense of why the evaluation has been initiated and consider this when they develop study objectives, hypotheses or research questions, the evaluation research design, and the methodology.

Study Objectives, Hypotheses, and Research Questions

In the preparation phase, the evaluation team formulates a problem statement, while in the second phase, the team develops study objectives, hypotheses, or research questions. Hypotheses and research questions operationalize objectives and provide specific guidance about what will be investigated. Hypotheses and questions limit the general area of investigation to specific topics that are manageable. With this framework in place, the team develops research designs and data collection procedures.

As an example, a possible research question for a problem statement discussing "how the library can reduce the time lag needed to catalog a monograph" might be:

- How much time do the various steps in cataloging a monograph take?
- Do certain types of monographs take longer to catalog than others?

For the same problem statement, possible hypotheses might include:

- In the monographic cataloging process, verifying the authority list for author name takes half the time of searching the title on OCLC
- The language of the monograph is significantly related to the length of time required to catalog the monograph.

Thus, one can see that hypotheses tend to be more specific than research questions, that hypotheses specify relationships between variables or levels of activities, and that they offer an informed view of what the evaluator suspects will be found relative to the problem statement. Furthermore, research questions are always stated as questions, whereas hypotheses are declarative sentences. Either an hypothesis or a research question is appropriate to help frame the evaluation.

The greater the knowledge that evaluators have about the problem area to be investigated, the more likely it is that they might use an hypothesis. However, in many cases the evaluation of a library service or activity is exploratory, i.e., it is a first attempt to identify which variables or factors related to that service or activity deserve greater scrutiny. Or, there are so many unknowns about the problem area that *specific* hypotheses limit the evaluation too greatly. In such instances, the use of research questions might be more productive.

Performance and Other Measures

At this stage of the evaluation process, it is a good idea to consider what measures are needed to describe the performance within a particular library area. For example, in the area of circulation, is "circulation per capita" an acceptable measure to gauge circulation performance? Or, perhaps another measure, such as "cost per circulation," would be a better indicator?

For some libraries, performance measures have either already been developed for specific types of library activities, or external governing agencies, such as a state library, have suggested performance measures and performance standards. When possible, the library should use performance measures and standards that have been previously established and validated in the profession.

Specific performance measures should be identified or developed that address the research questions and problem statements. It is essential to consider developing those measures at this particular stage in the evaluation process to ensure that the evaluation design and data collection activities generate data by which the measures can be computed. Chapter 8 provides additional information on developing performance measures and the role performance measures have in the evaluation process.

Evaluation Research Designs and Methodologies

Once evaluators know what is to be studied, they then decide how they will accomplish the evaluation. The evaluation design is simply a plan that outlines the procedures by which they can address the hypotheses and/or research questions. The design outlines the specific approach that will organize and select the subjects to be studied. As an example, the design might set up an experimental or quasi-experimental study.

The methodology is simply the manner in which evaluators actually collect the data. Data collection might involve the use of standardized tests, questionnaires, interviews (in-person or by telephone), etc. Careful attention must be given to the selection of an evaluation research design and method of data collection to ensure that the resulting data will be consistently gathered (reliable) and that they measure what they are supposed to measure (validity).

A key concept to remember during the development of the evaluation research design and methodology is *triangulation*—the use of a number of data collection methodologies and measures for the phenomenon being evaluated. Triangulation assists evaluators in ensuring that measures are valid if each of the various methods and measures reflect similar results. Triangulation is a fine-tuning of the research design and adds significant credibility to the results (Jick, 1983).

Implementation

The final activity during the second phase of the evaluation process is the actual implementation of the research design and data collection methodology. The implementation process calls for careful scheduling and planning of the evaluation, and may require considerable coordination among evaluators, the things to be evaluated, and the resources necessary to support the evaluation.

Planning/scheduling charts. Planning charts, such as PERT, flow process, and GANTT charts provide a basis for staff to understand what is to be done, when it is to be done, and how various parts of the evaluation relate to each other. Furthermore, planning charts, such as Figure 2-2, assist the person responsible for the overall evaluation to control and monitor the evaluation.

A GANTT chart (see McClure et al., 1987) "tasks out" or "proceduralizes" the implementation process by indicating (1) the tasks to be done, (2) who will do those tasks, and (3) the time frame for the completion of each task. Additionally, such charts include information about the resources that will be necessary for the accomplishment of various tasks and benchmark dates indicating when the tasks will be completed. Careful planning and scheduling of Phase II of

Figure 2-2. Planning Chart

Task	Person	Month (or week)											
		1	2	3	4	5	6	7	8	9	10	11	12
1.													
2.													
3.													
4.													
5.													
6.													
7.													
8.													
9.													
10.													
11.													
12.													
Notes and Explanations:													

the evaluation process make the third phase, organizational development, much easier and more efficient.

The pretest. A preliminary activity of implementation may be a pretest or pilot of the evaluation design and data collection methodology. A "pilot" suggests a "dry run" of the procedures called for in the evaluation design, while the "pretest" usually indicates an administration of the data collection instrument to a small sample of the people or objects to be studied.

Both the pretest and a pilot have similar objectives, including to:

- Determine the amount of time necessary to administer the data collection instrument and/or process, and assess the appropriateness of the instrument or process
- Determine the cost of developing the data collection instrument and/or process, and assess the appropriateness of both
- Identify weaknesses, problems, or inaccuracies with the data collection process or instrument
- Attempt to identify any "unanticipated consequences" resulting from the data collection process
- Ensure that the data actually collected address the research questions or hypotheses.

Investment in conducting a short pretest or pilot will usually provide excellent returns by saving evaluators extra time later. Such an approach identifies areas of the evaluation design that can be improved *before* it is too late, and allows evaluators to exercise tighter controls over the design. The result should be improved reliability and validity of the data.

Formative review within the design. Implementation of the evaluation design and data collection method can include either formative or summative evaluation, or even both. In one sense, the inclusion of these two types of evaluation methods will be determined during the development of the evaluation objectives and research design. A key component of evaluation research is the use of formative evaluation techniques, i.e., ongoing measures that *monitor* both the success of the evaluation as well as the quality of the services or activities being evaluated.

For instance, if library staff members attempted to evaluate the quality of the video cassette collection, formative evaluation could:

- Monitor the cost, quality, accuracy, timeliness, and/or other factors related to the evaluation design and data collection process on a regular basis. Staff could modify any procedures found inappropriate, ineffective, or inefficient (improvement of evaluation research)
- Revise and modify the evaluation design so that the program, collection, or

administration of the video cassette collection can be improved, *while* the evaluation is in process (improvement of library operations).

Figure 2-1 indicates both options with a dotted line, or feedback loop, from "programs," "collections," and "administration" to formative evaluation.

Frequently, either the evaluation research process or the actual programs, collections, or administration of library activities can be improved immediately, and on-the-spot, without having to resort to formal administrative review. Indeed, the intent of formative evaluation is to encourage library staff who work directly with the activity under investigation to *intervene* immediately in the activity once an area for improvement has been identified.

Many evaluation research designs employ approaches that are summative or assess the quality of an activity or service on a post-hoc or after the fact basis. Indeed, for many library programs, collections, and administrative activities, summative evaluation techniques adequately assess the activity. Formative review of the evaluation research design assists evaluators in enhancing "the evaluability of a program" or in making "it possible to examine other program components and goals/effects and/or to implement [a] more rigorous research methodology" (Rutman, 1980, p. 163).

Analysis of Data

The data resulting from evaluation are unintelligible until they are analyzed, summarized in terms of their descriptive and inferential characteristics, and interpreted. Typically, evaluators analyze data in terms of descriptive statistics (e.g., frequencies, percentages, and histograms) as a means to simplify, reduce, and report the basic nature of the data collected. On the other hand, inferential statistics (e.g., regression analysis and analysis of variance) enable evaluators to predict and infer characteristics of a population from the sample studied (see Hernon et al., 1989, Chapters 5–9).

Data analysis and interpretation address the evaluation questions, hypotheses, and objectives. Two pitfalls that occur in data analysis are that evaluators (1) do inadequate or inappropriate data analysis, or (2) do not know when to quit analyzing data. The latter can occur if they think that additional analysis, if done differently, more thoroughly, or with greater precision, will produce results more to their liking.

PHASE III: ORGANIZATIONAL DEVELOPMENT

The final phase of the evaluation process identifies specific strategies to improve the quality of library programs, collections, and administration; and to implement those improvements for increased overall organizational performance. During this phase, evaluators make value judgments about *how well* existing services and activities operate and *what* services and activities the library should offer. Many librarians ask the "how well" question, but they fail to consider the "what should be done" question. The "what should be done" question requires careful consideration and re-evaluation because libraries compete directly with other providers of information services and products.

Results and Recommendations

The results of the data analysis, simply stated, are summaries that address the evaluation questions and/or hypotheses, and provide recommendations for what should be done about the findings. Results should be concise. Administrators and others interested in the evaluation may want detailed information about the data and *the process* by which they were analyzed. More likely, however, they are interested in the "bottom line," or what exactly the evaluators determined.

Summarizing the results of an evaluation study almost always implies an attachment of value judgments and interpretations based on assumptions and limitations. Making such assumptions does not always imply a deficiency in the research; it does, however, require that every effort be made to identify *explicitly* these assumptions so that others can recognize possible limitations of the evaluation (Blalock, 1982).

Evaluators should develop alternative recommendations instead of simply offering one recommendation, because a list of alternative suggestions:

- Forces comparison among those alternatives concerning which might be "best," as judged by criteria such as cost, time, equipment needs, staff ability to perform the activity, and feasibility
- Encourages creativity, innovation, and a fresh perspective on how to improve the service or activity under consideration.

Furthermore, the stating of alternatives may be a catalyst for others reading the recommendations to develop their own approaches to improve the service or activity under consideration.

Reporting

The stating of results and the development of alternatives are *not* the same as reporting those findings and alternatives. Evaluators usually assume that individuals in the organization will use the results and consider the alternatives, that existing management style and organizational climates support the development of new strategies, and that library staff have the skills and competencies necessary to implement such strategies. However, such assumptions may not always be valid.

In short, reports and other means of communication about the evaluation process must be specifically tailored for the:

- Intended audience
- Expected level of understanding the audience already has about the topic
- Amount of time available to decision makers to consider the content of the report
- Magnitude of change being recommended.

Other more tangible factors, such as the format of the report, the use of clear and easy-to-read graphics, and a readable and pleasing writing style, must also be considered.

A key consideration in the reporting of an evaluation study is who should get what type of report? Constituencies that might be addressed during the dissemination process include, for example:

- Decision makers
- Library staff
- Funding agents
- Library users
- Program participants
- Communities and community leaders.

Matching information presentation formats to decision making styles significantly facilitates the decision-making process (Bybee, 1981). If the report and/or presentation of the findings are unintelligible, the evaluation is not likely to have a significant impact. Thus, the means of dissemination, such as reports, should match the decision-making and cognitive styles of those individuals expected to read the report and take action on it. Some general guidelines to accomplish this include (1) keeping the report as short as possible, (2) eliminating technical jargon, (3) having a preliminary draft of the report proofread and copyedited by someone with similar responsibilities and background as the intended audience, and (4) adding a brief executive summary to the report.

Clearly, evaluators should make every effort to write and present the report in order to *encourage* action—the making of a decision about what, specifically, to do about the problem and how to *implement* that decision. For this reason, it is important to (Weiss, 1972, pp. 110–128):

- *Clarify the role of the report writer*: The writer should explain his/her role in the evaluation, discuss the objectiveness of the evaluation, and stress actions that can be taken as a result of the evaluation

- *Reduce organizational resistance to the recommendations*: Stress the feasibility, benefits, and practicality of the recommendations
- *Disseminate report findings to appropriate individuals*: Key opinion leaders, decision makers, and administrators must be aware of the report if they are to take action on it
- *Be explicit about implementation of recommendations*: It is not enough to offer recommendations. The evaluator should offer suggestions that are clear, feasible, and practical for the implementation of those recommendations
- *Avoid evaluation reports that show no clear findings*: If the evaluation results in unclear, contradictory, or obviously inaccurate findings, revise the research design and methodology and redo the evaluation before reporting findings.

Factors, such as the timing of the release of the report and political considerations about who will provide an oral report and who will take action on the report, are important and affect the administrative use of the report.

Administrative Review and Implementation of Interventions

The administrative review of the evaluation occurs in a complex milieu, and any action or interventions that are taken will be based on at least four key factors:

- *Politics*: Decision makers will consider the action(s) to be taken against political criteria having to do with the use of power within the library as well as between the library and external factors, such as the governance board, clientele, and public relations. Decision makers might favor actions that enhance the library's power, usually in terms of further control over resources, resolving matters related to personnel, or putting a "good face" on a difficult situation
- *Budget*: Decision makers will consider any action to be taken in terms of (1) available resources for support of that action, (2) the total amount of resources necessary for taking that action, and (3) what actions can be sacrificed if the resources are channeled to this particular activity
- *Increased effectiveness and/or efficiency*: The action must have a high probability of increasing the degree to which the library's goals and objectives are accomplished and/or the degree to which resources are used productively
- *Feasibility*: The recommendations will be considered in terms of feasibility and practicality; any actions taken must be based on a clear sense that change, in fact, can be accomplished and that the organization will not waste time, staff, or other resources on changes that have little likelihood for success.

Evaluators must realize that recommendations which improve the effectiveness and efficiency of the organization may not, in themselves, be implemented because of political, budgetary, or feasibility considerations.

More specifically, the administrative review process should include input from various levels of the library staff. Although responsibility for the interventions to be taken as a result of the evaluation rests with the administration, the administrative staff ought to solicit input, in the form of suggestions, critical comments, alternatives, and additional ideas from those individuals who will be directly affected by any action taken in this area. The administration can use mechanisms, such as group meetings, written reviews, and informal discussions, to obtain that input.

Comparing the possible alternatives for intervention to (1) existing organizational goals and objectives, and (2) the results of the evaluation in terms of various library performance measures (see Chapter 8) is also essential. The meaning of the evaluation must be considered in the context of library goals and objectives and possible actions to be taken. If, for instance, the evaluation determines that video cassettes comprise only 1% of all library circulations, but there are no objectives having to do with increasing access to, awareness of, or circulation of video cassettes, then perhaps change is unnecessary. Change or new strategies should be concentrated only on those areas where *priorities* have been established, as evidenced by stated goals and objectives.

The results of an evaluation study must be placed in the context of the availability of other library management information. The complexities of administering today's library necessitates two approaches. The first is a conceptual approach by which the library identifies, collects, and presents information for decision making. The second is a practical approach by which procedures, techniques, and equipment are coordinated to provide staff with information necessary for decision making. In short, management information systems (MIS) and decision support systems (DSS) enable the results of the evaluation to be considered in light of other library activities and priorities (see Chapter 7).

Intervention or any planned effort designed to produce intended changes in a target population or study subjects is the capstone of evaluation (Rossi and Freeman, 1982, p. 16). This notion of intervention represents a significant difference between basic and applied research and evaluation or action research. Simply studying a problem and collecting data that help to describe it, or assist the researcher to better understand it, is not enough. An *intervention* strategy is needed to *change* the activity and produce increased performance.

During phase three, organizational development, evaluators design and implement interventions (see Figure 2-1). The design of intervention strategies is the creative, imaginative, and perhaps most challenging aspect of the evaluation process because it is at this point where library staff redirect and change the activities in the library. To conduct evaluation research without the design, development, and implementation of intervention or change strategies is to short-circuit the entire evaluation process.

Implementing the intervention is primarily a matter of planning and establishing procedures or tasks to be accomplished, determining who is responsible for those tasks, developing a time frame for the accomplishment of the tasks, establishing a budget for the changes agreed upon, and monitoring the change activities to make certain that they do, in fact, occur. Use of a GANTT chart can be helpful here as well as during the implementation of the evaluation research design and methodology.

Another critical component of the implementation process at this stage is to build in criteria to *evaluate* the new strategy—either through the use of performance measures or by establishing *in advance* criteria for determining the success of the activity. For instance, if the decision is to increase access to video cassette tapes, and the strategy selected to accomplish this objective is to improve bibliographic control over them, then a measure and performance standard for the success of the action might be to "complete cataloging and classification of video cassettes within 14 days of their receipt."

At this point, the evaluation process has now come full circle. The results of a specific evaluation process (outputs) provide resources (inputs) for interventions and other evaluations. Provision of such information for decision support aids library planning. The implementation of interventions is simply the continuation of the library's ongoing attempt to determine the effectiveness and efficiency of various activities and services and to develop strategies that will improve overall organizational effectiveness and efficiency.

POLITICS OF EVALUATION

Evaluation should take place in areas that are *actionable* and where there is at least a potential for designing and developing an intervention strategy that can improve the performance in that particular area. Intervention strategies should be designed to *maximize* performance on stated goals and objectives.

In the conduct of evaluation studies, it is important to separate issues related to the *quality of the activity* from those concerning the *value of the activity*. Numerous library activities can be accomplished with high quality, and, indeed, an evaluation of such an activity can document the degree to which that activity is effective and efficiently performed. However, just because an activity has high quality and excellent measures of effectiveness and/or efficiency, it is *not* the same as saying that activity has "value."

The value of a library service or activity depends on a host of factors—most of which have to do with the political process. Evaluation is conducted in a complex political context, and many evaluators are not well prepared to either guard against political ramifications or exploit them to advantage (Guba and Lincoln, 1981, p. 22). Considering evaluation within the political realities of libraries defies easy description and explanation. At the minimum, however, evaluators should be aware of:

• What individuals initiated or supported the evaluation study?

- What do the individuals involved in the area under evaluation have to gain or lose as a result of the process?
- How does the operation of this particular area in the library relate to organizational priorities and goals?
- What is the larger "agenda" of external officials/agencies (e.g., the state library) regarding the library?
- Who are the "powerful" individuals in the organization, and how do the results of the evaluation relate to *their* interests and activities?

Finally, those conducting evaluation studies within an organization that employs them would be well advised to have a clear understanding of *their* political power base, status, and authority prior to taking on evaluation responsibilities.

This brief discussion regarding the politics of evaluation is not intended to discourage people from engaging in the evaluation process. Rather, it raises an issue that, in itself, can account for the success or failure of an evaluation study. Indeed, the evaluation process is simply an aspect of organizational planning and decision making—and the political considerations at work in those activities are much the same as those affecting the evaluation process (see Chapter 13).

DISCUSSION ITEMS

1. Distinguish between a researchable and a nonresearchable problem meriting evaluation.
2. Who should conduct an evaluation study in a library, and what competencies should these people possess?
3. Provide an example of a study objective, hypothesis, and research question.
4. Differentiate between a pretest and a pilot study.
5. Locate an example of a pretest and pilot study in library literature, and critique each article.
6. Develop a GANTT chart for completion of a hypothetical study. (See McClure et al., 1987, for a sample GANTT chart.)
7. Discuss possible reasons why an evaluation report might have minimal affect on library administrators.
8. What steps can the evaluators take to increase the likelihood that an intevention is developed to improve the effectiveness and efficiency of the area being evaluated?
9. Summarize political factors about which evaluators must be aware.

Chapter Three
Exploiting the Literature on Evaluation

The evaluation component in organizational planning and decision making provides library staff with important feedback: (1) to improve the total effectiveness of the organization as a service agency, and (2) to better respond to the needs and wants of library clientele. Evaluation is change-oriented and presumably leads to improved decision making, programs, services, and activities. As McClure (1978, p. 462) observes,

> Failure to include evaluation as part of the library planning process may result in the creation of a self-serving bureaucracy, increased distance between information and users, ineffective allocation of resources, poor credibility with governing bodies, reinforcement of status quo, and, most important, the continuance of programs that should have ended because they no longer contribute to the accomplishment of organizational goals and objectives.

From a systems perspective, evaluation might examine inputs (i.e., resources), processes, outputs, or outcomes. Outcomes differ from outputs (services provided) in that outcomes are the impact of the outputs on the environment. For example, if reference librarians initiate extensive instructional programs on the use of the library, the output may be better-educated users who have substantial competence about the services that the library offers. The outcome of the instructional programs, however, may be a marked increase in the use of the library's resources—materials and services. If there are not enough materials or staff to accommodate the additional demand, the outcome may be dysfunctional to library goals and objectives. Typically, the library as an organization fails to consider the outcomes or impacts of its programs on the environment.

Evaluation is both a research and political process for assessing programs, services, or activities. Evaluation should have practical consequences. It generates information useful for judging the worth of a product, program, service, or activity, or for determining social utility. Library evaluation tends to concentrate on measuring the extent to which organizational goals and objectives are met.

Evaluation is "disciplined inquiry" or systematic investigation in that a problem is objectively examined and definite conclusions reached (Worthen and Sanders, 1973, p. 10). These conclusions might enable library staff to revise an ongoing program or service, or determine the extent to which a completed program or service met staff expectations.

Figure 3-1. Examples of Works on Research Methods, Statistics, and Questionnaire Design

RESEARCH METHODS

Ary, Donald, Lucy C. Jacobs, and Asghar Razavieh. *Introduction to Research in Education*. New York: Holt, Rinehart and Winston, 1985.

Backstrom, Charles H. and Gerald D. Hursh. *Survey Research*. Evanston, IL: Northwestern University Press, 1963.

Blalock, Hubert M. and Ann B. Blalock. *Introduction to Social Research*. New York: Prentice-Hall, 1982.

Borg, Walter R. and Meredith D. Gall. *Educational Research*. New York: Longman, 1983.

Brinberg, David and Joseph E. McGrath. *Validity and the Research Process*. Beverly Hills, CA: Sage, 1985.

Busha, Charles H. and Stephen P. Harter. *Research Methods in Librarianship: Techniques and Interpretations*. New York: Academic Press, 1980.

Cooper, Harris M. *Integrating Research: A Guide for Literature Reviews*. Newbury Park, CA: Sage, 1989.

Fink, Arlene and Jacqueline Kosecoff. *How to Conduct Surveys*. Newbury Park, CA: Sage, 1985.

Fitz-Gibbon, Carol Taylor and Lynn Lyons Morris. *How to Analyze Data*. Beverly Hills, CA: Sage, 1987.

Fowler, Floyd J., Jr. *Survey Research Methods*. Newbury Park, CA: Sage, 1988.

_____ and Thomas W. Mangione. *Standardized Survey Interviewing*. Newbury Park, CA: Sage, 1989.

Frey, James H. *Survey Research by Telephone*. Newbury Park, CA: Sage, 1989.

Jorgensen, Danny L. *Participant Observation*. Newbury Park, CA: Sage, 1984.

Katzer, Jeffrey, Kenneth H. Cook, and Wayne W. Crouch. *Evaluating Information: A Guide for Users of Social Science Research*, 3rd edition. Reading, MA: Addison-Wesley Publishing Co., 1990.

Kraemer, Helena C. and Sue Thiemann. *How Many Subjects: Statistical Power Analysis in Research*. Newbury Park, CA: Sage, 1987.

Krueger, Richard A. *Focus Groups*. Newbury Park, CA: Sage, 1988.

Lavrakas, Paul J. *Telephone Survey Methods*. Newbury Park, CA: Sage, 1987.

Majchrzak, Ann. *Methods for Policy Research*. Beverly Hills, CA: Sage, 1984.

McCracken, Grant. *The Long Interview*. Newbury Park, CA: Sage, 1988.

Morgan, David L. *Focus Groups as Qualitative Research*. Newbury Park, CA: Sage, 1988.

Powell, Ronald R. *Basic Research Methods for Librarians*. Norwood, NJ: Ablex, 1985, 1990.

Selltiz, Claire, Lawrence S. Wrightman, and Stuart W. Cook. *Research Methods in Social Relations*, 3rd edition. New York: Holt Rinehart and Winston, 1976; Louise H. Kidder and Charles M. Judd, *Research Methods in Social Relations*. New York: Holt & Co., 1986.

continued

Figure 3-1.—(Continued)

Spector, Paul E. *Research Designs*. Beverly Hills, CA: Sage, 1981.
Swisher, Robert and Charles R. McClure. *Research for Decision Making*. Chicago, IL: American Library Association, 1984.
Yin, Robert K. *Case Study Research*. Newbury Park, CA: Sage, 1989.

STATISTICS

Blalock, Hubert M., Jr. *Social Statistics*, 2nd edition. New York: McGraw-Hill, 1979.
Hafner, Arthur W. *Descriptive Statistical Techniques for Librarians*. Chicago, IL: American Library Association, 1989.
Hernon, Peter et al. *Statistics for Library Decision Making*. Norwood, NJ: Ablex, 1989.
Huck, Schuyler W., William H. Cormier, and William G. Bounds, Jr. *Reading Statistics and Research*. New York: Harper and Row, 1974.
Jaeger, Richard M. *Statistics: A Spectator Sport*. Beverly Hills, CA: Sage, 1983.
Langley, Russell. *Practical Statistics*. New York: Dover, 1971.
Siegel, Sidney. *Nonparametric Statistics for the Behavioral Sciences*. New York: McGraw-Hill, 1956.

QUESTIONNAIRE DESIGN

Berdie, Douglas R. and John F. Anderson. *Questionnaires: Design and Use*. Metuchen, NJ: Scarecrow, 1986.
Converse, Jean M. and Stanley Presser. *Survey Questions: Handcrafting the Standardized Questionnaire*. Beverly Hills, CA: Sage, 1986.
General Accounting Office. *Developing and Using Questionnaires*. Washington, D.C.: GPO, 1986.
Sudman, Seymour and Norman M. Bradburn. *Asking Questions*. San Francisco, CA: Jossey-Bass, 1983.

Evaluation uses the methods and strategies of social science research, but applies them in a specific context: problem solving and managerial decision making. "*Research* can provide a much needed contribution to rational decision-making—especially when program outcomes are complex and difficult to judge" (Van Maanen, 1979, p. 32). Clearly, evaluation is the application of the research process to an investigation that examines library effectiveness and efficiency.

The purpose of this chapter is to identify key writings on evaluation, both within and outside library and information science. The chapter provides a context for evaluators wishing to have background information on the topic of evaluation. Figure 3-1 lists key publications that cover research methods, statistics, and questionnaire design.

CHARACTERISTICS OF KEY SOURCES

Figure 3-2 identifies examples of works outside of library and information science that deal with evaluation. Evaluation is an important type of study in public administration, public policy, education, psychology, and sociology. The literature reflects these various perspectives. Librarians, library educators, and library school students may not be interested in the actual problems discussed in these writings. Nonetheless, they might benefit from an examination of the research designs, methodologies, and indicators of reliability and validity used. They might also be interested in the types of problems amenable to evaluation and in discussions of the political context in which evaluation takes place.

Rossi and Freeman (1989), who might be considered as writing the premier textbook on evaluation, indicate that evaluation research "is the systematic application of . . . research procedures for assessing the conceptualization, design, implementation, and utility of . . . programs, services, and operations" (p. 18). The purpose of such research therefore is to investigate and improve the planning, monitoring, effectiveness, and efficiency of programs, services, and operations (Rossi and Freeman, 1985, p. 19). The book, now in its fourth edition, provides an overview of the purposes, uses, types, designs, and methodologies used in social science evaluation. Each chapter contains examples of the principles discussed and places evaluation in a social context.

Van Maanen (1979) provides a detailed overview of program evaluation for "practicing administrators—organizational 'insiders' wishing to evaluate programs (whose very formation may be their own doing)" (p. 30). He stresses that "an adequate understanding of the 'all' that is involved in the evaluation process" will only come from extensive reading of the types of works listed in the four figures of this chapter and from actually attempting to conduct evaluation studies, perhaps under the direction of a seasoned evaluator (p. 30). Van Maanen (Ibid.) does insert an important reminder (p. 31):

> Evaluation is only one input among many to policy makers. Other factors are always involved in change decisions (e.g., costs, public receptivity, participant reactions, ideological climate, and so on). Above all, these decisions require certain value commitments. The system for attaching values to facts is, fundamentally, a political one and it is inherently a part of any program evaluation environment. Yet, undertaking an evaluation effort may in itself be an important step in the right direction—even if policy recommendations are eventually ignored. For instance, evaluation may provide data which will reduce uncertainty as to what's really happening inside the program and begin to clarify the pluses and minuses of various decisions. In a way, it may allow us to see the values and preferences of the decision-makers more clearly.

It is important to keep this caveat in mind when developing and implementing evaluation efforts.

Figure 3-2. Examples of Non-Library Works on Evaluation

ARTICLES

Frankel, Barbara. "On Participant-Observation as a Component of Evaluation: Strategies, Constraints, and Issues," *Evaluation and Program Planning: An International Journal*, 5 (1982): 239–246.

Maynard-Moody, Steven. "Program Evaluation and Administrative Control," *Policy Studies Review*, 2 (February 1983): 371–390.

Van Maanen, John. "The Process of Program Evaluation," *The Grantsmanship Center News*, 27 (January/February 1979): 29–74.

BOOKS

Alkin, Marvin C. *A Guide for Evaluation . . . Decision Makers*. Beverly Hills, CA: Sage, 1985.

Anderson, Scarvia B. and Samuel Ball. *The Profession and Practice of Program Evaluation*. San Francisco, CA: Jossey-Bass, 1978.

Brinkerhoff, Robert O. and Dennis E. Dressler. *Productivity Measurement*. Newbury Park, CA: Sage, 1989.

Conner, Ross F. *Methodological Advances in Evaluation Research*. Beverly Hills, CA: Sage, 1981.

Datta, Lola-Ellin and Robert Perioff, eds. *Improving Evaluations*. Beverly Hills, CA: Sage, 1979.

Fitz-Gibbon, Carol Taylor and Lynn Lyons Morris. *How to Design a Program Evaluation*. Beverly Hills, CA: Sage, 1987.

Guba, Egon G. and Yvonne S. Lincoln. *Effective Evaluation*. San Francisco, CA: Jossey-Bass, 1981.

————. *Fourth Generation Evaluation*. Newbury Park, CA: Sage, 1989.

Herman, Joan L., Lynn Lyons Morris, and Carol Taylor Fitz-Gibbon. *Evaluator's Handbook*. Beverly Hills, CA: Sage, 1987.

House, Ernest R. *Evaluating with Validity*. Beverly Hills, CA: Sage, 1980.

Kimmel, Allan J. *Ethics and Values in Applied Social Research*. Newbury Park, CA: Sage, 1988.

King, Jean A., Lynn Lyons Morris, and Carol Taylor Fitz-Gibbon. *How to Assess Program Implementation*. Beverly Hills, CA: Sage, 1987.

Kosecoff, Jacqueline B. *Evaluation Basics*. Beverly Hills, CA: Sage, 1982.

Leistritz, F. Larry. *Social Impact Assessment and Management: An Annotated Bibliography*. New York: Garland Publishing, 1986.

Levin, Henry M. *Cost-Effectiveness: A Primer*. Beverly Hills, CA: Sage, 1983.

Morris, Lynn Lyons, Carol Taylor Fitz-Gibbon, and Marie E. Freeman. *How to Communicate Evaluation Findings*. Beverly Hills, CA: Sage, 1987.

Morris, Lynn Lyons, Carol Taylor Fitz-Gibbon, and Elaine Lindheim. *How to Measure Performance and Use Tests*. Beverly Hills, CA: Sage, 1987.

Figure 3-2.—(*Continued*)

Palumbo, Dennis J., ed. *The Politics of Program Evaluation.* Newbury Park, CA: Sage, 1987.

Patton, Michael Quinn. *Creative Evaluation,* 2nd edition. Newbury Park, CA: Sage, 1987.

_____. *How to Use Qualitative Methods in Evaluation.* Newbury Park, CA: Sage, 1987.

_____. *Practical Evaluation.* Beverly Hills, CA: Sage, 1982.

_____. *Qualitative Evaluation Methods.* Beverly Hills, CA: Sage, 1980.

_____. *Utilization-Focused Evaluation,* 2nd edition. Beverly Hills, CA: Sage, 1986.

Rossi, Peter H. and Howard E. Freeman. *Evaluation: A Systematic Approach.* Newbury Park, CA: Sage, 1989.

Rutman, Leonard. *Evaluation Research Methods: A Basic Guide,* 2d edition. Beverly Hills, CA: Sage, 1984.

_____. *Planning Useful Evaluations: Evaluability Assessment.* Beverly Hills, CA: Sage, 1980.

Stecher, Brian M. and W. Alan Davis. *How to Focus an Evaluation.* Newbury Park, CA: Sage, 1987.

Struening, Elmer L. and Marcia Guttentag. *Handbook of Evaluation Research.* Beverly Hills, CA: Sage, 1975.

Weiss, Carol H. *Evaluation Research.* Englewood Cliffs, NJ: Prentice-Hall, 1972.

_____, ed. *Evaluating Action Programs.* Boston, MA: Allyn and Bacon, 1972.

Worthen, Blaine R. and James R. Sanders. *Educational Evaluation: Theory and Practice.* Belmont, CA: Wadsworth Pub. Co., 1973.

SERIALS

Evaluation Practice. Newbury Park, CA: Sage, 1979– . Quarterly. Formerly called *Evaluation News.*

Evaluation Review. Newbury Park, CA: Sage, 1977– . Bi-monthly. Formerly called *Evaluation Quarterly.*

Evaluation Studies Review Annual. Beverly Hills, CA: Sage Publications, 1976– . Annual.

Long Ranging Planning. Elmsford, NY: Pergamon Press, 1968– . Bi-monthly.

Managerial Planning. Oxford, OH: Planning Executives Institute, 1952– . Bi-monthly.

New Directions for Program Evaluation. San Francisco, CA: Jossey-Bass, 1978– . Quarterly.

Figure 3-2 underscores that Sage Publications, Inc. (Newbury Park, CA) is the leading and most prolific publisher of monographs on the topic of evaluation. Clearly, the writings depicted in the figure cover numerous aspects of the evaluation process and underscore that evaluation is of concern to a diverse range of social science activities.

Figure 3-3 provides examples of library literature related to evaluation. As the

Figure 3-3. Examples of Library Works on Evaluation

ARTICLES

Buckingham, B.G. "Planning/Evaluation Cycle in the Library Media Center," *Catholic Library World*, 54 (March 1983): 514–516.

Childers, Thomas and Nancy A. Van House. "The Grail of Goodness: The Effective Public Library," *Library Journal*, 114 (October 1, 1989): 44–49.

Cohen, Lucy R. "Conducting Performance Evaluations," *Library Trends*, 38 (Summer 1989): 40–52.

DeProspo, Ernest R. "Personnel Evaluation as an Impetus to Growth," *Library Trends*, 20 (July 1971): 60–70.

_____. "Potential Limits and Abuses of Evaluation," *School Media Quarterly* (Summer 1975), pp. 302–306.

DuMont, Rosemary and Paul DuMont. "Measuring Library Effectiveness: A Review and an Assessment," in *Advances in Librarianship*, Volume 9. New York: Academic Press, 1979, pp. 103–126.

"Collection Evaluation," *Library Trends*, 33 (Winter 1985), entire issue.

"Evaluation of Library Services," *Library Trends*, 22 (January 1974), entire issue.

"Evaluation of Reference Services," *The Reference Librarian*, 11 (Fall/Winter 1984), entire issue.

Friedman, A.M. "From Objectives to Strategies: Completing the First Cycle," *Public Libraries*, 22 (Summer 1983): 64–67.

Goleff, C.J. "Introduction to Evaluative Research," *Colorado Libraries*, 9 (December 1983): 16–18.

Hansel, P.J. "Administrative Perspective in the Evaluation Process," *North Carolina Libraries*, 42 (September 1984): 8–11.

Hobson, Charles J., Robert F. Moran, Jr., and Arena L. Stevens. "Circulation/Reserve Desk Personnel Effectiveness," *The Journal of Academic Librarianship*, 13 (1987): 93–98.

Kantor, Paul B. "Quantitative Evaluation of the Reference Process," *RQ*, 21 (Fall 1981): 43–52.

Katzer, Jeffrey. "The Evaluation of Libraries: Considerations from a Research Perspective," *Drexel Library Quarterly*, 13 (July 1977): 94–101.

Lindsey, J. "Performance Evaluation: Worth the Cost?," *North Carolina Libraries*, 42 (September 1984): 18–22.

Lynch, M.J. "Measurement and Evaluation," in *ALA Yearbook*, Volume 8. Chicago, IL: American Library Association, 1983, pp. 175–176.

Martell, Charles. "Achieving High Performance in Library Work," *Library Trends*, 38 (Summer 1989): 73–91.

Neal, James G. "Employee Turnover and the Exit Interview," *Library Trends*, 38 (Summer 1989): 32–39.

Perspectives on Library Measurement. Entire issue of *Drexel Library Quarterly* devoted to Planning and Evaluation, Vol. 13, no. 3 (July 1977).

Figure 3-3.—(*Continued*)

Taylor, R. "Employee Perspective in Evaluation Process," *North Carolina Libraries*, 42 (September 1984): 12–14.
Vincelette, Joyce P. and Fred C. Pfister. "Improving Performance Appraisal in Libraries," *Library & Information Science Research*, 6 (April-June 1984): 191–203.

BOOKS

Beeler, M. G. F., Jerry Grim, John P. Herling, Stephen James, Miles W. Martin, and Alice Naylor. *Measuring the Quality of Library Service*. Metuchen, NJ: Scarecrow Press, 1974.
Blazek, Ron, ed. *Achieving Accountability: Readings on the Evaluation of Media Centers*. Chicago, IL: American Library Association, 1981.
Conroy, Barbara. *Library Staff Development Profile Pages: Guide and Workbook for Library Self-Assessment*. Granby, CO: Country Printer, 1979.
Cronin, Mary J. *Performance Measurement for Public Services in Academic and Research Libraries*. Washington, D.C.: Association of Research Libraries, 1985.
DeProspo, Ernest R., Ellen Altman, and Kenneth E. Beasley. *Performance Measures for Public Libraries*. Chicago, IL: American Library Association, 1973.
Evaluating Bibliographic Instruction: A Handbook. Chicago, IL: American Library Association, ACRL, Bibliographic Instruction Section, 1983.
James E. Rush Associates. *Library Systems Evaluation Guide*. 8 vols. Powell, OH, 1983–1984.
Kantor, Paul B. *Costs of Preservation Microfilming at Research Libraries*. Washington, D.C.: Council on Library Resources, 1986.
_____. *Objective Performance Measures for Academic & Research Libraries*. Washington, D.C.: Association of Research Libraries, 1984.
Lancaster, F. W. *If You Want to Evaluate Your Library. . .* Champaign, IL: University of Illinois, Graduate School of Library and Information Science, 1988.
_____. *The Measurement and Evaluation of Library Services*. Washington, D.C.: Information Resources Press, 1977.
Library Effectiveness: A State of the Art. Chicago, IL: American Library Association, Library Administration and Management Association, 1980.
Lindsey, Jonathan A. *Performance Evaluation*. Phoenix, AZ: Oryx Press, 1986.
Lynch, Mary Jo. *Library Data Collection Handbook*. Chicago, IL: American Library Association, 1981.
Performance Evaluation in Reference Services in ARL Libraries. SPEC Kit #139. Washington, D.C.: Association of Research Libraries, 1987.
Robbins, Jane and Douglas Zweizig. *Are We There Yet? Evaluating Library Collections, Reference Services, Programs, and Personnel*. Madison, WI: University of Wisconsin, School of Library and Information Studies, 1988.
Rubin, Richard. *In-house Use of Materials in Public Libraries*. Urbana, IL: University of Illinois, Graduate School of Library and Information Science, 1986.

continued

Figure 3-3.—(Continued)

Van House, Nancy, Beth Weil, and Charles R. McClure. *Measuring Academic Library Performance.* Chicago, IL: American Library Association, 1990.

Van House, Nancy, Mary Jo Lynch, Charles R. McClure, Douglas Zweizig, and Eleanor Jo Rodger. *Output Measures for Public Libraries,* 2nd edition. Chicago, IL: American Library Association, 1987.

figure indicates, entire issues of a journal have been devoted to "collection evaluation," the "evaluation of library services," the "evaluation of reference services," and other aspects of library services.

Perusal of the monographic literature depicted in the figure indicates two significant works by Lancaster (1977, 1988). The 1977 book identifies a wide range of library research studies that have evaluated document delivery services, reference services, resource sharing, costing (cost-benefit and cost-effectiveness), and so forth. For each topical area, Lancaster discusses study findings and their implications, but he neither assesses individual studies nor shows readers how to conduct an evaluation study. The 1988 publication offers more specific guidance on how to conduct specific types of evaluation.

James E. Rush Associates (1983–1984) produced eight volumes that illustrate how to evaluate different library operations. For example, the manuals encourage the development of a decision support system useful for planning, budgeting, personnel management, accounting and financial analysis, establishment and maintenance of policies and procedures, inventory control, statistical analysis and projection, marketing and promotion support, and reporting.

Robbins and Zweizig (1988) provide a reprint of the series "Are We There Yet?" published in *American Libraries* from October 1985 to March 1986. The manual centers on a continuing education course offered through the University of Wisconsin-Madison and reprints the seven course readings. Robbins and Zweizig discuss the preparation of descriptive studies on selected aspects of library collections, reference services, programs, and personnel evaluation. They encourage the collection of management data that are not too difficult to gather. The purpose of the manual is to encourage librarians to engage in evaluation and to get them started. Once involved, however, they should refer to a more comprehensive text on the topic.

Library literature (see Figure 3-3) contains fewer monographs and has a broader spread among publication dates. The monographic literature of library and information science is not as current and generally does not convey the latest developments in social science research as do the types of writings depicted in Figures 3-1 and 3-2. Additional comparison between Figures 3-2 and 3-3 suggests that no publisher in library and information science dominates the publication of monographs on evaluation.

There is also no journal devoted exclusively to library planning and evaluation. Perhaps the closest equivalent journal in library and information science is *Library & Information Science Research* (Ablex). Each issue of this quarterly journal contains an editorial, articles, and reviews of dissertations and monographs. The articles sometimes have practical application and provide insights useful for planning and implementing an evaluation study.

ABSTRACTS AND INDEXES

There are four basic indexes to the literature of library and information science: (1) *Library Literature*, (2) *Information Science Abstracts* (ISA), (3) *Library and Information Science Abstracts*, and (4) *Resources in Education*. *Library Literature* indexes journal articles, books, pamphlets, microforms, films and filmstrips, library school dissertations, and research papers by author and subject. It does not include a separate subject heading entitled "evaluation." However, evaluation is a subheading for subject headings such as:

* "Use Studies—Evaluation"
* "Research in Information Sciences—Evaluation"
* "Reference Services—Evaluation"
* "Libraries—Evaluation."

In addition, evaluation studies might be discovered under subject headings such as:

* "Output Measures"
* "Performance Appraisal."

Not all of the works listed under these subject and subordinate headings would be considered as evaluation research. Instead, many of the writings comprise an opinion piece, assessment of the literature, an explanation of relevant terminology, and so forth. Even the research literature varies in quality. Quantity is more abundant than quality.

Information Science Abstracts offers classified indexing and title keyword indexing of journal articles, conference proceedings, technical reports, ERIC documents, and books. *Library and Information Science Abstracts* covers books, periodical articles, dissertations, reports, and conference proceedings on an international basis. Both indexes include a subject heading, "Evaluation," but do not limit their coverage to research studies.

The Educational Resources Information Center (ERIC), sponsored and financed by the U.S. Office of Education, was created: (1) to improve the national dissemination of education resources and research-related materials, and (2) to provide bibliographic control over government-funded educational reports. Reports and other sources accepted by an ERIC clearinghouse are abstracted in the monthly *Resources in Education*. Many of the documents are available from the ERIC Document Reproduction Service in microfiche or paper copy. Certainly, many of the reports and other works included in the ERIC database do not comprise evaluation research, but a person conducting an evaluation study might still find relevant literature there.

Resources in Education includes a subject heading for "Evaluation" and:

- "Evaluation Appraisal"
- "Evaluation Criteria"
- "Evaluation Methods"
- "Evaluation Needs"
- "Evaluation Problems"
- "Evaluation Research"
- "Evaluation Utilization"
- "Evaluative Thinking"
- "Evaluators."

In addition, investigators might check this indexing/abstracting service under headings such as:

- "Library Personnel"
- "Library Services"
- "Research Libraries"
- "Research Design."

A careful perusal of the *ERIC Thesaurus* can suggest a number of index terms useful for obtaining information about library evaluation.

All the indexes, excepting *Library Literature*, are available online. *Library Literature*, *Library and Information Science Abstracts*, and *Resources in Education* are available on CD-ROM. Having direct access to a database, evaluators can combine search terms and narrow the range of potentially useful titles. This is especially important when using *Resources in Education* because many of the titles included are not library-related; they pertain to primary and secondary school education.

Investigators should be aware of the years covered by the CD-ROM or online database and adjust their search strategies accordingly. For example, the Wilson Company does not offer *Library Literature* in CD-ROM prior to October 1984. Evaluators should also update their literature searches by checking the latest periodical issues.

In 1969, ERIC officials created *Current Index to Journals in Education* (CIJE) to serve as a reference guide for articles published in education-related periodicals. This index supplements the four previously mentioned ones and reports a wide diversity of evaluation studies. Depending on the topic under investigation, evaluators might also examine the writings listed in:

- *Business Periodicals Index*
- *Dissertation Abstracts*
- *Education Index*
- *Hospital Literature Index*
- *Psychological Abstracts*
- *Social Sciences Citation Index*
- *Sociological Abstracts.*

Checking the sources mentioned in this section enables evaluators to obtain access to *published* literature. Individual libraries and funding agencies/ organizations, however, frequently produce internal reports involving the completion of an evaluation study. Furthermore, library school students and others might have written pertinent papers. As becomes apparent, investigators should be cautious in making a claim that the literature review contained in their report is *comprehensive* of the entire literature, published and unpublished.

BIBLIOGRAPHIES AND TEXTBOOKS

In addition to consulting Lancaster (1977, 1988) and the types of works depicted in Figures 3-2 and 3-3, evaluators completing a literature review might consult bibliographies and general textbooks in library and information science. For example, they might consult bibliographies and textbooks on bibliographic instruction, management, reference services, technical services, collection development and management, and so forth. Bibliographies may provide annotations for cited works, while the textbooks presumably identify the more important literature.

The advantage of consulting bibliographies and textbooks is that novice evaluators might obtain quick access to some very useful evaluation studies. They can check the footnotes and bibliographies attached to these works, and then use the indexing and abstracting services to update and expand their literature search.

IMPORTANCE OF KEY WRITINGS ON EVALUATION

Literature regarding evaluation is available in a number of different contexts:

- Methods and techniques for conducting evaluation from the larger social science arena

- Examples of evaluations completed on specific topics in library and information science
- Issues and concerns about evaluation, the importance of evaluation in organizational development, and philosophical debates about its role in library and information science.

Regardless of the specific context, evaluators can profit by reviewing this literature and exploring the existing evaluation knowledge base. This exploration should be initiated *before* they design methodologies and data collection techniques to conduct a study.

Equally as important, library evaluation efforts should profit from the knowledge gleamed from studies conducted in other social science disciplines. Numerous other evaluators have considered topics such as user needs, quality of services, and effectiveness of programs and services. Although such studies may not have been done in a library setting, much can be learned and adapted from these studies for use in a library context. A number of possible applications have been incorporated into the discussion of the evaluation process provided in Chapters 2 and 4.

DISCUSSION ITEMS

---

1. Compile a bibliography of the research studies completed on the topic of library staff *burnout*. Be sure to include the relevant literature from related disciplines and professions.
2. Which indexes were most useful? Why?
3. Assess and compare the methodologies used by these studies.
4. Can you find examples of unpublished research on staff burnout?
5. Does the literature suggest the need for further research on staff burnout?
6. Repeat steps 1–5 for an evaluation study examining student willingness to approach a reference librarian again for further assistance.

Chapter Four
The Steps in Conducting an Evaluation Study

Social science research often represents an investigation characterized by certain activities: (1) reflective inquiry, i.e., identification and justification of a problem, conducting a literature search to place the problem in proper perspective, and formulation of a logical structure, objectives, hypotheses, and research questions; (2) adoption of appropriate procedures, i.e., research design and methodologies; (3) the collection of data; (4) data analysis and interpretation; and (5) presentation of findings, conclusions, and recommendations for future study. Evaluation, a type of research, relies on the same five components.

The purpose of this chapter is to provide an overview of the steps involved in the conduct of an evaluation study. As such, this chapter details the information provided in Chapter 2. Chapters 5 and 6 amplify on this discussion, while Chapters 10 and 11 provide condensed versions of evaluation papers that employ the steps identified in this chapter.

REFLECTIVE INQUIRY

Problem Statement

The term *problem statement* contains two components: the problem itself, and its explanation in form of a statement, not a question. In a research study, a problem statement has two purposes. It shows that a problem exists, suggests the benefits to be derived from an investigation of the problem, and justifies the importance of that problem to a specified audience—library administrators, funders, journal or book series editors, or readers of the study. Once a problem has been shown to exist, the statement remains unchanged. In contrast, researchers might adapt the justification to spark the interests of a particular target audience.

Within any given topical area (see Figure 4-1 for examples), numerous problems theoretically exist. The purpose of the problem statement is to show that the topical area lends itself to evaluation research and that the problem is both significant and unique. (Of course, in some instances, a study might only replicate existing research and provide additional insights.) The problem must be clearly stated, specific, manageable, and written to stimulate reader interest. Of

Figure 4-1. Some Suggested Broad Areas and Subareas for Research*

Library use and nonuse

- Who uses the library?
- Among the population of possible users who does not use the library?
- What kinds of uses are made of the library and by whom?

Catalog use

- Who uses the library card [or online] catalog?
- What kind of searches are made and what is their frequency?
- What kinds of searching errors are made?
- What type of library catalog is optimal?
- How adequate are subject headings?

Availability of materials

- How can the need for duplicate copies of library materials be predicted?
- Who uses interlibrary loan? How effective is this service?
- What is the effect of different loan periods on the availability of materials?
- To what extent do censorship and related repressions affect the availability of certain materials?
- Do cooperative projects among libraries increase the availability of materials?

Fines for overdue materials

- How effective are library fines as deterrents to overdues?
- Are there alternatives to fines?

Browsing in the library

- How important is browsing to library clientele?
- How does browsing function?
- Could browsing be eliminated in particular instances?
- What is the effect of closed stacks on the research process?

Microforms

- How can user acceptance and utilization of various microforms be increased?

Figure 4-1.—(Continued)

- What are the unique problems of microform usage in libraries?
- How can microform collections and services be evaluated?

Selection of materials by patrons

- Why do children select a given book or other medium of expression?
- Why do adults select certain kinds of library materials?
- Can certain characteristics of a medium of communication be identified, such as color, cover design, etc., that influence the selection of a given book or other piece of library material?
- What are the implications of these selection characteristics?

* This figure is a partial reprinting of Table 1-1 in: Charles H. Busha and Stephen P. Harter, *Research Methods in Librarianship* (New York: Academic Press), pp. 22–23. Copyright 1980. Reprinted with permission.

course, the researcher should have the knowledge, skills, and resources to conduct the study.

In library and information science, the existence of the problem typically centers around either a knowledge void or conflicting evidence. A knowledge void refers to the absence of existing research on the topic, while conflicting evidence indicates that previous research was divided into distinct camps, each of which sharply disagrees on the findings and/or research strategies employed. The purpose of the new research is to attempt to resolve the differences between/among the camps.

The problem statement indicates the central focus of the research or evaluation. The subsequent components of the reflective inquiry and the procedures expand on this modest beginning and significantly clarify and delimit the scope of the study. Often novice researchers state the problem in terms of a question or by saying that the purpose of the study is to accomplish a particular task. In fact, neither of these approaches comprises a problem statement. A statement of purpose indicates what the study will accomplish, but does not place that goal in the context of a problem.

A mere question does not show conflict or that something is unsettled, perplexing, vexing, distressful, and in the need of investigation. For illustrative purposes, suppose that two people do not get along. There is definitely a conflict or problem. Does the resolution of that problem, however, require the conduct of research, or might there be other ways to resolve the conflict? The problem statement must clearly indicate the former.

Evaluation, as already noted, comprises a special type of research. Evaluators have greater latitude in the formulation of a problem statement. They can either use the research approach for writing the statement or ask a question. Sometimes, library managers do not know if a problem, in fact, exists. They want to examine a topical area and see if there is a significant problem. A question accomplishes this purpose. Still, there must be ample justification for why the question is important to decision making and merits priority attention within the organization.

An example of a problem statement might be:

> Over the past two decades, approximately 30 separate studies in academic and public librarianship have used unobtrusive testing to determine the *correct answer fill rate* for questions asked of reference staff. Unobtrusive testing of library reference services, however, has not examined the *correct answer fill rate* for staff members of state libraries.
>
> Two primary benefits would result from such a study. First, the effectiveness with which state libraries handle factual and bibliographic questions can be assessed and linked to a performance measure, *correct answer fill rate*. Second, the investigators can offer recommendations and strategies for improving the effectiveness of state libraries as disseminators of information.

This problem statement takes the form of a knowledge void.

That void, however, should be amply explained. The purpose is to set up the objectives and hypotheses/research questions so that it is apparent that subsequent stages of reflective inquiry emerge from the stated problem. In other words, evaluators might state that research has neither examined the *correct answer fill rate* nor the question negotiation and referral ability of general reference and documents staff. The problem statement thereby delimits the scope of the intended research.

Because problem statements do not introduce terms unfamiliar to readers or open to different interpretations, the evaluator must identify the major concepts discussed (unobtrusive testing, performance measures and *correct answer fill rate*, and library effectiveness) and ensure that these are explained either in a background section or in the literature review.

Figure 4-2 offers another example of a problem statement. In this case, the library staff are unsure if a significant problem, one meriting corrective action, exists. The research would be exploratory and offer an opportunity for staff to examine a supposition.

Literature Review

The literature review supports the problem statement and the declaration of a knowledge void or conflicting evidence. The review, however, has other responsibilities as well. It assesses the research designs and methodologies that previous evaluators have used to define and attack a similar problem. The literature review section does not summarize study findings. Rather, it evaluates the research in the context of the problem statement, the study design, and methodology. It notes major variables that previous research has found to be either

Figure 4-2. Example of a Problem Statement for an Evaluation Study*

Background: Library staff members are concerned that once original materials (book chapters and periodical articles) have been photocopied and returned to the collection, students will see what is on reserve, but consult the original material as opposed to the photocopy placed on reserve. Consultation of the original material might take the form of mutilation or theft, so that they do not have to compete with other members of the class for the reserve room copy.

Problem
Statement: If volumes located in the stacks, but comprising the original source from which the reserve copy is made, are being mutilated and pages cut out, then accessibility to the original material decreases. In addition, staff members widely suspected that students relocate or hide materials of high use in the stacks, further limiting accessibility in seeking the original material.

The extent to which these factors comprise a severe problem, however, has not been investigated. The literature of library and information science does not suggest how prevalent such a problem might be. It is therefore believed that an exploratory study might examine the topic and determine the magnitude of the problem. If it is severe, correct remedies might be proposed and implemented.

* Source: Lynn Andros, formerly a student in the Graduate Library School, University of Arizona, Tucson.

relevant or not relevant. The section alerts the evaluators and the readers of the report about danger signs encountered by previous research. For example, if past studies have used a mailed questionnaire but only achieved a return rate of 10–25%, should not the proposed study do something different in order to obtain a substantially higher rate of return?

The search for relevant literature extends to internal library reports, studies, and data, and to the published writings. These writings encompass conference proceedings, reports contained in the ERIC database, journal articles, and monographs (see Chapter 3). Perhaps the state library or an organization, such as the Association of Research Libraries, as well, has sponsored a study of value to the evaluator. The search for relevant literature, as is evident, may be far-reaching and initially time-consuming. It may be especially difficult to find high-quality studies in the literature of library and information science. Katzer (1989, p. 83) has compared the search for quality studies to looking for "nuggets in a sparse vein."

Logical Structure

The logical structure provides the framework within which the problem will be investigated. For an evaluation research study, the structure identifies and clarifies the theories, concepts, critical variables, and knowledge implicit in the problem statement. "Sound theoretical knowledge about the problem area from which the research task originated is necessary to the conduct of meaningful inquiry, no matter what the subject of the project may be" (Busha and Harter, 1980, p. 17). The structure validates the framework in terms of the anticipated advantages and outcomes. It also offers the context for viewing and understanding the objectives.

The logical structure, in effect, articulates how all parts of the puzzle fit together. The structure, in part, might be compared to a restaurant menu. The menu lists everything that the restaurant offers. After careful examination of the menu, we then decide what to order. The decision about what we order becomes the objectives, hypotheses/research questions, and research design. The structure for a research study also identifies theoretical considerations to be addressed.

Evaluators use the literature to round out the logical structure and to ensure that the menu is complete. They can then discuss possible selections with library managers, staff, and funders. Together, they might make the selections ensuring that the choices fit together conceptually and within the proposed budget.

Figure 4-3 illustrates the framework for a study of library users and nonusers. Evaluators might be less interested in theoretical aspects unless they intend to place the investigation in a larger context of information needs and information-gathering behavior. In such an instance, the evaluators would identify where people turn to for the resolution of an information need. Libraries thereby become only one of many institutional providers that they might use (Chen and Hernon, 1982). Even if the evaluators did not use this framework, they would want to employ some framework to organize conceptually how the various parts of the study fit together and which aspects they should examine.

It might be noted that evaluation research rarely probes all facets proposed in the figure. Evaluators have choices. Assuming that the study will ultimately revolve around the use of a questionnaire, the selections from the diagram indicate topical areas for inclusion in the questionnaire. For example, there might be one section probing the purposes for which students use the library and another section covering students' reasons for nonuse of the library.

Study Objectives

Study objectives narrow the focus of the problem statement and indicate those aspects of the problem that will be examined. They operationalize those compo-

Figure 4-3. Diagram of Components for a Study of Library Use and Nonuse

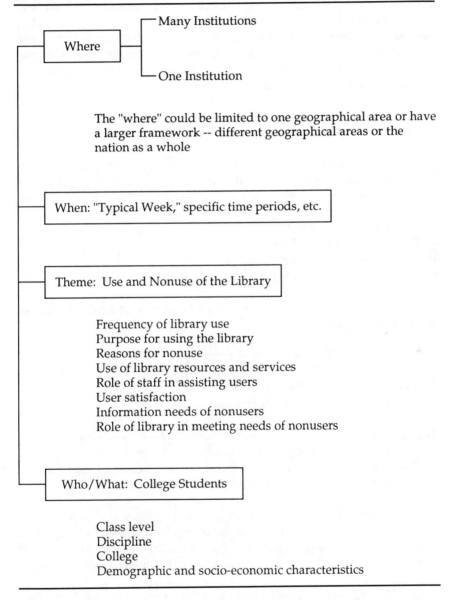

Where
— Many Institutions
— One Institution

The "where" could be limited to one geographical area or have a larger framework -- different geographical areas or the nation as a whole

When: "Typical Week," specific time periods, etc.

Theme: Use and Nonuse of the Library

Frequency of library use
Purpose for using the library
Reasons for nonuse
Use of library resources and services
Role of staff in assisting users
User satisfaction
Information needs of nonusers
Role of library in meeting needs of nonusers

Who/What: College Students

Class level
Discipline
College
Demographic and socio-economic characteristics

nents of the logical structure that the study will explore. Objectives provide the conceptual framework for the formulation and testing of hypotheses and research questions.

Every objective has two components: an action verb and the content or object of that verb. In library and information science, basic research involves conceptualization (i.e., developing a theory or model), while applied research tests and refines that theory or model. Action research attempts to support decision making in particular library settings. Evaluation studies typically involve depicting and relating (comparing or contrasting). When library staff members test learning interventions (bibliographic instruction programs), they are actually comparing or contracting the impact of an intervention. As a result, objectives for evaluation research might be cast as:

- To depict (describe, determine, identify, etc.)
- To relate (compare or contrast).

Objectives examine each part of the logical structure. They start with the central box or theme and then relate one box to another. Using Figure 4-3 as an example, the evaluator might focus on the following components of the theme:

- Frequency of library use
- Purpose for using the library
- Reasons for nonuse of the library
- Information needs of nonusers.

The evaluator indicates the selection of each of these components by choosing the following objectives:

- To identify the frequency of library use
- To determine the purpose for using the library
- To depict the reasons for nonuse of the library
- To identify information needs of nonusers.

The verb chosen does have a specific meaning. Evaluators should carefully consider whether they want only to "identify" as opposed to "describe."

Next, the evaluator compares the theme, use and nonuse of the library, to students and formulates the next set of objectives:

- To compare the frequency of library use by discipline and class level
- To compare the purpose for using the library by discipline and class level
- To compare the reasons for nonuse of the library by discipline and class level
- To compare the information needs of nonusers by discipline and class level.

Finally, the evaluator compares the theme to the "where" category. If the study takes place at one institution, there are no comparison objectives. On the other hand, if the study takes place at two universities, the following comparisons become possible:

- To compare the frequency of library use by academic institution
- To compare the purpose for using the library by academic institution
- To compare the reasons for nonuse of the library by academic institution
- To compare the information needs of nonusers by academic institution.

As is evident, one study may result in the formulation and examination of multiple objectives.

Hypotheses/Research Questions

Hypotheses flow from the conceptual framework and can represent a narrowing of objectives. They provide a framework for viewing and reporting study findings. Hypotheses are subject to testing and are expectations about the nature of things based on generalizations about the assumed relationship between variables. Hypotheses enable evaluators, on the basis of sample data, to determine whether or not something about the population is likely to be true or false.

Rossi and Freeman (1989, pp. 129–133) discuss the types of hypotheses applicable to impact modeling, or the translation of concepts into a plan of action. Figure 3-1 offers examples of research methods textbooks that include additional coverage of hypotheses.

The greater the knowledge that evaluators have about the problem area to be evaluated, the more likely that they will engage in hypothesis testing. In many cases, however, the evaluation of a library service or activity is exploratory, i.e., it is a first attempt to identify which variables or factors relating to that service or activity deserve greater attention. Or, there are so many unknowns about this problem area that specific hypotheses would limit the evaluation too greatly. In such instances, the use of research questions to guide the evaluation is likely to be more productive than the use of hypotheses.

Formulation of hypotheses and research questions involves a three-step process that (1) includes the selection of key questions appropriate to the objectives, (2) defines major components of study variables, and (3) identifies relationships, if appropriate, between variables. Hypotheses reflect a highly sophisticated conceptual framework for the study, while research questions indicate a less sophisticated and more exploratory framework.

Returning to the previous section and to the discussion of Figure 4-3, each objective should translate into one or more hypotheses and/or questions. For example, the objective "to depict the reasons for nonuse of the library" might become a question: "For what reasons do students not use the library?" Another objective, "to compare the reasons for nonuse of the library by academic institution," might become an hypothesis: "There is a statistically significant correlation among the reasons (at the .05 level) between the students at the two institutions." In contrast to the articulation of a directional hypothesis, evaluators might use a null hypothesis stating that no relationship between the variables studied exists.

PROCEDURES

The procedures refer to the study design and the methods by which the evaluators will study the problem. The procedures grow out of the reflective inquiry. Too often, novice evaluators initially decide to use, let us say, a mailed questionnaire and shape the reflective inquiry and design to support their decision. In fact, a questionnaire might not be the most appropriate choice. Methodological decisions should come later and not be part of the problem statement, unless the purpose of the research is to test a methodology.

Design

In *Designing Evaluations*, the General Accounting Office (1984, p. 1) explains that:

> According to a Chinese adage, even a thousand-mile journey must begin with the first step. The likelihood of reaching one's destination is much enhanced if the first step and the subsequent steps take the traveler in the correct direction. Wandering about here and there without a clear sense of purpose or direction consumes time, energy, and resources. It also diminishes the possibility that one will ever arrive. One can be much more prepared for a journey by collecting the necessary maps, studying alternative routes, and making informed estimates of the time, costs, and hazards one is likely to confront.
>
> It is no less true that front-end planning is necessary to designing and implementing an evaluation successfully. Systematic attention to evaluation design is a safeguard against using time and resources ineffectively. It is also a safeguard against performing an evaluation of poor quality and limited usefulness.

Chapter 5 provides detailed treatment of evaluation designs, primarily those applicable to an experiment that seeks to control conditions and engage in hypothesis testing. Chapter 3 discusses the evaluation literature and the types of writings that provide guidance in using other types of evaluation designs. Chapters 10 and 11 complement the discussion and provide practical examples of studies not using an experimental approach.

Evaluators might use case studies that focus on a specific target group and attempt to describe the subject's behaviors and the relationship of these behaviors to selected environmental variables or conditions. Such studies allow evaluators to probe in-depth, identify variables and propositions that can serve to direct additional research, and "develop insight into basic aspects of human behavior . . . [and] may lead to the discovery of previously unsuspected relationships" (Ary, Jacobs, and Razavieh, 1985, p. 323).* Case studies are useful for both

---

*Quoted from *Introduction to Research in Education*, Third Edition, by Donald Ary, Lucy Chester Jacobs, and Asghar Razavieh. Copyright © 1985 by Holt, Rinehart and Winston, Inc., New York. Reprinted by permission of the publisher.

exploratory evaluations and for descriptive and explanatory purposes. They provide an important tool for evaluators.

Evaluation design involves the examination of the "theme" of the problem statement (the center box in Figure 4-3) in the context of the other boxes or study components. The design questions whether sampling procedures will be used and how the sample will be drawn (see Hernon et al., 1989). More precisely, the evaluators ask and answer the following questions as part of design considerations:

- What is the population under investigation?
- How will a sample be drawn from the population?
- How large will that sample be?
- Where and when will the study be conducted?

In answering these questions, evaluators must interact with library managers and determine the extent to which the study provides research or management data.

Management or research data. The conduct of evaluation studies might be viewed from two different perspectives: management and research. The management perspective focuses more on utility of the findings to decision making and planning, rather than on understanding the phenomenon at a more basic conceptual level. Clearly, managers often have different requirements than do researchers. Most studies conducted in the social sciences are "error bound," which is to say that, regardless of the safeguards used, there is unexplained "error." The issues to be addressed in this context are:

- Identification of the likely sources of error
- Determination of how much error is acceptable, in a management context, for the collection of data useful for library planning and decision making.

Katzer, Cook, and Crouch (1990) discuss the various types of error and offer suggestions to minimize these errors. But, "statistical and sampling error" should not be confused with the utility of data for decision making and planning.

Management studies should attempt to produce as high quality data as possible. Yet, they might produce impressions open to wide interpretation. The more attention accorded to research strategies and data collection procedures, the more likely that more than impressionistic data will emerge. Perhaps an analogy might be useful. When taking a photograph with a sophisticated camera that requires complex settings, many people might be satisfied with a picture in which the primary target is off-center and perhaps somewhat out of focus. The question is "How much off-center and out of focus is the photographer willing to accept?" Of course, we might all like to have high-powered research data, but realistically we might be willing to accept something less. How much less?

Methodology

Simply explained, methodology is the means by which the evaluator collects data. Chapter 5 offers examples of different evaluation methodologies that have been used in library and information science.

Reliability and Validity

As shown in Chapter 5, reliability and validity concerns apply to both the evaluation design and methodology. Reliability seeks to determine the degree to which the data are consistent; consistency is the extent to which the same results are produced from different samples of the *same* population.

Validity refers to the extent to which study findings are generalizable to a population (external validity) or to which the study accurately measures what it purposes to measure (internal validity). Internal validity also asks whether the evaluator has the *correct* interpretation of the findings, or whether other factors, variables, or conditions had been considered or acknowledged.

If the reliability and internal validity of the data are limited, so too is the degree to which the findings can be generalized outside a particular setting. However, in many instances, evaluators will have little desire or interest in generalizing findings beyond their particular library.

As this brief discussion indicates, evaluators must be sure that decision makers understand reliability, internal validity, and external validity issues. External validity should be of less concern than ensuring that the study is examining what it intends to study. For example, some libraries are concerned about missing material and automatically equate missing material with stolen material. In fact, material might be misshelved, awaiting reshelving, etc., and not stolen. Evaluators should avoid the careless characterization of material as "stolen," if their methodologies do not enable them to isolate on one type of missing material, that which is stolen. Otherwise, the data have limited validity.

DATA COLLECTION, ANALYSIS, AND INTERPRETATION

Hernon and Richardson (1988) and Hernon et al. (1989) discuss data collection and the use of microcomputers and statistical software for analyzing large datasets. These works also discuss the use of statistics and data interpretation. Evaluators may want to collect data of greater usefulness than simply "descriptive" data. However, sophisticated data analysis and interpretation necessitate greater knowledge of the research process, types of data (nominal, ordinal, interval, and ratio), and decision making regarding the type of statistics most appropriate to the study (Swisher and McClure, 1984; Hernon et al., 1989).

REPORT WRITING

The real test of evaluation research is its impact on library decision making. The ultimate product, be it written or delivered orally, is less a contribution to existing knowledge in the literature than a tool to further change, planning, and decision making. The report therefore must be written to aid librarians in making formative and summative decisions about library activities and services.

The results of evaluation research must be communicated in such a way so as to assist decision makers and not to detract from decision making. Chapter 12 amplifies on this point and encourages greater attention to the presentation of findings and their value to improved library activities and services.

CHARTING PROJECT MANAGEMENT

A GANTT chart represents one type of project management. Project management software permits the identification and monitoring of project tasks. As needed, resources (e.g., people and money) can be shifted from one task to another, to ensure that deadlines and objectives are met. Further, different tasks can be compared and priorities constantly re-evaluated. Library decision makers may want to use such software. On the other hand, they could produce a handwritten or typed chart that highlights the tasks. A number of easy-to-use project management software tools are available and can greatly enhance the effectiveness of project design, tasking, and monitoring.

EXAMPLES FROM TWO STUDIES

This section highlights two studies, their reflective inquiry and procedures. Readers seeking more detailed insights into the study components, including indicators of reliability and validity, should examine the studies themselves—Hernon and McClure (1987b) and Hernon and Pastine (1977).

Unobtrusive Testing

Problem statement. Unobtrusive testing treats library staff as subjects and examines the accuracy of the responses that they make to reference questions. Such tests have explored government documents and general reference service, but they have not compared reference desk service between two library types and between staff members in two areas of the library.

Four primary benefits would result for the proposed study: (1) the effectiveness with which both library types provide access to U.S. government publications could be assessed; (2) recommendations and strategies could be offered for improving the effectiveness of depository libraries as providers of government publications and their information content; (3) library school educators teaching a course(s) in government documents, general or advanced reference, or the literature of the social or physical sciences could access their approach to teaching effective reference interviews and search strategies; and (4) the linking of findings to performance measures should have great appeal to those academic and public libraries adopting or planning to adopt such measures.

Literature review (part of it). Studies have shown that library personnel are not as successful in answering factual and bibliographic questions, posed either inperson or by telephone, as they suppose (see Hernon and McClure, 1987b, for a list of these studies). Typically, these studies have asked general reference staff members a few questions relating to government affairs. These questions, however, did not always prove easy to answer. In 1981, we administered, both by telephone and inperson, 20 pretested questions to government documents staff at 17 academic depository libraries in two states (McClure and Hernon, 1983).

Of all the studies using unobtrusive testing, this one produced the lowest percentage of correct answers. This finding alone suggests the need for further exploration and for drawing upon a larger geographical base. It also suggests that library administrators and educators should examine ways to enhance the ability of staff to answer questions correctly, to engage in referral services for questions which cannot be answered, and to determine patrons' actual information needs.

Logical structure. The study revolves around the use of unobtrusive testing to examine staff responses to questions of a factual and bibliographic nature. Such testing dates back to the 1960s when it was used in sociology, journalism, and librarianship (see Hernon and McClure, 1987b). *Correct answer fill rate*, which compares the number of questions answered correctly to the number asked, is a performance measure that has been shown to have face and construct validity (Ibid.).

As discussed in the problem statement, the evaluation study will examine the answers provided by the staffs of two library types and departments. For consistency with the existing body of research, the study will examine general reference and government documents departments and personnel in academic and public libraries.

The study might examine libraries in a particular community, state, or geographical region(s), or the nation as a whole. The decision was to make the study national in scope and to collect data in the spring, 1985.

Objectives. The objectives of this study are to:

- Identify the accuracy with which staff members from academic and public libraries answer pretested questions of a factual and bibliographic nature
- Identify the extent to which staff negotiate reference questions (will they elicit that a U.S. government publication is sought)

- Identify the factors contributing to the successful and unsuccessful answering of questions by depository library staff in terms of the reasons for incorrect answers, the extent and accuracy of referrals, the difficulty of the questions asked, and the duration of the reference process
- Compare the number of correct answers, as well as the reasons for incorrect answers, by library type, department, and geographical region
- Test general reference staff members from both academic and public libraries and assess the extent to which they identify a reference question as involving the use of government publications, and refer these questions to personnel of a separate documents department.

Hypotheses. For the purpose of this investigation, the objectives can be translated into formal hypotheses, guiding the collection and analysis of data. Examples of the hypotheses include:

- There is no statistically significant difference (at the 0.05 level) between:
  a. *Correct answer fill rate* of academic versus public library documents personnel
  b. *Correct answer fill rate* of academic versus public library general reference personnel
  c. *Correct answer fill rate* of academic documents and general reference staff members
  d. *Correct answer fill rate* of public documents versus general reference staff members
- There is no statistically significant difference (at the 0.05 level) between:
  a. *Correct answer fill rate* and the number of referrals made
  b. *Correct answer fill rate* and the accuracy of those referrals
  c. *Correct answer fill rate* and the ability to negotiate reference questions and determine that a government document was really sought.

These hypotheses apply to the first and fourth objectives. The second and third objectives might be refined as research questions. The final objective might be cast in terms of hypotheses, because it involves a comparison between two library types and departments.

Research design. Because this section only highlights the research design, readers requiring more detailed information should consult Hernon and McClure (1987b).

Twenty-six GPO depository libraries (13 academic and 13 public) were selected for investigation. Relying on the division of the United States used by the U.S. Bureau of the Census, the evaluators collapsed the 50 states into four geographical regions: the Northeast, Midwest, South, and West. Excluding the Northeast, this study examined eight libraries (four academic and four public) from each of the other three regions.

Using the *Statistical Abstract of the United States*, which the Bureau of Census produces, the evaluators generated a list of cities with a minimum of 100,000 inhabitants (as based on data derived from the 1980 Census of Population and Housing). Using *Government Depository Libraries*, produced by the U.S. congressional Joint Committee on Printing and the Government Printing Office, the evaluators had access to a current list of depository libraries. The evaluators produced a list of depository libraries for each city or town. Next, they listed those cities with at least 100,000 inhabitants having a minimum of one public depository library and one general academic depository library.

The evaluators randomly selected four cities from each census region and a public and academic library from each city. When a city had more than one general academic depository library, the evaluators selected the actual test site by consulting a table of random numbers.

The evaluators selected two libraries in the West as pretest sites and administered the questions unobtrusively to documents and general reference personnel at these libraries under actual test conditions. The test afforded a final opportunity to review the questions and testing procedures. Because no changes in the questions or in the administration procedures resulted, the evaluators incorporated data from both visits into the study findings.

Methodology. As already discussed, data were gathered from the use of unobtrusive testing. Hernon and McClure (1987a, b) assess the strengths and weaknesses of such testing and describe this method in detail.

Student Perceptions of Academic Librarians

This section highlights Hernon and Pastine (1977), a study centering on a knowledge void.

Problem statement and literature review. Studies have focused on faculty attitudes regarding librarian-faculty relationships and the extent of faculty awareness about the services that librarians offer. Librarians are often more aware of faculty than of student perceptions. In regard to student utilization of libraries, an examination of library literature indicates that the following points are repeatedly discussed and/or questioned: (1) assessments of student ability to use libraries, (2) how often and why students enter libraries, (3) the types of materials that students utilize, and (4) whether students believe that library use affects their scholastic achievement. The proposed research explores an area that the published research has neglected: student perceptions about the roles, duties, and functions of academic librarians.

Librarians do not completely comprehend the nature and extent of student perceptions about them and their role in the educational process. With the trend toward independent study, bibliographic instruction, and the application of psychology to reference desk service, precise knowledge of student perceptions and receptivity to the services that librarians provide is needed. Prior to upgrading students images of librarianship, the extent and types of misperceptions merit identification.

The findings of the studies previously identified illustrate the need for research methodologies aimed at more than just actual library users. Surveys should not rehash the same points but seek a deeper understanding of basic student perceptions. Line (1963, pp. 116–117) summarizes the need for in-depth research when he states:

> the use of attitude scales instead of rather crude categories is clearly desirable. Again, more satisfactory criteria of adequate or successful use of the library are required if librarians are to discover how far the barriers and difficulties they know to exist affect library use. A more sophisticated study could tell us much more about the library as the student sees it, and possibly help the librarians to see it with different eyes.

Logical structure. For a number of years, perception studies have frequently been conducted in the social and behavioral sciences. This investigation operates within the theoretical framework set by these studies and distinguishes between perceptions and attitudes.

The current investigation will center on the perceptions of college students about the role, duties, and functions of *librarians*. The focus therefore is on librarians as a subset of library staff. Can/do students distinguish between professional librarians and other members of the staff?

Similar to Figure 4-3, this study could examine students at one or more academic institutions. It might also include and contrast undergraduate and graduate students, full and part-time. As another possibility, special students might be examined.

Objectives and research questions. The objective is to delineate and codify student perceptions by type. The research questions are:

- Do students perceive the role of librarians, clerical, or student assistants as the same? The purpose of this question is to study student ability to distinguish among jobs
- Do students perceive librarians as service-oriented rather than teaching-oriented? The evaluators are interested in major accountabilities
- Do students believe that librarians do less than they actually do in terms of duties? The evaluators are interested in student awareness of the extent of librarian job duties.

Research design. The study population consisted of full-time students carrying at least 12 semester credit hours at the University of Nebraska at Omaha during the spring semester, 1975. Staff at the university computer center provided a computer program that randomly selected 700 names and addresses from current enrollment lists based on a proportionate percentage of names from each class level.

Although class level became the basis for sampling, data collection would explore the following variables: age (those 30 years old and younger, and those over 30), subject area (humanities, social sciences, physical sciences, and unclassified), gender, student purposes for using the library, the number of hours spent each week in using the library, and whether students had ever received a library lecture conducted through the classroom or a library orientation tour.

Methodology. The evaluators employed two methods of data collection: (1) questionnaire, and (2) interview. Interviews served as a cross-check on the questionnaire findings, as interview questions were taken directly from the questionnaire.

EVALUATION BASICS

The material presented in this chapter suggests the importance of a generalized approach for conducting evaluations. Chapter 2 summarizes such an approach. While evaluators may not complete each of the steps outlined in Figure 2-1, and different levels of effort might be applied to some of the steps rather than others, a general approach can be followed for conducting evaluations.

While "cookbook" strategies for conducting evaluations inevitably require fine-tuning and modification in light of specific and unique organizational needs and constraints, the basic steps for conducting any evaluation remain much the same. A key to conducting successful evaluations is following the *basic* steps, but modifying and refining those steps in light of local circumstances.

Novice evaluators would do well to work, initially, with a mentor, or someone who has had some experience in conducting evaluation research. The experience from each evaluation effort will make the next study easier to complete. Finally, it is well to remember that all evaluation research is likely to contain error. Despite the evaluator's best efforts, some error will creep into the evaluation. Understanding evaluation research basics, following a generalized model to conduct the evaluation, and seeking advice and counsel as novice evaluators conduct evaluation, however, can significantly reduce the amount of error.

DISCUSSION ITEMS

---

1. Develop a problem statement relating to burnout of library staff.
2. For the study of burnout, develop the rest of the reflective inquiry.
3. Write the procedures section for the burnout study.
4. Do the procedures provide for the collection of reliable and valid data?
5. Review the research design from the vantage point of both management and

research data. Which type of data would you actually collect if you were in charge of conducting the study. Discuss.

6. Define reliability and validity.
7. What might be some indicators of reliability and validity for the two example studies discussed in the last section of this chapter?
8. Provide the remaining hypotheses and research questions for the example on unobtrusive testing of general reference and government documents staff members in academic and public libraries.
9. Diagram the logical structure for the two examples, unobtrusive testing and student perceptions of academic librarians. As needed, examine Hernon and McClure (1987b, Chapters 2 and 3), and Hernon and Pastine (1977). Discuss the framework once it has been assembled.

Chapter Five
Evaluation Designs and Data Collection Techniques

A design provides the conceptual framework or plan for how and when data will be collected to address study objectives, research questions, and/or hypotheses. Thus, the design specifies who or what will be evaluated and under what conditions, the schedule for data collection, and whether the target population or a sample will be investigated. If a part of the population (a sample) is selected, the design identifies its composition and the criteria for selection of its members (see Figure 5-1). The design for an experiment often controls for extraneous variables and eliminates alternative hypotheses.

A methodology derives from the problem under investigation, study objectives, and the research questions or hypotheses. A methodology specifies the data collection instrument(s) and justifies the approach used to attack a problem. The purpose of this chapter is to provide an overview of evaluation designs and methodologies. Evaluators can select those designs and methodologies most appropriate for attacking local problems. Chapters 10 and 11 place designs and methodologies in a practical context—illustrative studies actually conducted in libraries to aid local decision making.

Part of the decision concerning which design and methodology to employ is based on whether library staff want to describe activities or attitudes (conduct a survey or observe use patterns), identify relationships between variables (test for correlations), or determine whether a particular treatment did or did not produce a change (undertake an experiment). Since much of the published literature discusses survey research, this chapter emphasizes experimentation and related methodologies; however, the chapter suggests instances where survey and correlational studies might be implemented.

The chapter contains four sections: (1) a classification of evaluation research, (2) criteria of relevance (internal and external validity, and reliability), (3) selected evaluation designs, and (4) selected methodologies, with an additional discussion of criteria of relevance. This introduction to methodologies provides a framework for Chapters 10 and 11.

CLASSES OF EVALUATION RESEARCH

Evaluation: A Systematic Approach (Rossi and Freeman, 1989), now in its fourth edition, provides a conceptual overview of evaluation research and designs. The

Figure 5-1. Evaluation Design: An Action Plan for Addressing Specific Research Issues

Who Is Studied
- Will it be the target population itself or sample of that population (how is the sample drawn so that it is representative of that population)?

- What variables or characteristics of the sample or population are important for hypothesis testing (e.g., age, class level, sex, or ethnic group)?

- Should any of these variables be *controlled* (at what level and how)?

- Will any of these variables *mask* other variables?

How will the sample or target population be studied
- What type of general design will be used (experimental, quasi-experimental, etc.)?

- Which specific design will be selected (e.g., Solomon Four)?

- How will study groups be randomized, matched, etc.?

Data collection
- When will the data be collected?

- By what means (methodology)?

Addressing Threats to Data
- What steps have been taken to ensure data reliability, validity, and utility?

first edition (Rossi, Freeman, and Wright, 1979) classified evaluation research into four categories, while the latest edition reorganized these categories into the ones depicted in Figure 5-2. Each category suggests a different level or type of evaluation study and design.

Performance measures comprise a means of determining the degree to which objectives are accomplished, services provided, and materials made available. They can be applied to each of the three types of evaluation activity outlined in the figure. Any performance measure employed, however, should be reliable, valid, and useful for effective library planning and decision making (see Chapter 8).

The classification of evaluation activities, combined with the use of performance measures, assists library staff members in deciding which library services and activities lend themselves to formal investigation. Further, a variety of methodologies can be used. Because program planning is useful in designing a prototype program or system, evaluators may conduct a community or needs assessment during this phase. In addition, the library reviews and modifies, as necessary, its goals and objectives.

Figure 5-2. Three Major Classes of Evaluation Research*

I. *Program Conceptualization and Design*
   This class relates to program planning and addresses the following types of questions:
   - Is a . . . problem appropriately conceptualized?
   - What is the extent of the problem and the distribution of the target population?
   - Is the program designed to meet its intended objectives?
   - Is there a coherent rationale underlying it?
   - Have chances of successful delivery been maximized?
   - What are the projected or existing costs?
   - What is the relationship between costs and benefits?

II. *Monitoring and Accountability of Program Implementation*
   This class deals with the following questions:
   - Did the program reach the specified target population?
   - Do the intervention efforts match the program design?
   The purpose is to ensure that the program provides the resources, services, and other benefits specified in the project design. Monitoring examines what occurred, while accountability compares "what is" to "what should be."

III. *Assessment of Program Effectiveness and Efficiency*
   This class addresses the extent to which a program produces the desired outcomes and examines program benefits in relation to their costs. Program utility encompasses both program impact (whether "a program causes change in the desired direction") and program efficiency. This class deals with the following questions:
   - Is the program effective in achieving its intended goals?
   - Can the results of the program be explained by some alternative process that does not include the program?
   - What are the costs to deliver services and benefits to program participants?
   - Is the program an efficient use of resources, compared with alternative uses of the resources?

* Peter H. Rossi and Howard E. Freeman, *Evaluation: A Systematic Approach*, pp. 44–52. Copyright 1989. Sage, Newbury Park, CA, 1989. Reprinted with permission. See also Rossi, Freeman, and Wright (1979, p. 33) for additional questions regarding the classification of evaluation research.

Program monitoring examines the extent of awareness that a target group has of a particular service or program, and reviews the scope of that program or service. The intent is to narrow or broaden the scope as necessary and to provide feedback to program conceptualization and design. Both program conceptualization and program monitoring can make extensive use of surveys, and do not require the controls exercised with impact assessment and the examination of program efficiency. Impact studies may require a sophisticated design so that a possible cause and effect relationship cannot be attributed to extraneous variables. "The critical issue in impact evaluation is whether or not a program produces effects different from what would have occurred either without the intervention or with an alternative intervention" (Rossi and Freeman, 1989, p. 231).

This chapter emphasizes the types of designs and methodologies useful for analyzing *impacts*. Library decision makers might be interested in economic efficiency and issues of cost-benefit and cost-effectiveness. To conduct an efficiency study, library staff members must determine direct and indirect, as well as immediate and long-term costs. The difference is that in one a monetary value is assigned to a program, service, or activity (cost-benefit), while in the other a precise monetary value cannot be calculated (cost-effectiveness).

Regardless of which category of evaluation research is undertaken, library staff must ensure that a study can be replicated and its validity verified. Evaluation is not merely a one-time examination of the effectiveness or efficiency of a particular program or service. Instead, evaluation is an ongoing, cyclical process whereby programs and services are examined individually and collectively to monitor interrelationships and to ensure that stated goals and objectives are met.

Replication necessitates that accurate and complete records be maintained, that consistency in findings be available from sample to sample of a target population (reliability), and that data collection instruments, in fact, measure what they are supposed to measure (validity). Reliability and validity should be addressed when evaluators develop both research designs and methodologies. Too often these concerns receive insufficient attention. In instances where staff want to generalize study findings to a larger setting, they must include appropriate safeguards in the design to ensure the collection of high-quality data.

CRITERIA OF RELEVANCE

Criteria of relevance refer to reliability and validity issues. Any evaluation design, as well as the data obtained from an evaluation study, most likely contain inherent limitations and potential biases. By the use of random assignment to control and experimental groups, employment of statistical analyses, and attention to issues of validity, these limitations usually can be minimized and their possible impacts reduced. Library personnel conducting an evaluation project must be aware of such factors and take the necessary precautions—especially when producing *research* as opposed to *management* data.

Internal validity, which concerns itself with the extent to which researchers measure what they intend to measure, raises a key issue: Valid for what purpose? As Cronback has noted, the measuring instrument is not validated. Rather, the *use* of that instrument for a particular purpose is: "one validates . . . an interpretation of data arising from a specified procedure" (1971, p. 447). External validity examines the generalizability of the design and findings to a population.

Internal Validity

Internal validity is concerned with whether a treatment caused "any change in the outcome as measured" (Mark and Cook, 1984, p. 75). Conclusions regarding causal relationships become possible when threats to validity have been rendered implausible. More simply, internal validity indicates that the program or service did, in fact, produce the observed outcome.

Evaluation studies explore relationships between (and among) variables. Variables, which comprise "things that are measured and represent the concepts studied" (Spector, 1981, p. 11), exist in different forms:

- A *dependent* variable explains, or is used to measure, observable behavior (e.g., an attitude change). This variable is dependent on or influenced by the independent variable
- An *independent* variable, which is frequently equated with the treatment, is manipulated so that its effect on the outcome and dependent variable can be observed. The independent variable determines, influences, or produces the change. In those designs dealing with a determination of casual relationships, the causes become independent variables and the effects are dependent variables. When variables are not manipulated, a distinction between cause and effect becomes impossible
- *Control* variables are held constant or randomized so that their effects are neutralized or "controlled." Examples include age and sex.

For an excellent discussion (offering examples of these as well as other kinds of variables) see Chapter 4 of Tuckman (1978).

Internal validity "is essentially a problem of control"—eliminating those variables which suggest alternative explanations or which prevent the identification of causal relationships (Ary, Jacobs, and Razavieh, 1985, p. 261). Campbell and Stanley (1963, and 1966, p. 5) have identified the following eight factors as possible threats to the internal validity of an evaluation or research design:

- *History* raises the issue that some factor, other than the independent variable, accounted for the change in the dependent variable. For example, the length

of time between conducting the pretest and posttest may have a detrimental effect
- *Maturation* suggests that the change resulted from biological or psychological processes, which occurred over time, and not from the treatment itself. As with history, maturation becomes more of a concern the longer the period between the pretest and posttest
- *Pretesting* may affect the dependent variable; pretesting may alert participants or educate them about the topic under investigation. Therefore, if subjects are administrated a posttest, their performance may reflect a marked improvement due to the fact that they were pretested; improvement may not be a result of manipulation of the independent variable. For this reason, some of the evaluation designs discussed later in the chapter either avoid the use of a pretest or administer a pretest to one control group but not to another
- *Measuring instruments* or observational techniques, rather than the treatment itself, might account for change in the dependent variable, if they are not sufficiently compatible. Further, the validity of the study findings may have been influenced by the fact that the evaluators as observers, raters, graders, interviewers, and coders gained experience, became tired, obtained a more complete understanding of the project, or eased their expectations of test subjects
- *Statistical regression* "refers to the tendency for extreme scores to regress or move toward the common mean on subsequent measures" (Ary, Jacobs, and Razavieh, 1985, p. 262). The assignment of subjects to a particular test group on the basis of extreme views may affect study findings. Extreme scores from a sample may well move toward the common mean, as repeated samples are drawn. The change may be interpreted as a consequence of the treatment employed, when, in fact, the change resulted from statistical regression
- A nonrandom assignment of *subjects* to groups might signify that the groups were dissimilar from the beginning. Therefore, any change might be attributed to the differential selection of subjects, rather than the actual treatment received
- *Mortality* refers to the possibility that some subjects may have dropped out of the study after completion of the pretest but before the administration of the posttest. In such instances, every effort should be made to identify any common patterns or characteristics to ensure that any difference between a group's pretest and posttest scores cannot be attributed to the loss of subjects
- More than one of the seven possible threats might be active at once and produce an *interaction*. This is especially likely in those cases where subjects were not randomly assigned to groups and the evaluation was based on existing, intact groups.

Chapter 4 of *Unobtrusive Testing and Library Reference Services* (Hernon and McClure, 1987b) provides an example of an experimental design that attempted to control for a range of factors to increase internal validity. Individuals were randomly assigned to intervention groups, and the evaluators took precautions to ensure that outside factors did not have an impact on the investigation of study objectives and the interpretation of hypotheses and research questions.

External Validity

External validity, which is concerned with the generalizability or representativeness of study findings, addresses the question "To what extent are the findings generalizable to the *population* or other *environmental settings*, within known limits of sampling error?" While internal validity can be enhanced by random assignment to treatment or control groups, external validity addresses the representativeness of the sample compared to the larger population. As Lincoln and Guba observe, "the criteria of internal and external validity are placed in a trade-off position by their definition." Elaborating on this point, they explain that "if, for the sake of control (internal validity), strenuous laboratory conditions are imposed, then the results are not generalizable to any contexts except those that approximate the original laboratory" (1985, p. 291).

External validity examines: "(1) the fit between the desired target population and the sample actually achieved at the end of an evaluation, and (2) whether the treatment effect is similar across various kinds of persons, settings, and times" (Mark and Cook, 1984, p. 71). Thus, external validity is threatened if the sample studied does not match characteristics of the target population or if the evaluator does not discover an interaction between the treatment and its impact on what was studied (Ibid.).

The external validity of a study can be increased by the use of sampling techniques that examine characteristics similar to those of the target population. Such techniques might be based on random sampling, stratified random sampling, quota sampling, or another method (see, for example, Chapter 6 and/or Slonim, 1960; General Accounting Office, 1986; and Powell, 1985, pp. 69–79 for a discussion of sampling techniques). A sample might draw together individuals of diverse backgrounds, achievement levels, aptitudes, or places of residence or work.

For example, a cross-institutional study of academic libraries in the South might include schools representing different degree programs, affiliations, geographical locations (e.g., suburbs, inner city, and rural settings), as well as those known as centers of learning and as "party" schools. The more diverse the spectrum of libraries and institutions included, the greater the opportunity there is to gauge the effect of a treatment across subgroups of students and settings. However, the more components to the sampling frame, the larger the sample size must be. In addition, more factors must be controlled and monitored.

Library staff are often less concerned with the generalizability of evaluation findings to other institutions or geographical settings. Instead, they want to generalize their findings to a part of the clientele served by the library (e.g., all the college students enrolled in freshman English or all the residents of a particular neighborhood) or to the entire community of current and potential library users.

Certain factors can threaten the external validity of a study. As was already noted, these are grouped into either population or ecological validity. The former is concerned with generalizability to subjects of other populations and whether the characteristics of the subjects receiving a particular treatment inhibit generalizations to other groups. For example, programmed instruction that an academic or public library has developed to explain the use of an online catalog might be more effective for people of a particular grade, educational, or reading level, or for people having certain abilities.

Population validity is also an important concern in those instances in which the population from which evaluators select subjects differs from the population to which they want to generalize. For example, library staff might test programmed instruction on high school students but want to generalize the findings to all user groups. To display wider generalizability, the programmed instruction would have to be tested on different user groups.

Ecological validity addresses the generalizability of study findings to other environmental conditions (e.g., changes in physical setting, time of day, or evaluators). Threats to this type of validity exist when:

- Insufficient insights into the design and procedures of a study exist to permit replication
- Participants' awareness that they are receiving special treatment encourages them to either perform better than they normally might or respond in a certain way (the Hawthorne effect)
- The behavior, expectations, or appearance of the evaluators affects participants' performance or responses to data collection instruments
- The perception of a treatment as new or unusual influences participant motivation and performance.

Change resulting from the treatment may decline as the novelty of that treatment decreases. For example, students unfamiliar with computers might be attracted to computer-assisted instruction explaining the use of reference aids (e.g., abstracting/indexing services such as *Psychological Abstracts*). However, as student opportunity to own or use microcomputers increases, the attraction of computer-assisted instruction may substantially decrease. In addition, a pretest may facilitate learning, increase participants' awareness about the problem under investigation, or give subjects an opportunity to reflect about the issue.

LeCompte and Goetz (1982) summarize the threats to external validity by their effect on:

- *Selection*: Study findings only pertain to a single group, or the researcher selects groups to study for which the findings do not apply
- *Setting*: Study findings pertain to the context under investigation
- *History*: Unique historical experiences may militate against comparisons
- *Constructs*: The constructs under investigation may be peculiar to the group studied. This category refers to the inferences drawn from conceptual evidence. Conceptual confirmation is important when empiricial confirmation of validity is difficult or impossible to determine (see also Lin, 1976, p. 173).

Evaluators wanting to generalize their study findings should incorporate strategies in the study design and method that minimize threats to both internal and external validity, to the best extent feasible.

Reliability

Reliability is the extent to which the same results are produced on repeated samples of the same population. Reliability is concerned with replication and the consistency, stability, or accuracy from measurement to measurement. Common methods used to test for reliability include: *test/retest*, *alternative form*, and *split halves*.

For the test/retest method, the same test is administered to the same individuals or group after a certain period of time. Based on the two sets of scores for each person, a correlation coefficient is computed. A high relationship between the two indicates data reliability (see Hernon et al., 1989, Chapter 8). The problem, though, is that threats to internal validity (e.g., history, pretesting, and maturation) may arise.

With the alternative form method, the same people encounter two testing situations. In approximately two weeks after the completion of the initial test, perhaps they are given an alternative form of the same test. Since the same test is not administered both times, a person's recall of the original test situation is lessened. The problem with this method is that it is difficult to construct two parallel forms of the test having the same purpose.

Unlike the other methods, the split-half method can be conducted on one occasion. One approach is to have two or three questions that measure the same variable on one test and then, from all of the responses, determine the degree to which each person answered all three questions correctly. This way, evaluators can have reliability estimates on different variables on the same test.

Another approach is to divide the total number of test items in half, with the correlation of the scores between the two halves offering the estimate of reliability. The division of a test into half is comparable to the development of an alternative form of the same test. To use this method, however, data collection measures one variable. When a class receiving bibliographic instruction is administered a set of 20 questions related to knowledge of the card catalog and basic indexes, a correlation between the first and second 10 questions for each student indicates reliability for the test scores.

The methods discussed in this section examine internal consistency, or the interrelationships among the components of a data collection instrument. If different people score a test, or code the data collection instrument for computer or manual analysis, a purpose of reliability is to determine that they did, in fact, score or code in a similar manner. This type of reliability is called scorer (or interscore) reliability. Specific statistical tests (e.g., Cronbach's alpha and Kuder- Richardson formula 20 and 21) test for reliability. For further discussion of reliability, or examples of the various statistical tests, see works such as Ary, Jacobs, and Razavieh (1985, pp. 229–237) and Borg and Gall (1983).

EVALUATION DESIGNS

This section emphasizes the employment of experimental, quasi-experimental, and descriptive designs, but does not detail or diagram any of these designs using statistical terminology. The purpose, rather, is to present each of them simply so that library staff can make comparisons and determine which ones might have the most application to their situation.

The designs discussed in this section examine *impact assessments* and whether an intervention or treatment produced its intended effect. They look at the impact of the treatment, or independent variable, once all confronting effects (those masking the true effects of an intervention and competing with the intervention measures to explain any changes, in the target population, which occurred after the program began) have been removed or controlled.

Impact evaluation must be systematic and rigorous if the effects of both measurement errors and chance are to be minimized and the estimate of effectiveness maximized (Rossi and Freeman, 1982, p. 165). Figure 5-3 graphically depicts the components required for measuring the impact of a program or service. Taking measurement error and chance into account necessitates an understanding of elementary statistics and concepts such as standard deviation—the amount of variation of a sample mean from the mean of the population (see Hernon et al., 1989, Chapter 5).

Formative and summative evaluation may require different designs, because one provides feedback to modify or improve a program or service in operation, while the other examines the effectiveness and efficiency of a completed activity. Depending on the particular objective, the evaluation design might lead to a survey for measuring opinions, attitudes, or perceptions; an experiment for gauging the impact of a treatment; correlations for investigating the amount of variation between similar factors; or a comparison whereby evaluators observe consequences and examine the data for plausible causation.

The choice of an appropriate design also depends on constraints of time,

Figure 5-3.   The Components of Impact Assessment*

IMPACT = Net outcome or results attributed
to the intervention

MINUS

Confounding factors (extraneous variables that obscure or
exaggerate the actual effects of an intervention).
Confounding factors involve threats to reliability
and validity, internal and external

PLUS OR MINUS

The effect of chance, random fluctuations; or
measurement error

* Adapted from Rossi and Freeman (1989, Chapter 5, "Strategies for Impact Assessment")
and (1982, p. 174). Peter H. Rossi and Howard E. Freeman, *Evaluation: A Systematic Approach.*
Copyright 1989. Sage, Newbury Park, CA, 1989. Reprinted with permission.

finances, human and material resources, and political concerns. Based on the
evaluators' assessment of the constraints, they select the design most appropriate
to the problem, objectives, and level of available expertise. If they cannot meet
the requirements of an experimental design, they might opt for a quasi-
experimental design; such a design offers neither complete control over the
scheduling of experimental conditions nor the ability to randomize subjects (Ary,
Jacobs, and Razavieh, 1985, p. 282). If a quasi-experimental design is too labor
intensive, evaluators might prefer the survey approach and a description of
attitudes, etc. A survey indicates if recipients of a treatment believe that they
benefited from that treatment. A survey also assesses their general awareness of a
program or service, suggests the extent to which they used the program or service
and if they might use it in the future, and provides insights into information
transfer and what they believed they learned.

Experimental and quasi-experimental designs frequently require the use of a
control group. A control group consists of subjects who either do not receive the
treatment or intervention, or receive the usual or standard treatment, while the
experimental group is selected for special treatment. Control groups perform a
useful purpose; they invite comparison to the group receiving treatment and offer
support to the conclusion that observed change resulted from the treatment and
not the normal maturation process which occurs with individuals and organizations (or to other validity threats as well).

Library staff exploring the impact of a program or service might not have access to a sufficient number of study participants to justify the inclusion of a control group and a couple of treatment groups. For example, 21 reference personnel from two departments of one library participated in an experiment testing the impact of two treatments upon their reference desk performance (see Hernon and McClure, 1987b, Chapter 4). Inclusion of a control group would have required even more participants. Many libraries, however, may lack the personnel, resources, or time to conduct large scale testing using a control and different treatment groups.

Instead of employing a control group, evaluation studies might use a *comparison group*, which seek to determine whether a particular treatment produced the desired outcome more effectively, or more efficiently, than an alternative method. The purpose, therefore, is to test and compare different methods, and to see which is the most effective or efficient. Depending on the particular objectives, a third type of group might be employed. Two groups having different competencies, attitudes, or perceptions might be selected and contrasted.

An example of the use of *contrasting groups* would be to take a group of professional, library reference staff members and to contrast their ability to answer a set of factual and bibliographic reference questions, with a group of paraprofessional personnel. The purpose is to see which group answers the questions more accurately and quickly. If paraprofessional personnel perform well, library administrators might assign fewer librarians to reference desk service or have professionals concentrate more on time-consuming and complex questions, and less on directional and ready reference questions.

Experimental Design

An experimental design aids in ruling out rival explanations and extraneous variables, and is the most likely to protect against threats to internal validity. To have a truly experimental design, library staff must be able to assign subjects to control, comparison, or contrasting groups *randomly*, manipulate the independent variable (intervention) and observe its effect on the dependent variable (subjects), decide which groups will be measured, and determine the timing of the observation or measurement.

Randomization ensures that the groups under investigation are similar and that any difference between them is due to the treatment (independent variable) and not to the participants themselves, e.g., their age, sex, or level of education. Randomization may be achieved by either random selection or random assignment. In the former, each person in the population has an equal chance of being selected to participate in the study, while the latter involves the random placement of subjects in a control or treatment group.

Rossi and Freeman (1989, pp. 304–306) summarize limitations on the use of randomized experiments. They note, for instance, that such studies are costly

Figure 5-4. Impact of a Program/Service Involving an Experimental Design

IMPACT =

Outcome of experimental group receiving the treatment

MINUS

Outcome of the control group

MINUS

Threats to internal and external validity

PLUS OR MINUS

Fluctuations attributed to chance and
measurement error

and time-consuming to conduct, require extensive controls on selection and treatments, and may not have significant generalizability. Yet such research is the flagship of evaluation and offers the best conclusions in regard to the different classes of evaluation research (see Figure 5-2).

Instead of using randomization, evaluators might achieve equivalence by systematic assignment from serialized lists, provided that the ordering of these lists does not produce bias (Rossi and Freeman, 1989, p. 287; 1982, p. 211). By this method, students might be assigned to a group based on whether their college identification number ended in an odd or even digit. However, prior to using this method, the evaluators would have to determine that the institution did not assign numbers to students in a biased way. For example, they would want to ascertain, prior to adopting this method, that female students did not receive odd numbers and male students the even numbers (Ibid.).

Figure 5-4 characterizes how the impact of a study using an experimental design is determined. The outcome for either the experimental or control group might be determined by measuring the differences between the scores of the pretest and posttest, and then taking into account threats to internal validity, chance, and measurement error. Having this depiction in mind, library staff can decide:

• Whether the experimental method and its requirements are most appropriate
• The type of experimental design to employ

- The need to control threats to validity and determine the amount of fluctuation attributed to chance.

Various types of experimental designs exist and have potential application to libraries and information centers. These designs either use a combination of pretest and posttest, or bypass the pretest in preference to a posttest. They may also employ one or more control and experimental groups, and vary the type of test given with each.

With the *pretest-posttest design*, evaluators randomly assign subjects to a control and experimental group, and administer a pretest to both groups. Some time after the experimental group has received the treatment, they give both groups a posttest. The outcome in *mean* scores for both groups, minus the factors identified in Figure 3-4, indicates the extent of program effectiveness. Mortality, whereby participants drop out, is probably the major, potential problem (Figure 5-5, part A). Evaluators must ensure that both the pretest and posttest are administered in the same way, and that both groups have minimal contact with each other.

A variation of this design would be to have both groups receive different treatments, but not to use one as a control group. The differential effects of both forms of the treatment would then be compared (Figure 5-5, part B). For example, library staff participating in bibliographic instruction programs might not have a control group. Instead, they might compare computer-assisted instruction to print program instruction (e.g., guides or workbooks).

Library staff wanting to use a control group might be interested in a variation of the first design. Because pretests may affect participants' behavior or attitudes in some way, the pretest-posttest design might be modified so that the control group only receives either the pretest or posttest (Figure 5-5, part C). It is also possible that neither the control nor experimental group would take the pretest. The two groups might even be exposed to different forms of the same treatment, with the measurement being in the form of a posttest.

The *Solomon four-group design* is based on the premise that the pretest sensitizes participants to the treatment. If this premise has merit, study results cannot be generalized (external validity) and the treatment could not be administered to people who had not received the pretest (internal validity). With this design, subjects are randomly assigned to four groups. Two of these groups receive the treatment and the posttest, while a third experimental group benefits from the treatment, but completes both the pretest and posttest. A control group receives both tests as well (Figure 5-5, part D). This design controls for threats to internal validity.

Another option is a *pretest-posttest design for many groups*, whereby subjects are randomly assigned to three or more groups. Each group, then, receives the pretest, a treatment, and the posttest (Figure 5-5, part E). Again, variations in the administration of the pretest and posttest are possible. There might be a com-

Figure 5-5. Types of Experimental Designs

PART A: Pretest/Posttest Design (with Control Group)

	Pretest	Treatment	Posttest
Experiment	yes	yes	yes
Control Group	yes	no	yes

Impact of Program/Service is the difference from the posttest and pretest for the experimental group and the difference from the posttest and pretest for the control group. Evaluators should consider threats to validity, chance, and possible measurement errors.

PART B: Pretest/Posttest Design (without Control Group)

	Pretest	Treatment	Posttest
Experiment A	yes	yes	yes
Experiment B	yes	yes	yes

Impact of Program/Service is the difference from the posttest and pretest for Experiment A and the difference between the posttest and pretest of Group B. Evaluators would consider threats to validity, chance, or possible measurement error.

PART C: Pretest/Posttest Design (with Control Group). The control group, however, does not receive both the pretest and posttest.

	Pretest	Treatment	Posttest
Experiment	yes	yes	yes
Control Group	maybe	no	maybe

(The control group receives *either* the pretest or the posttest, but *not* both.)

Impact of Program/Service is the difference between the posttest and pretest for the experimental group, and a comparison of this score to the pretest or posttest of the control group. Evaluators would also consider threats to validity, chance, or possible measurement error.

PART D: Solomon Four-Group Design

	Before	Treatment	After
Experiment 1	no	yes	yes
Experiment 2	no	yes	yes
Experiment 3	yes	yes	yes
Control Group	yes	no	yes

Impact of Program/Service is determined from a comparison of pretests and posttests, as well as a comparison of the four posttests. Evaluators would be sensitive to threats to validity, chance, or possible measurement error.

Figure 5-5.—*(Continued)*

PART E: Pretest-Posttest Design (for Many Group)

	Pretest	Treatment	Posttest
Experiment 1	yes	yes	yes
Experiment 2	yes	yes	yes
Experiment 3	yes	yes	yes

Impact of Program/Service is determined from a comparison of the three pretests and posttests, as well as the posttests by themselves. Evaluators would be sensitive to threats to validity, chance, and measurement error.

---

parison of "the original 'model' program and a naturally evolving version of it." Program participants could be divided into two subgroups, "one of which remains stable and the other of which is encouraged 'to improve continually' on the basis of best opinion" (Weiss, 1972, p. 65). As noted by Weiss (Ibid.),*

> The experimental method does not require a stable program. It can be used even when the program meanders. If there is interest in the effects of a program under developmental conditions or in its usual nonstandardized form, randomized designs are perfectly suitable for studying outcomes.

Additional experimental designs are possible; however, these involve the use of sophisticated statistical measures (factorial and repeated measures). Their sophistication, both in terms of design and statistical manipulation, may well be beyond the budget, time constraints, and skills of many librarians. For these reasons such designs will not be presented here. However, authors such as Kerlinger (1973, 1986) and Kirk (1968) describe them.

As this section has stressed, experimental designs most typically require the random assignment of subjects to groups. For some problems confronting evaluators in library and information science (other than those relating to the preservation of library materials), randomization is not feasible. Instead, evaluators must work with intact groups or place participants in groups by matching them on some attribute. However, with matching, evaluators can only be certain that the participants in each group are similar to the characteristic matched. Further, the threats to internal validity increase. For these reasons, library staff must carefully select the appropriate design, be aware of its strengths and weaknesses, and determine if they want management or research data.

---

* Carol H. Weiss. *Evaluation Research: Methods for Assessing Program Effectiveness*, pp. 65. Copyright © 1972. Prentice-Hall, Englewood Cliffs, NJ. Reprinted by permission.

Quasi-Experimentation

Evaluation designs rarely occur in a laboratory setting but do address practical questions. An experiment monitors change or the impact of the independent variable (treatment) on the dependent variable. Evaluators exercise control when they make observations or take measurements, and when they give a treatment to a group. When the random assignment of subjects to a group does not occur, and increased validity threats are potentially present, evaluators engage in quasi-experimentation. They probe, but do not prove, causal relationships. Inferences presume that a particular interpretation of the data is the most plausible. If both relevant theory and sound procedures have been followed, the likelihood of alternative explanations has been significantly reduced. A causal relationship is accepted as provisionally true, until or unless a better explanation later emerges.

Where the quasi-experimental design is weak, the findings are subject to varied interpretation. In such cases (especially for summative evaluation of an entire program or service), evaluators might adopt a multiple methods approach and employ different methods of data collection.

In quasi-experimental designs, evaluators match groups so that the groups share some similar characteristics. Matching is done on either an individual or aggregate basis. The former is usually preferable because greater attention is given to the characteristics matched; however, greater knowledge about individuals and their characteristics is required. Matching on an individual basis, therefore, becomes more time-consuming and costly.

Matching is not a substitute for randomization. Misleading results may emerge when the participants represent different populations. The possibility of *statistical regression* becomes a major threat to internal validity. Another danger is self-selection, or letting people choose to participate or enter a group. Self-selection is likely to produce people dissimilar from others in the population (Weiss, 1972, pp. 70–72). Weiss offers relevant observations and points out that a true experiment requires the assignment of volunteers to control and experimental groups.

Matching on the basis of one or more attributes ignores the impact that other attributes might have. As Weiss (1972, pp. 69–70) notes, there might be matching on age, sex, race, and IQ, but the important factor (motivation) might have been unmatched. However, if the key characteristic for matching was known beforehand, there would probably be no need to carry out the study. To enhance the statistical precision of the study, evaluators might match on some attributes and then initiate random assignment to a group.

If matching is not feasible, evaluators use intact groups (e.g., classes). These groups should be as similar as possible, with the similarities verified by a pretest. Still, evaluators must keep in mind various threats to internal validity, such as pretesting, and compensate for them.

The description of experimental designs in Figure 5-4 is also applicable here.

The impact of the program or service is determined from the outcome minus the validity threats, the measurement error, and the fluctuations attributed to chance. As has been emphasized, the likelihood of an outcome being influenced by threats to validity, and chance, increases with quasi-experimentation or the descriptive designs presented later in the chapter. Experimental designs tend to have high validity, while quasi-experiments have moderate validity, and other designs have limited validity.

Quasi-experimental designs frequently use pretest and posttest measures in a time series so that treatments are removed or reintroduced at different times. Similar to the pretest-posttest control group, described in the section on experimental designs, the *nonequivalent control group* compares two similar groups before and after the exposure of one group to a treatment (Figure 5-6, part A). Although the groups are intact and participants are not randomly assigned to a group, evaluators can randomly assign a treatment to one group.

Evaluators might take intact groups and randomly assign participants to two subgroups, each of which receives a different treatment. Perhaps one group is investigated prior to the treatment. Both groups receive the treatment, but only the one which was not pretested is measured or observed after the treatment.

Measures such as these offset the major threats to internal validity—selection and statistical regression. The intent is to make the comparison group as similar to the experimental group as possible. The greater the number of similarities (e.g., enrolled in alternative sections of the same course taught by the same instructor, or performing in a similar fashion on a pretest), the better is the comparison between the groups. Any lack of similarity between the groups understates or overstates the program outcome, and should be incorporated in the analysis of the findings.

A *time-series design* involves the taking of repeated observations or measurements before and after the treatment has been given (Figure 5-6, part B). In this way, any change in the dependent variable is observed over time, and evaluators have access to longitudinal data. Repeated testing serves as a check to some threats of internal validity—maturation, testing, and statistical regression—but not to history; some factor other than the treatment might have served as the change agent.

There are a number of variations of the time-series design. Many of these do not require the use of a control group; however, the presence of such a group reduces threats to internal validity. For example, prior to and after the initiation of one treatment, evaluators draw repeated measurements in order to document any change in the dependent variable. Evaluators either periodically reinstate the same treatment or follow it with subsequent treatments. Furthermore, after they apply the first treatment, evaluators might give the second one without removing the first treatment.

An interrupted time-series employing "switching replications" enhances external validity and controls for most threats to internal validity. Two nonequiva-

Figure 5-6.   Depiction of Designs for Quasi-Experiments

PART A: Nonequivalent Control Group

	Pretest	Treatment	Posttest
Experiment	yes	yes	yes
Control	yes	no	yes

Impact of Program/Service is determined from finding the difference between posttest and pretest for the experimental group and comparing this score to the difference between the posttest and pretest for the control group. Evaluators must consider threats to validity, measurement error, and chance.

PART B: Time-Series Design

	Pre-test	Treat-ment	Post-test	Pre-test	Treat-ment	Post-test	Pre-test	etc.
Experiment	yes	yes	yes	yes	yes	yes	yes	....
Control Group	yes	no	yes	yes	no	yes	yes	....

Impact of Program/Service is determined by giving the experimental group and the control group repeated pretests and posttests, and then comparing the scores of the two groups. Evaluators would also consider threats to validity, measurement error, and chance.

PART C: Pretest/Posttest Design

	Pretest	Treatment	Posttest
Experiment 1	yes	yes	yes
Experiment 2	yes	yes	yes
Experiment 3	yes	yes	yes
Experiment 4	yes	yes	yes

Impact of Program/Service is determined by taking the posttest and pretest scores for each group, determining the differences, and comparing them. Evaluators would also consider threats to validity, measurement error, and chance.

lent groups thereby receive the treatment but at different times. By continuing the process and rotating treatments between the two groups, each group at different points serves as the control (Mark and Cook, 1984, p. 113).

Figure 5-6, part C, suggests that evaluators might compare the effectiveness of different treatments through the use of both a pretest and posttest. Because this design does not employ a control group, evaluators are more interested in an analysis of different treatments than in a comparison of treatments to a control group that did not receive a treatment.

Descriptive Designs

The *pseudoexperimental* is another type of design. Lacking built-in controls, it cannot rule out rival explanations for change, or the lack of change, in the dependent variable. This design also does not provide satisfactory controls to minimize threats to internal validity. However, for small projects for which quickly and inexpensively gathered data are needed (especially those comprising *formative* evaluation research), this design may have some merit. If the project has importance and is *summative* in nature, and if there is sufficient time to collect and analyze the data, staff might use one of the aforementioned, more rigorous designs.

Three examples of pseudoexperimental designs are the *one-shot case study*, *one-group pretest and posttest*, and the *intact-group comparison*. The first design is descriptive, exposes a group to a treatment, and measures the impact. The problem with this approach is that there is no control or comparison group and that evaluators must surmise the attitudes, competencies, etc., of the group before the treatment.

With the one-group pretest and posttest, observations are made before and after the group received the treatment. Although this approach marks an improvement over the previous design, it neither offers a control group nor satisfactorily minimizes threats to internal validity. As a result, rival explanations for the change, or the lack thereof, in the dependent variable are not eliminated.

The intact-group comparison involves the location of two intact groups, the administration of a treatment to one group but not the other, and the administration of a pretest and posttest to both groups. The control group might receive only the pretest or posttest. The weaknesses to this design are twofold: (1) subjects are not randomly assigned to groups, and (2) the groups may not be equivalent. If change in the dependent variable occurs, rival interpretations are not eliminated.

Other descriptive designs involve the use of a survey, observation of a phenomenon, or examination of historical records. All of these involve the identification and isolation of a problem; the development of a hypothesis; the collection, classification, and analysis of data; and the attempt to eliminate alternative explanations.

Many descriptive designs involve *case studies*, which represent an intensive, in-depth investigation of an individual, practice, or procedure to discover those variables important to its history or development. Evaluators can take the results gathered from case studies and see if the interpretation made is applicable to other situations (Yin, 1984, 1989). Where this approach is used, staff, nonetheless, should be cautious about drawing inferences to other groups.

In some cases, library staff members cannot assign subjects to a group or manipulate the independent variable. Perhaps, the changes in the independent variable have already occurred, and they want to study historical records to discern its effect on the dependent variable. Obviously this type of study requires some insights into the evaluation design that was employed and the validity threats possibly encountered.

Ex post facto studies require caution in the interpretation of results. Nonetheless, in some instances, staff members want to explore previously implemented services and programs prior to the implementation of a new program. For example, they might want to implement a current awareness service for faculty members. However, in the planning stages, they discover that previous staff, five years ago, had experimented with such a service. Therefore, prior to the implementation of the new service, they would want to investigate the historical records in an effort to determine if the experiment had been successful—or if not, why?

DATA COLLECTION TECHNIQUES

The methodologies used to generate the collection of data emerge from the problem statement, objectives, and hypotheses/research questions under investigation. Other influencing factors might be constraints of time, money, and staff. Numerous possible methodologies exist and have application to evaluation research. The purpose of this section is to: (1) highlight basic methodologies, (2) raise key issues relating to the use of statistics (selection of the appropriate test for data analysis, the level of significance, and types of errors), and (3) further discuss criteria of relevance (validity and reliability), but in the context of methodologies.

Basic Techniques

Figure 3-1 identifies research methods textbooks that present and assess different methodologies. One section of that figure suggests writings that discuss the development of survey instruments.

Common methods for data collection include:

- *Testing (standardized or locally developed tests).* Examples of writings using this methodology include Toifel and Davis (1983) and Hardesty and Wright (1982)
- *Self-rating of a project's impact from participants.* The success of numerous conferences is often determined from the opinions of participants about which meetings they liked and disliked. Johnson and Mann (1980) identify examples of studies based on a self-assessment process implemented by library staff
- *Assessment of a program's effectiveness by experts making site visits.* McCart (1983) used a modification of this approach. She employed social judgment

analysis; she studied policy decisions and drew inferences based on the types of judgments that people might have made in a given situation. A more direct use of this methodology is where library staff invite outside experts, perhaps persons familiar with medical literature, to evaluate a specific collection and offer recommendations for improving its quality

- *Response to a questionnaire or interview.* Alzonton and Van Pulis (1984), and Urquhart and Schofield (1972), are among the many researchers who have employed a questionnaire or conducted an interview
- *Focus group interviews.* These comprise a type of group interview whereby people come together and provide information on highly focused issues or problems. Group members interact and the researcher assumes the role of an impartial moderator (Krueger, 1988; Morgan, 1988)
- *Observation of behavior and the impact of that behavior on programs and services.* For example, Kenney (1966) used a similar approach to investigate the use of a card catalog. Participant observation, a type of observation, has the observer being accepted by those observed. In other words, those observed go about their normal routines while accepting the presence of the observer. Jorgensen (1989) shows the application of this methodology for describing everyday activities
- *Unobtrusive evaluation* (or the testing of staff members unaware that they are being tested). Using this methodology, Myers and Jirjees (1983) studied academic reference librarians, while McClure and Hernon (1983) examined documents personnel in academic libraries. Hernon and McClure (1987b) unobtrusively tested general reference and documents personnel in both academic and public libraries
- *Obtrusive evaluation* (or the testing of staff members who are fully aware that they are being tested). Examples of studies using this methodology include Bunge (1967), Weech and Goldhor (1982), and Pizer and Cain (1968)
- *Analysis of logs or diaries maintained by participants.* A number of studies have employed this methodology; for example, see Kantor (1981), Gouke and Pease (1982), and McClure, Hernon, and Purcell (1986)
- *Analysis of historical and current records.* Relying on existing records necessitates some insights into the reliability and validity of the data. For an analysis of one instance in which the data lacked reliability and validity and how this affects planning and decision making, see Hernon, McClure, and Purcell (1985, Chapters 6 and 7). Authors who have based studies upon the analysis of existing records include, for example, Getz and Phelps (1984), and Waldhart (1984)
- *Queuing or the monitoring of traffic patterns (e.g., observing the flow of traffic at reference, periodical, and circulation desks).* Halperin (1977) and Lee (1966) discuss queuing theory and its application to library and information science
- *Transactional analysis (e.g., analysis of records resulting from participants'*

use of online catalogs or other computer services). Examples of this means of data collection include Quigley (1944), Cooper (1983), Tolle (1983), and Borgman (1983)

- *Content analysis.* Documents representative of an issue or topic are gathered and their content is classified and analyzed. Examples using this methodology include Fitzgibbons (1976) and Wilson (1982). However, for an extensive discussion of this methodology see Holsti (1969) and Weber (1985)
- *Bibliometrics, including citation analysis.* Bibliometrics "denotes the quantitative study of phenomena of 'documentary discourse,' such as authorship, publication, reading, and citation." It includes studies relating to "the growth of the literature on a given subject," "patterns in the distribution of publishing productivity by individual authors," "how articles on any subject are dispersed across journals," "the 'obsolescence' of literature," "the epidemiology of ideas as reflected in technical literature," "and the study of networks in scholarship as evidenced by analyses of who cites whom" (Buckland, 1983, p. 166). See Frost (1989), and the appendix of Hernon's (1984) investigation into the information-gathering behavior of academic historians includes examples of citation analyses.

Lancaster (1977, 1988) identifies and describes a number of studies that have used many of the above-mentioned methodologies. In addition, Westbrook (1989) describes four techniques for assessing reference service: observation, interviews, surveys, and content analysis.

The category *response to a questionnaire or interview* comprises survey research and produces data collected from the use of:

- A mailed questionnaire or other type of distributed questionnaire (e.g., left in student mailboxes or handed to people either entering or leaving the library)
- A telephone interview
- An in-person interview.

Evaluators can conduct interviews with one or more individuals at the same time. In some instances, evaluators benefit from group interaction. For example, they might be charged with the development of a course evaluation form. As part of the process, they might gather students in a group and ask them to comment on individual questions—their wording, interpretation, and significance. During the interview, an evaluator serves as a neutral moderator and does not interject personal views.

In other instances, evaluators might interview people in sets and use the responses from each set to formulate questions for subsequent interviews. Interviewing therefore is progressive; insights gained from one set of interviews guide the formulation of questions for the next set of interviews.

In addition to the data collection techniques already discussed, evaluators might analyze relevant policies, procedures, laws, regulations, and guidelines. For example, an evaluation of the depository library program administered by the U.S. Government Printing Office might examine structural changes in that program and in the role that regional depositories play. In this case, evaluators would have to consider existing laws and the aborted congressional attempt to revise existing law in the 1970s.

Evaluators might conduct an environmental scan or review of social, environmental, demographic, economic, and technological patterns and trends. For example, evaluators asked to do a futurist study suggesting likely uses of a public library by the year 2000 would want to know who are the present users and what are their uses. With such knowledge, they could investigate census and other data useful in making projections. The study might also employ a nominal group or Delphi technique,[1,2] whereby different opinion leaders are involved in futurist consensus building of the most likely public library uses. Group members might comment on each set of conceivable uses—its strengths, weaknesses, and likelihood of being present by the turn of the century. Evaluators would take the accumulated data into account in making their projection.

Summary of Basic Methods

Figure 5-7 takes some of the methods discussed in the previous section and summarizes their strengths and weaknesses. The purpose is to illustrate that no single methodology is flawless. Rather, evaluators must review various methodologies and determine the one(s) most relevant to the particular study.

Indeed, multiple data collection strategies related to specific research questions are usually the best approach to take. For example, library staff investigating the use of manual and online catalogs might examine completed transactions (transaction analysis), survey users (questionnaire or interview), observe search behavior and patterns, or develop tests for participants to complete (reflecting actual use patterns).

Library staff providing reference service might:

- Analyze the types of questions asked during specific time intervals (such studies *must* indicate that the data are reliable and that the overwhelming majority of questions were, indeed, captured; in other words, they must show

---

[1] The nominal group technique can overcome the reluctance of people to express their views in a group setting. According to Anthony (1985, p. 47), it "generates independent views and a greater degree of meaningful participation." Anthony (Ibid.) outlines the steps involved in the process.

[2] The Delphi method "is another way to obtain structured responses from a group of experts to construct a forecast or to solve a problem" (Anthony, 1985, p. 48). In contrast to the nominal group technique, "it is used with people who are geographically dispersed over a fairly wide area and cannot readily get together for a face-to-face meeting" (Ibid.). Anthony (Ibid.) also identifies the steps involved in the use of this method.

Figure 5-7. Assessment of Selected Methodologies

Method*	Strengths	Weaknesses
Analysis of Records	Records are nonreactive, allow historical comparisons, and provide baselines for comparisons	There may be confidential restrictions
	Records already exist; they need not be created	May be incomplete, out-of-date, and inaccurate
		Changes in record-keeping may make comparisons over time invalid
		May not be able to determine how records were compiled
		Purpose of record-keeping often differs from purpose of evaluation
Citation Analysis	Provides an indicator of use—cited works	Source from which citations are drawn might selectively index journals and articles—indexing policy
	Does not involve interaction with subjects	No assurance that all materials used are cited
	Profiles the literature used in the research process	No assurance that all cited materials are used
	Can define and monitor changes in fields	Errors and inconsistencies may exist in completeness of bibliographic citations
		Materials used may have been those available or known to the author rather than the so-called best material available
Group Interviews	Discloses group dynamics and extent of consensus	May suppress individual differences and intensify group loyalties
	Can stimulate discussion and reactions. Shows interaction patterns	Tends to result in conformity
		May result in manipulation by an influential participant
In-person Interviewing	Permits in-depth probing of issues, etc.	Expensive to conduct and can be time-consuming to set up and administer interviews
	Permits interaction between evaluator and subject	Requires well-trained interviewers
		Requires intensive data collection
		May produce self-reported data

Figure 5-7.—(Continued)

Method*	Strengths	Weaknesses
Mailed Questionnaire	Survey large number of people	Produces self-reported data
	Cost may be less than conducting interviews	Data often lack depth in comparison to data generated from interviewing
	Are self-administered	No assurance that intended person actually answered the survey
		Might have low response rate
Obtrusive Evaluation	Assess staff responses to actual set of reference questions	Staff are aware that they are being studied
	Probe staff variables, e.g., professional or paraprofessional status	Only examines accuracy of responses and length of time spent in the search
Participant Observation	Observe subjects in their natural setting—everyday work situations	May be difficult to blend in so that subjects forget evaluator's presence
	Can be treated as an insider	May not be given access to all the needed information
Standardized Test	The form has been certified; its reliability and validity have been assessed	Copyrighted tests may be expensive
	The data collection form has already been developed	May not have been written for the intended population
Telephone Interviewing	May be cheaper to conduct than in-person interviewing	More conceptual topics are difficult to probe via phone
	Able to talk to those unable to meet in person	Not everyone will agree to a phone interview
	Can be conducted at any time	Requires intensive data collection
	Can have geographical coverage or a national sample	Can be difficult to reach subjects, interest them in the study, and obtain their cooperation for a detailed interview
		Requries well-trained interviewers
		Not everyone has a phone
		The population may involve people with unlisted phone numbers
Unobtrusive Evaluation	Assess staff responses to a set of reference questions, as well as staff question negotiation skills,	Such evaluation is still controversial

continued

Figure 5-7.—(Continued)

Method*	Strengths	Weaknesses
	the offering of referral, and other variables	
		Only looks at reference desk service
		Does not examine patron satisfaction

*For any of these methods, evaluators may have to know sampling, question and schedule construction, data analysis techniques, and other technical matters. Evaluators might profit from an examination of Tables 3–3, 3–4, and 3–5 in Marshall and Rossman (1989, pp. 78, 102–104). Table 3–3 matches research questions with data collection techniques, while the other two tables identify the strengths and weaknesses of different data collection techniques.

that the questions which were not gathered and analyzed do not differ significantly from those collected and scrutinized)
- Engage in obtrusive or unobtrusive testing (examining the number of questions answered correctly, reference interview skills, search strategies, and willingness of patrons to request assistance again from the members of the library staff)
- Compare online searching skills of staff, or analyze outreach programs (e.g., current awareness services and bibliographic instruction programs).

Staff involved in collection development activities might investigate document delivery capabilities (the ability to supply clientele with needed resources effectively and efficiently) and pursue methods to increase the circulation of needed source material (e.g., experimenting with variations in loan periods and the number of copies purchased for high circulation monographs). Staff might also investigate problems related to economic efficiency and automation, and explore methods for improved preservation of resources. For example, they might experiment with different atmospheric conditions and methods for the extinguishing of fires. Additional experiments might focus on crime reduction or elimination (e.g., the prevention of theft and source mutilation).

Two key points from this section are: (1) numerous techniques for collecting data are available, and (2) multiple data collection strategies should be used whenever possible. Evaluators should not select one particular technique because it is "easily available" or "its one I already know how to do." Indeed, too much evaluation is already based on surveys. The selection of a data collection technique should be considered in terms of strengths and weaknesses (see Figure 5-7), the degree to which it assists in answering research questions accurately, and practical considerations such as the technique's cost and/or time requirements.

Statistics and Significance

This chapter has emphasized the context in which methods of statistical analysis are performed. The more sophisticated the study design and methodology, the more likely that a fuller range of statistical tests have application. Because this book does not present different types of descriptive and inferential statistics, readers might profit from an examination of works such as Hernon et al. (1989), Swisher and McClure (1984), and Huck, Cormier, and Bounds, Jr. (1974). Such books identify various research/evaluation designs, suggest possible threats to internal validity for each, indicate which methods of statistical analysis are most appropriate, explain the proper use and interpretation of statistics, and offer examples from the literature for purposes of clarification.

Prior to the collection of data, evaluators should identify which statistical tests to use and the most appropriate level of statistical analysis. Common levels include the .05 or .01, meaning that the evaluators are willing to accept the probability that erroneous findings could result (and be due to chance) in either 5 times or 1 time in 100 trials. Setting the level of significance involves a judgment about the relative importance of two types of errors.

A *Type I* error raises the risk of concluding that there is a significant effect when one does not actually exist. In other words, the evaluators assume that the treatment produced change in the dependent variable when, in fact, no change had occurred. With a *Type II* error, the evaluators failed to detect an actual program effect; a change in the dependent variable went undetected (Katzer, Cook, and Crouch, 1982, pp. 50–67).

For example, library staff members who analyze data with a level of significance at .10 (they are willing to chance being correct in 90 of 100 trials) set a broad criteria for statistical significance. They may be increasing the likelihood of making a Type II error, while decreasing the probability of identifying a Type I error (a false, negative error). Since it is generally too costly to attempt to control both types of errors, library staff members must decide which is the more important to control and set the level of significance accordingly (see Hernon et al., 1989).

Criteria of Relevance

Validity. Because validity issues arise with both evaluation designs and methodologies, this section amplifies on criteria of relevance. Data collection instruments (such as questionnaires, interviewing forms, and tests) must measure what they are intended to measure. In this regard, the following three types of validity merit brief mention:

Figure 5-8. Validation of a Library Skills Test for Different Purposes*

Purpose	Type of Validity	Questions to Be Asked
Achievement test for college freshmen	Content	How well does the test sample what the students learned?
		How well does a standardized test cover what was taught in the library skills program?
Aptitude test to predict performance in a library skills program for college freshmen	Criterion-related (predictive)	How well does the test predict achievement in the freshman program?
Diagnostic test to identify problems in library use	Criterion-related (diagnostic)	How well does the test diagnose current difficulties in library use?
A test to measure library skills comprehension	Construct	How well does the test measure comprehension of library use? Do the data support hypotheses about library use comprehension?
		Does a test on the use of a card catalog really measure effective and efficient use rather than one's ability to read test items?

*This figure is adapted from *Introduction to Research in Education*, Third Edition, by Donald Ary, Lucy Chesar Jacobs, and Ashghar Razavieh, p. 224. Copyright © 1985 by Holt, Rinehart and Winston, Inc., New York. Reprinted by permission of the publisher.

- Content
- Criterion
- Construct.

Figure 5-8 shows the purpose of each type and illustrates the questions each considers.

Content validity is concerned with the representativeness of the measuring instrument in describing the content which it is intended to measure. This type of validity is more easily applied to practical considerations than to abstract or theoretical concepts. The central question is "How well does the content of the instrument represent the entire universe of content which might be measured?" (Ary, Jacob, and Razavieh, 1985, p. 214). *Face validity*, which represents the evaluators' appraisal that the content reflects what they are attempting to measure, comprises a type of content validity. Face validity is also judgmental and subject to interpretation.

Criterion-related validity compares scores on the data collection instrument to certain criteria known or commonly believed to measure the attribute under study. The purpose is to determine the extent to which the instrument treats a criterion. Any criterion must display (Ary, Jacobs, and Razavieh, 1985, pp. 216–217):

- "Relevance" ("represents successful performance on the behavior in question")
- "Reliability" ("a consistent measure of the attribute over time or from situation to situation"), and the "absence of bias" ("the scoring of a criterion measure should not be influenced by any factors other than actual performance on the criterion").

A problem with the application of criterion validity is that many types of behavior cannot be converted into an appropriate criterion.

There are two types of criterion-related validity: *predictive* and *diagnostic*. The purpose of the former is to estimate or predict a future outcome, while the latter type diagnoses the existing or current state of a subject. The central difference between the two relates to the time when the data depicting the criterion are collected. To qualify as predictive validity, the correlation between the test scores and the criterion comes at a later time. Diagnostic validity requires that the correlation not be delayed, but made at approximately the same time. The following example should clarify the distinction.

If library staff members administer a library skills test to students completing the required freshman English course, diagnostic validity is determined by a correlation of test scores with, perhaps, the grade that the students received on a term paper that required use of the library. Predictive validity involves a correlation of their test scores with the grade from a term paper in a subsequent class. Perhaps library staff might correlate test scores with the term paper assigned in the freshman English class and later correlate their scores with a term paper in a subsequent class. Longitudinal data gathered under a suitable design definitely aid the determination of predictive validity.

Construct validity, which has the most generalized application of the three types of validity discussed here, questions whether the theoretical construct or trait is actually measured. For example, does a study of creativity, motivation, anxiety, or self-actualization actually measure that trait? One way that the question can be answered is to correlate items on locally produced tests to those on standardized tests. If the correlation is high, one assumes that the new instrument measures what is intended (the construct).

In an experimental or quasi-experimental study, change occurring, in a predictable fashion, in the group receiving the treatment but not in the control group, indicates that the construct has been measured. Evaluators might identify the actual components of the desired construct (e.g., motivation), search the data collection instrument for indicators of that construct (check for content validity), and determine if the instrument adequately reflects the full dimensions of that construct. They might also take two dissimilar groups and test whether their performance on the same instrument differs.

Mark and Cook (1984) elaborate on these methods and identify specific steps that evaluators can follow to improve construct validity. For example, they recommend the careful explication of constructs, an examination of the published literature for a clarification of components and a determination of which have the greatest potential value, and the employment of a pilot test prior to implementation of the formal evaluation project. They further point out that "construct validity accumulates over many studies, as evidence grows about the pattern of relations among numerous research operations" (Ibid., p. 75).

Suppose that evaluators want to examine the perceptions that undergraduate college students have of librarians, their duties, functions, and professionalism. One method of determining validity would be to use contrasting groups, one consisting of students, preferably those labeled as nonusers of the library, and the other contains members of the professional library staff. The perceptions between both groups would probably be quite different. Therefore, a questionnaire might be administered to 10 students qualifying as nonusers and to 10 librarians selected by consulting a table of random numbers. Using a statistical test (e.g., the Mann-Whitney U Test, which shows whether two independent groups were drawn from the same population—see Hernon et al., 1989), the evaluators could determine if there were differences in the responses of both groups and the magnitude of those differences. Statistically significant differences would lend support to the ability of the questionnaire to measure those characteristics it was designed to measure.

Hernon and McClure (1987a) assess the reliability, validity, and utility of unobtrusive testing. They also call for further methodological refinement of such testing. Murfin and Gugelchuk (1987) designed a reference transaction assessment instrument to evaluate the outcome of reference service in terms of patrons' perceptions of success. They extensively reviewed their data collection instrument for construct validity, external validity, and reliability. Such careful construction of an instrument could serve as a model for other researchers, regardless of the area of librarianship that they examine.

This discussion should not conclude with the impression that all validity issues can be reduced to the precision of statistical analysis. Guba and Lincoln (1981) emphasize that evaluation must include the human factor and that, where relevant, evaluators must address issues that lack statistical precision. For example, they might investigate the implementation of a current awareness service by which faculty members are alerted to new government publications received by the library. A critical issue revolves around whether the faculty, as a whole, know what a government publication is. Consequently, a questionnaire might contain an item or two eliciting examples of government publications that they regularly use, or request a list of a faculty member's scholarly writings. These writings could then be examined for examples of government publications. As an alternative, the evaluators might interview a sample of the faculty and look for government publications in their offices, or question them about their understanding of current issues and problems confronting the production and distribution of government publications.

Library staff should see that their data collection instrument has reliability and that study participants would be consistent in their response, if they were tested again. Indicators of a high correlation or association between a test and retest confirm the quality of the data collection instrument.

A high response rate on a questionnaire does not guarantee that all segments of the target population are adequately represented. If possible, evaluators should collect data on nonrespondents and determine if they differ significantly from respondents. For example, a survey of academic libraries could easily be supplemented by a search for descriptive information on each library and academic institution from standard reference sources. Data on the size of the budget, volume counts, highest degree offered, institutional affiliation (private or public), etc., could be compared for responding and nonresponding libraries to see if statistically significant differences emerge. If they do, the evaluators would have to increase the number of responding libraries and re-examine respondents and nonrespondents to see if the statistically significant differences have been eliminated. When there is no significant difference, generalizability of the findings to the target population is strengthened.

In some cases, evaluators may want to draw a sample of nonrespondents and to contact them directly (either by mail or telephone). Their responses could be compared to those of the respondents. Again, comparisons between the two groups that do not indicate statistically significant differences strengthen the degree to which study findings can be generalized to the target population.

Reliability. As already noted, this criterion seeks to determine the degree to which data are consistent; consistency is the extent to which the same results are produced from different samples of the same population. Thus, if a survey question seeks to determine the number of microfiche that a library holds, one would expect an identical answer regardless of who the respondent is. If two librarians at the same institution were asked "How many microfiche do you presently have?" and one said 11,756, and the other reported 3,986, then data related to microfiche holdings are not likely to be reliable. Unreliability, then, occurs when the data or the instrument do not produce the same results twice for the same population or sample.

Reliability can also be injured if two respondents interpret a question differently. For example, if a staff member at one library interprets the question "How many microfiche do you have?" as how many are there within that department, but a person at another library interprets the question to mean the number of microfiche in the entire library collection, the resulting data are likely to be unreliable.

Inconsistent coding and inappropriate analysis of data also can cause reliability problems. Such problems typically occur either when the researcher has to interpret "open-ended" questions and categorize them for analysis, or simply through coding errors (e.g., a response that should have been coded as a "2" was coded as a "3").

Vagueness and the lack of clear definitions for key terms in questions also contribute to unreliable data. For example, a question probing whether the library has adequate facilities and equipment to serve handicapped library patrons is likely to produce unreliable data. The degree of "adequacy" is open to individual interpretation. Rewording the question, for example, to ask "Can patrons in wheelchairs physically access materials in the periodicals collection" is more specific and more likely to produce reliable data about access to the collection by the handicapped.

OPTIONS, CHOICES, AND TRADEOFFS

The various designs identified in this chapter represent a small number of those possible. Even for the ones identified, various modifications are possible. Perhaps the key word for designs is *adaptability*; they can be modified to fit local needs and to lessen threats to internal validity. The time-series design, for example, is one of the most useful quasi-experiments, because it is "possible to see whether the measures [taken] immediately before and after the program are a continuation of earlier patterns or whether they mark a decisive change" (Weiss, 1972, p. 68).* The major, internal validity threat to the time-series is history. However, the implementation of a multiple time-series, whereby regular and periodic measurements are taken over time, reduces this threat to internal validity.

With the time-series design, outcome results are gathered at regular intervals; they need not be taken solely after the completion of a treatment. The collection of data may prove useful to library administrators wanting feedback on a program currently under operation. Of course, evaluators should be aware of any impact that data collection had on the subjects. Such impacts might include their willingness to participate and provide honest and full responses.

In many cases, library staff can neither make a random assignment nor engage in a true experiment. They should still undertake an evaluation project, especially for objectives labeled as priorities for the library, and explore another design, preferably one with reliability and validity safeguards. It is important to remember that "we-are better off being able to rule out some possible explanations for observed effects than not rule out any" (Weiss, 1972, p. 72).*

---

* Carol H. Weiss. *Evaluation Research: Methods for Assessing Program Effectiveness*, p. 68. Copyright © 1972. Prentice-Hall, Englewood Cliffs, NJ. Reprinted by permission.

* Carol H. Weiss. *Evaluation Research: Methods for Assessing Program Effectiveness*, p. 72. Copyright © 1972. Prentice-Hall, Englewood Cliffs, NJ. Reprinted by permission.

There is no one prescribed design or methodology for addressing a given library problem. Instead, library evaluators have to explore the local situation, the goals and objectives related to the program or service under review, and select the most appropriate design and methodology. The selection will not be made entirely in terms of research principles. Instead, the evaluator has to address political factors as well as financial, staff, and time constraints. Once evaluators have selected the design and methodology(ies), they should be able to defend the choice and provide the library with the most valid and reliable data possible under the circumstances.

Internal validity demonstrates "the linkage between variables" and supports a researcher's "interpretation of the evidence" as "the only proper one" (Krathwohl, 1985, p. 57). Nevertheless, researchers never actually prove a proposition can be accepted with absolute certainty;*

> any single test does not prove the proposition is true—it merely adds one more piece of evidence that the proposition has not yet been disconfirmed. Although theoretically the process of escaping disconfirmation is never-ending, in effect what is happening is that each piece of evidence lowers the uncertainty about the relationship until it crosses the knowledge threshold. Even after the relationship has crossed that threshold, there might still be some as yet untested instance in which it would be disconfirmed. That is why all scientific knowledge is held as tentatively true. (Ibid., p. 60)

A determination that internal validity exists is based on a combination of judgments that the study, as conceived and executed, is consistent with theory, accepted knowledge, and previous research. Furthermore, the study should employ a sound research design so that the results cannot be accounted for by any other reasonable explanation.

Because external validity is concerned with generalizability, it can be difficult to gain sufficient insights into a proposition to permit sufficient generalizations from samples. To make generalizations, evaluators must have a detailed knowledge of the population to demonstrate the wider application of their data. Clearly, if evaluators must make a choice, they should demonstrate internal validity rather than external validity.

Decisions concerning which evaluation design and methodology to employ must address issues of internal and external validity, as well as the significance of the problem to the accomplishment of library goals and objectives. Designs therefore comprise one step in developing and implementing an evaluation study. However, they comprise a step that interacts with all the others and forms a vital link in the process of producing data useful for library planning and decision making.

---

* David R. Krathwohl, *Social and Behavioral Science Research*. Copyright © 1985. Jossey-Bass Publishers, San Francisco, CA. Reprinted with permission.

When developing the study design and method, evaluators often realize that they must make decisions for how best to conduct the evaluation in the context of tradeoffs. If they allocate additional resources and time to improving the internal validity of the data, perhaps they will have fewer resources and less time to increase the external validity of the data. Such tradeoffs in evaluation designs are inevitable. The key, however, is that evaluators make conscious decisions about which:

- Design and methods they will use
- Strategies will improve the quality of the data.

They must also recognize the limitations and assumptions under which they will collect the data.

DISCUSSION ITEMS

---

1. How do design and methodology differ?
2. What types of questions do studies on "impact assessment" address?
3. What types of questions should evaluators address when they develop a research design?
4. Define "internal validity" and "external validity," and suggest "threats" to each?
5. How do "experimental" and "quasi-experimental" designs differ?
6. Take a survey published in library and information science and critique the reliability and validity of the instrument.
7. Compare the use of unobtrusive and obtrusive testing for a study on the effectiveness of public service personnel in answering questions of a factual or bibliographic nature? Also identify an experimental and quasi-experimental design that could be used to gauge the effectiveness of the public service staff in answering these questions.
8. Assume that your supervisor asked you to conduct a study that examines patterns by which the public uses the online catalog and that you plan to analyze the logs of completed transactions. What are some possible threats to internal and external validity that you would have to address prior to reaching conclusions and addressing your hypotheses or research questions?
9. Assume that your director asked you to monitor the questions asked at the central reference desk for the next six months. What steps would you take to ensure data reliability and validity?
10. Assume that the library director has asked you to determine the extent to which library clientele may have mutilated the periodicals from which

articles have been placed on reserve. The director fears that placement on reserve may provide certain students with an incentive to bypass the reserve copy and remove articles from the periodicals themselves for their personal use. Identify the issues and questions that you would raise in selecting an appropriate evaluation design and methodology. Also indicate the steps you would take to ensure reliable and valid findings.

Chapter Six
Sampling*

For thousands of years, people have been basing judgments about a large group of objects on their observations of a few of them. Prehistoric humans probably decided whether the berries on a bush were edible by tasting a few of them (with possibly fatal results). At harvest time, farmers judged the quality and expected yield of a wheat field by rubbing the husks off a few ears of grain pulled from various parts of the field. People have used sampling techniques, such as spot checking, for many years. The great improvement in the last 50 years or so has been the development of statistical sampling. We now have ways of drawing and analyzing samples to produce more objective information of better quality. We can also be more explicit about the limitations of this information.

Sampling could be necessary, regardless of the type of data collection method used, e.g., questionnaires, interviews, and subjects in focus groups. And in some instances, the evaluation study may not need to sample; that is, the evaluators can collect data from all the information sources within the larger population, e.g., all 28 participants in a bibliographic instruction project. But the evaluators will not want to collect data from all 1,800 freshmen who used the library this semester (for example), but would prefer to gather data from a sample of that population.

Knowledge of the sampling process is important to evaluators for a number of reasons:

- There rarely is adequate time and resources available to collect data from all the information sources within a particular population
- Identifying a "good" sample is one of the best ways to ensure the quality of the data and improve the accuracy of findings (see previous chapter)
- There are different ways to sample a population and the evaluator must be able to determine which type of sample is best for a particular type of evaluation.

Being able to sample a population rather than collect data from all information sources, to know "how many" sample sources are needed to have a certain level of confidence in the data, and to demonstrate the representativeness of that

* This chapter essentially is taken from General Accounting Office. Program Evaluation and Methodology Division. *Using Statistical Sampling*. Transfer Paper 6. Washington, D.C.: U.S. Government Printing Office, April 1986.

Figure 6-1.   Selected Works on Sampling

Cochran, W. G. *Sampling Techniques*. New York: Wiley, 1977.
Kalton, G. *Introduction to Survey Sampling*. Beverly Hills, CA: Sage, 1983.
Kish, L. *Survey Sampling*. New York: Wiley, 1965.
Kraemer, H. C. and S. Thiemann. *How Many Subjects*. Newbury Park, CA: Sage, 1987.
Scheaffer, R. L., W. Mendenhall, and L. Ott. *Elementary Survey Sampling*. Belmont, CA: Wadsworth, 1979.
Slonim, M. *Sampling in a Nutshell*. New York: Simon and Schuster, 1960.
Sudman, S. *Applied Sampling*. New York: Academic Press, 1976.
Williams, B. *A Sampler on Sampling*. New York: Wiley, 1978.

sample are all key factors that contribute to the success of any evaluation—assuming a sample is necessary.

A *sample* is a portion of a universe, and *sampling* refers to the methods for selecting that portion. Sampling is an element of project design, which, along with such other elements as data collection and methods of analysis, determines the soundness of the answers given to evaluation questions. Figure 6-1 offers a selected bibliography that complements this chapter.

REPRESENTATIVENESS: THE GOAL OF STATISTICAL SAMPLING

Statistical sampling produces a sample that is representative of a universe. However, samples of a universe differ from one another as well as from the universe itself. Hence, there should be an objective measure of the possible variation between samples and of the sample's relationship to the universe. With this information, it is possible to determine the amount of error that arises because a sample does not correspond exactly to the universe. This is an important feature of statistical sampling because evaluators can be precise about the error introduced by the sampling process. Decision makers can then decide whether the amount of error is tolerable when weighed against tradeoff factors, such as the cost of obtaining a larger sample that will have less error.

CONFIDENCE LEVEL

The level of significance is the predetermined level at which a null hypothesis is rejected. The level is an arbitrarily chosen probability that is used to decide whether a given sample is likely to have come from a given population. The most commonly used levels are .05 and .01. When librarians collect management data, they might increase the margin of error and accept, e.g., the .10 level.

The .05 level of significance corresponds to the .95 level of confidence. The .01 level is the same as the .99 level of confidence, while the .10 level equals the .90 level of confidence.

Evaluators either support or reject a null hypothesis on the basis of the level selected. For example, by setting the level at .05, they reject a null hypothesis if the probability is less than .05. The probability level may be reported as $p < .05$, with p meaning probability, and the symbol $<$ standing for "less than."

Evaluators should select a level of significance prior to data collection after they have examined the consequences of making a Type I error (rejecting a true null hypothesis) or Type II error (accepting a false null hypothesis as true). The final determination should also reflect the purpose for data collection—action research, publication, and so forth—and the margin of error that decisions makers and evaluators are willing to accept.

RANDOM SELECTION

The essence of statistical sampling is selecting a sample by some random (or chance) process. By randomizing sample selection, evaluators make sure that the sample represents the universe within the limits of sampling error, and they can measure the precision of the information yielded by the sample. Sampling error, or precision, is a measure of the expected difference between the value found in a statistical sample and the value of the same characteristic that would have been found by examining the entire universe. Sampling errors are always stated at a specific confidence level.

The term "random selection" does not mean a haphazard sample. Rather, to select randomly is to eliminate personal bias or subjective considerations from the choice of the sample items. Every item in the universe has an equal or known probability of being selected, and items are selected independently. Although the results obtained from different random samples drawn from the same universe differ, the differences stem from chance, not personal bias or other systematic factors.

The selection of a sample by some random method in order to obtain information or draw conclusions about a universe is referred to as "probability" or "statistical" sampling. Regardless of the name used to describe the method, there are two key elements:

- Each possible sample from the universe has a known (non-zero) probability of being selected
- The actual selection technique truly executes the random method.

This notion of "randomness" is a key concept underlying a number of sampling techniques.

SAMPLE DESIGN

Sample design involves the following steps:

- Defining the universe and the sampling units
- Choosing the sampling strategy and the type of sampling
- Determining the size of the sample.

Defining the Universe and the Sampling Units

The universe should be defined very carefully, because this is the entire collection or group of items to which estimates and inferences apply. Once the universe has been defined, evaluators must either obtain or develop a sampling frame. The sampling frame is the "things" or "objects" contained in the universe. For example, it might be a list of libraries, students enrolled in the college, public libraries in the state, geographic region, or nation, etc.

The sampling frame has several characteristics. First, it permits the sampler to identify and locate the specific item that is to be drawn into the sample, and to differentiate this item from all other items in the sampling frame. The frame also contains all the items in the universe. For example, if the universe has been defined as the work force in an academic library, the list of workers from which the sample is drawn includes all workers as of the date of the study, contains no duplicate entries, and offers no entries not found in the universe.

In addition, evaluators may want to define subdivisions of the universe. One type of subdivision is the stratum, a subpopulation obtained by dividing the universe into two or more mutually exclusive groups, or *strata*, which evaluators can do if they know in advance the number of sampling units in each stratum. Independent random samples are selected from each stratum in order to obtain more precise estimates or to emphasize certain portions of the universe, such as units with a high dollar value or a great potential for error. Often, the stratification system is based on the locations of the units of observation. Examples of strata are households classified as urban and rural, and public libraries classified by geographic location.

Another type of universe subdivision is the domain of interest. This type of subdivision is necessary when separate estimates are needed for each of a number of classes into which a universe may be divided, but evaluators do not know in advance the number of sampling units in each class. Thus, they must depend on the sample if they are to develop this information. An example of domain of interest is students at a university who intend to major in education.

Sampling units are often defined as persons or things we want to study—the units of the universe about which we need information. But sometimes, because of the arrangement of the universe, the lack of a list of items they want to observe, and practical considerations, evaluators may have to select a sampling unit that is larger than the item about which they want to obtain data. An example is selecting a household in order to determine library use patterns of its members. In this example, the item of interest, the household member, is called the "secondary sampling unit," and the larger unit, the household, is called the "cluster" or "primary sampling unit."

The primary sampling units must:

• Be mutually exclusive
• Include the entire universe.

This means that each unit being observed, the secondary sampling unit, must belong to one and only one primary sampling unit, and that the primary sampling units must cover the entire universe.

Choosing a Sampling Strategy

The choice of a census (everything), a judgment sample, or a statistical sample is a project-design decision of great importance. Besides project objectives, factors such as cost, precision, and the feasibility of drawing certain kinds of samples must be considered. Although this chapter concentrates on statistical sampling, a brief discussion of different sampling strategies is appropriate.

For some projects, a census is appropriate, as when individual items in the universe are very important in themselves or when the information to be obtained is critical and the universe is small enough to allow 100% sampling. On other occasions, the universe may be so small that sampling is not needed. Also, when all the data are already on a computer or machine-readable form, it may be no less efficient to analyze every item. This is because most of the work is in setting up the programs, not in processing the items, and because the computer must read every record before selecting the record for inclusion or exclusion. Aside from special cases, the main disadvantage of conducting a census is usually the high cost and extensive time requirements relative to other options.

Judgment sampling is not statistical or scientific sampling—it is discretionary. In this type of sampling, the evaluator bases the selection of a sample on knowledge or judgment about the characteristics of the universe. Haphazard samples—for example, grabbing a few items "at random"—are usually included in the category of judgment sampling.

Judgment samples have valid uses. When one need not generalize to a universe, a census or a statistical sample is not necessary and a small judgment sample might be cost-effective. The case-study approach might use judgment sampling (see Yin, 1989).

Sometimes the intent is to generalize, but it is not possible to obtain a suitable list of the universe. Statistical sampling is then not possible, and evaluators may be forced to use a judgment sample. Although not necessarily less accurate than probability samples in describing a universe, judgment samples lack three important characteristics of statistical samples:

- Random selection of the cases to be examined
- Precise determination of the sample size
- Objective evaluation of the sample results.

The key problem with using a judgment sample when evaluators want to generalize is that they have no way of knowing how near the results obtained are to the universe characteristics they are attempting to measure. A statistical sample's results, in contrast, can be computed and expressed in quantitative terms. Evaluators therefore can numerically measure the precision of the sample results and the probability that the sample estimate is within the calculated precision of the universe characteristic.

When the objective of a project is to draw conclusions about a universe of people or things, and when evaluators can list the universe, statistical sampling is the preferred method. (It is not necessary literally to "list" the universe. For example, it is possible to select randomly from the list of all conceivable telephone numbers without possessing a physical list of such numbers. Sometimes the list exists only in a conceptual sense.)

Because no individual's judgment is infallible, and because the ability to make effective judgments varies widely from individual to individual and even in the same individual from time to time, the evaluators' judgment and objectivity can always be questioned in judgment sampling. This is not so in statistical sampling, which is based on the widely accepted theory of probability, because the sample is scientifically selected and evaluated. Certainly, the complaint that evaluators looked at only the worse cases would have no merit.

Using statistical sampling, a third party can repeat a study and expect to reach comparable conclusions about the characteristics of the universe being measured. Although the study results may be interpreted differently, there can be no question about the facts. Likewise, statistical samples can be combined and evaluated even if they were taken by different persons. Evaluators working at different locations can participate independently in the same study, and the results from the several locations can be combined to develop one estimate. Also, a study started by one evaluator can be continued by another, without difficulty. Furthermore, if evaluators decide to extend the sampling, they can do so easily and combine the results.

Statistical sampling provides a means of objectively determining the sample size in order to provide results having the precision required for the universe being examined and the question being investigated. This approach usually results in a smaller sample than that found in judgment sampling. Because of the intuitive but incorrect belief that an adequate sample must always be a fixed percentage, say 5 or 10% of the universe, oversampling occurs frequently in judgment sampling. However, if the universe is small, using the intuitive approach of selecting a sample that is equal to a fixed percentage of the universe could yield a sample too small to produce reliable results. For example, if the universe consisted of 200 items and a 10% sample were drawn, the sample size would be only 20 items.

Determining the Type of Statistical Sampling

If a statistical sample is the choice, a further decision must be made among the possible types of statistical sampling methods. This section highlights five types that might be used: random, stratified, systematic, quota, and cluster sampling.

Random sampling. Random sampling, which is the simplest method of drawing a statistical sample, is the most common method of sampling, but sometimes is less efficient than other methods. The assumptions underlying the use of simple random sampling are that the population is homogeneous and is in one location, or the population can be sampled from a single list of sampling units if it is in several locations and if there is only moderate variation among the values of the items in the universe. No attempt is made to segregate or separate any portion of the population into separate groups before the sample is selected. Thus, each individual item in the universe has an equal probability of inclusion in the sample.

Random sampling ensures that the sample statistic is representative of the population parameter and that evaluators can determine the amount of difference between the two. The difference between the characteristics of a sample and those of the population from which the sample was taken is called *sampling error*. For random samples, evaluators can estimate this error. Sampling error is a function of the size of the sample; the error is the greatest when the sample size is small.

For many library-related projects, evaluators might use random number generators contained in microcomputer software. For example, StatPac, a statistical analysis software package, contains a random number generator. (See Table 6–1 of Hernon et al. (1989) for an illustration of the printout.) Note that StatPac generates the numbers, but does not place them in numerical sequence. For this reason, some evaluators might prefer to use other software.

Stratified sampling. Stratified sampling refers to the situation in which the universe is divided into two or more parts and a sample is selected from each part. The parts may be selected in proportion to their numbers in the population itself. In some instances, evaluators might use *disproportional* stratified sampling. When defining parts (strata) and setting stratum boundaries, evaluators should keep certain rules in mind. First, each sampling unit can be included in one, and only one, stratum. Second, the strata must not overlap. And, finally, the items in each stratum should be as much alike as possible in relation to the characteristic being measured.

Because the universe is divided into two or more parts (strata), evaluators can use a different procedure to select the samples in the various subuniverses. Depending on the arrangement of the items in the subuniverses and the numbering systems employed, they might use random number sampling in some of the strata and systematic selection in others.

Perhaps an example might clarify stratified sampling. Hernon (1979) studied social scientist's use of government publications at Midwestern academic institutions. He defined Midwestern states as Illinois, Indiana, Michigan, and Ohio, and social scientists as faculty members representing the disciplines of economics, history, political science, and sociology. He grouped academic institutions by highest degree: baccalaureate, master's, and doctorate. Furthermore, Hernon subdivided each group by institutional control (public or private). As a result, there were six groupings: baccalaureate public and private, master's public and private, and doctorate public and private. By random sampling institutions from each group, he obtained a list of 17 institutions to study.

The sampling process might have been more elaborate. For example, the institutions in each group could have been arrayed according to volume count of the library or enrollment of the institution. The purpose would be to select study sites to be further representative of each group. However, the inclusion of more elements in the sampling process increases the sample size necessary to investigate the objectives, hypotheses, and research questions.

Systematic sampling. Systematic sampling does not choose each member of the population independently. Once the first member of the population has been chosen, other members of the sample are automatically determined. For example, evaluators might decide to select (by use of a random number table) every 50th page of the telephone book and every 30th name on that page. Using this procedure they go through the telephone book until they have selected all the names needed.

As another example, assume that evaluators want to draw a sample of 200 items from a vertical file containing 10,100 items. Dividing the sample size into the universe size gives a quotient of 50.5. Rounding downward to the nearest whole number gives a sampling interval of 50. From a table of random digits, the first number between 1 and 50 is selected to obtain the starting point. (Note that since the sampling interval is a two-digit number, evaluators look at two-digit combinations in the table of random numbers.) Suppose the random starting number between 1 and 50 is 36. The evaluator starts with item number 36 and pulls every 50th item thereafter; the 36th item, 86th item, 136th item, and so on will constitute the sample.

Systematic sampling may be used when the sampling units are not numbered or when it would be too cumbersome to attempt to match the sampling units against random numbers. Some circumstances in which systematic selection might be advantageous include:

- The sampling units are long lists or pages of lists
- The sampling units are files on index cards that are not serially numbered, or if they are numbered, they are not in numerical sequences
- The sampling units are not suitably numbered and are intermingled with other items that are not to be included in the sample
- The sampling units are numbered in blocks of numbers, and some blocks are not used.

To obtain a sample size that is neither too large nor too small, evaluators must know or be able to estimate the universe size. Before using systematic selection, evaluators should make sure that the sample will be drawn from the entire universe. If the sample is to be drawn from a list of items, the list must be complete; if the sample is to be drawn from a file, all the folders must be in the file, or charge-out cards or a similar system must be used to mark the position of missing folders. Otherwise, the evaluators must make special arrangements to ensure that missing sampling units have the opportunity of being selected.

Once the sample has been selected, it is not permissible to substitute other items for sample items that are missing (that are out of the file or the like), or for sample items that may not have adequate supporting material to permit measurement. Every effort should be made to locate the missing items or supporting material. If they cannot be located, this fact should be noted and reported as one of the sample results.

Quota sampling. Quota sampling recognizes that evaluators may want to select a proportion of the population according to certain characteristics. For example, academic librarians might decide to base their sampling on class level and to take a proportion of undergraduate and graduate students at the university. For convenience, they might conduct the study prior to a school term at the time of course registration. As students leave the building upon completion of registration, library staff seek subjects based on class level. Once the staff have filled their quota of undergraduate and graduate students, and these students have answered the study questions, the evaluators terminate data collection. From such a study, evaluators would not label study participants as representative of the student population, rather they only discuss responding quotas.

Cluster sampling. Another type of sampling is cluster sampling, which is the selection of groups of items (or clusters) rather than the selection of individual items directly. Cluster sampling focuses on a naturally occurring group of individuals. Evaluators divide the population into subdivisions, clusters of smaller units. Some of these subdivisions, or clusters, are randomly selected for inclusion in the study. If the clusters are geographic subdivisions, this kind of sampling is known as *area sampling*. Examples of clusters are counties in a state and persons in a household. For an excellent discussion of cluster sampling, see Powell (1985, 1990).

Determining the Sample Size

A determination of sample size involves four concepts: sampling error, precision, confidence, and standard deviation. *Sampling error* is the extent to which the *means* of repeatedly drawn samples deviate from each other and presumably the population mean. By minimizing sampling error, evaluators increase the likelihood that the sample represents the population. *Precision* is the amount of sampling error that can be tolerated but that will still permit the results to be useful. This is sometimes called "tolerable error" or the "bound on error."

Confidence level is a measure of the degree of assurance that the estimate obtained from a sample differs from the universe parameter being estimated by less than the sampling error. Evaluators should decide on the confidence level prior to data collection (see Figure 6-2 for guidance). The decision should reflect the purpose of data collection and whether library decision makers want management or research data. Other related considerations are the costs and time required to obtain the sample data. If the precision is specified *too tight*, without considering cost and time, the sample size may be larger than is practical. Usually only limited resources (money, staff, etc.) and time are available for data collection. This must always be remembered when the estimate's precision is being specified.

To compute the precision, or sampling error, calculate the *standard deviation*, which is a numerical measurement of the dispersion or scatter of a group of values about their mean. Understanding this statistic is a key to understanding much of sampling. Hernon et al. (1989, pp. 56–58) discuss standard deviation and its computation.

Perhaps the most practical guidance that can be given for determining sample size is that the evaluator should specify the precision required, calculate the sample size needed to achieve this precision, and then estimate the cost or time required to collect the data for the computed sample size. If the cost is more than can be afforded, or the required time is more than can be allowed, the precision should be relaxed (sampling error should be allowed to increase) until the evaluators find an affordable sample size. An adjustment like this should be made by relaxing the specified precision, not manipulating the confidence level.

Examples showing how to determine sample size can be found in Hernon et al. (1989, pp. 78–81), Swisher and McClure (1984, pp. 103–128), Clark (1984), and Drott (1969). For research studies in the social sciences, the confidence level may be set at 95% (the .05 level), meaning that there is a 95% chance that the sample is distributed in the same way as the population.

Figure 6-2.   Computation of Sample Size Estimate*

FORMULA:

$$N = \frac{Z^2}{E} (P) (1 - P)$$

WHERE:

Z = CONFIDENCE LEVEL DESIRED
    90% = 1.65
    95% = 1.96
    99% = 2.58

E = ACCEPTABLE DEGREE OF ERROR
    .15 = PLUS OR MINUS 15%
    .10 = PLUS OR MINUS 10%
    .05 = PLUS OR MINUS   5%

P = ESTIMATED PROPORTION OR
    INCIDENCE OF CASES IN
    THE POPULATION—
    BETWEEN .01 AND .99

N = SAMPLE SIZE

EXAMPLE: PRIVATE TWO-YEAR COLLEGES ACCOUNT FOR 25% OF ALL TWO-YEAR COLLEGES. THE PROPORTION OF CASES OF PRIVATE COLLEGES IN THE POPULATION OF TWO-YEAR COLLEGES IS .25 (P = .25). IF YOU WANTED A CONFIDENCE LEVEL OF 95% (Z = 1.96) WITH A TOLERABLE AMOUNT OF ERROR NO GREATER THAN PLUS OR MINUS .10, YOU WOULD CALCULATE THE NECESSARY SAMPLE SIZE AS SHOWN:

$$N = \frac{1.96^2}{.10} (.25) \ (.75)$$

$$N = (19.6^2) \ (.1875)$$

$$N = 72$$

*This example is loosely based on the general discussion provided in Bruce W. Tuckman, *Conducting Educational Research* (New York: Harcourt Brace Jovanovich, 1978), pp. 205–206.

Let's clarify the discussion with an example. Assume that evaluators at a university with 3,000 full-time faculty members want to draw a random sample of the faculty and to survey them about their possible use of a proposed current awareness service. The evaluators have access to a current and accurate directory of faculty members and do not want to sample the faculty based on academic rank, department, or college. For the purposes of the study, they want to random sample the population.

The evaluators number the faculty in the directory from 1 to 3,000. Next they might turn to StatPac and program 4, "Determine Sample Size & Generate Random Numbers," on the utility disk. Having decided to produce management data at the 90% level, they determine that 1,081 faculty yield that confidence level ±2; 601 faculty correspond to ±3; and 370 faculty equate to ±4.[1] Upon review of study objectives and constraints, as well as managerial needs, the

---

[1] For comparative purposes, it might be noted that 95% ± 2 is 1,333, ± 3 is 787, and ± 4 is 500.

evaluators decide on a random generation of 601 faculty so that all 3,000 names have an equal and independent chance of inclusion in the study. Using the same StatPac program, they can generate a random number list and check off the corresponding names in the directory. They can compare this sample to the population on certain characteristics. The better the match, the greater confidence that the sample is representative of the population—full-time faculty at this one institution.

THE STRENGTHS AND LIMITATIONS OF STATISTICAL SAMPLING

In setting up a study, the question arises as to whether or not to sample. If the universe is small or the individual sampling units in the universe are very important, it is often advisable to examine every item in the universe. However, if the universe is large, a sample is preferred to a complete enumeration of the universe, because the information that is wanted can be obtained more cheaply, more quickly, and often more accurately, and in more detail. In some instances, only one of these benefits applies, and in some extreme situations, none does. These points deserve some explanation.

Sampling is usually cheaper than a complete review of the universe because, by definition, it usually deals with only a small group selected from the universe. The total cost of getting information includes a variable cost related to examining the individual items. By reducing the number of items to be examined, sampling permits a substantial reduction in that variable cost. However, a good sampling plan may add some costs that would not be present in a complete review. Although almost always much smaller than the savings, such costs should not be ignored. They usually cover developing the sampling plan, selecting the sample, monitoring the sample selection process, processing the data and calculating estimates and sampling errors, and providing special training or instruction necessary for completion of the previous steps.

With regard to speed, sometimes a recommendation must be prepared or a decision made within a relatively short time. No matter how good the quality, information is of no help unless it is received in time to be used in making a recommendation or arriving at a decision. The measurement or examination process takes time; so too does the summarization of results. Because a sample involves fewer items than a complete review, these processes can be done more quickly in order to make them more useful to decision makers.

Sometimes an attempt will be made to obtain more information from the sample than the study was originally designed to provide. An example of this is taking a sample that was designed to evaluate the effectiveness of a bibliographic instruction program as a whole and then attempting to develop estimates for different domains of interest (e.g., classifying students by class level, subject area, full- or part-time status, or age). In some cases, attempts to use a sample for purposes other than those for which it was designed can lead to estimates with sampling errors as large as, or larger than, the estimates themselves.

Similarly, many people believe that sampling may furnish less accurate answers than a complete analysis. In fact, the opposite view is probably more reasonable. The basis for this suggestion is the reduction in the risk of errors of measurement, recording, processing, and reporting. Because sampling involves the observation of fewer items, it frequently allows evaluators to use personnel who have been better trained to collect, process, and evaluate the data than would be practicable in a full examination of the universe. In fact, it has been found that measuring physical inventory by sampling is more accurate than counting and pricing every item. Also, because fewer observations are needed in sampling, the measuring process can be done more simultaneously. The result more likely represents correctly the status of the universe at a given time than would the result of a complete review, during which changes may take place. For instance, by the time the last item has been measured, the first one may have been consumed or materially changed.

By suggesting that sampling permits more detailed information to be obtained, we mean that if an attempt is made to measure all the items in the universe, it may be possible to make only one or a few observations on each sample item. However, if sampling is used and fewer items are measured, it may be possible to collect much more data about each item and thus develop more information about the universe.

Additionally, evaluators may discover during data collection that they are taking the wrong measurements, that additional data are needed, or that their objectives have been poorly defined. If sampling is used to collect the data, as opposed to making a complete enumeration, mistakes are easier to correct.

In sum, if statistical sampling is feasible and is carried out correctly, it usually has advantages over complete enumeration and nonstatistical sampling. Still, even if the evaluators avoid common sampling mistakes (see Hernon et al., 1989, p. 78) and design a study that meets all the requirements of good sampling, nonsampling errors might emerge. These are errors of measurement, e.g., response, coding, or interviewing errors (see Ibid., pp. 42–43).

Total error is a function of two independent sources of error—sampling and nonsampling error. Total error "cannot be substantially reduced unless both types are simultaneously controlled" (Blalock, 1972, p. 529). "A proper balance between sampling and nonsampling errors should . . . be maintained" (Ibid., p. 530).*

---

* Hubert M. Blalock, Jr., *Social Statistics*. Copyright © 1972, by McGraw-Hill Publishing Co., New York. Reproduced with permission.

SAMPLING AS A TOOL

The discussion in this chapter suggests that sampling is simply another tool that evaluators need to consider in the overall design of the evaluation study. By treating sampling as a tool, evaluators can increase the overall quality of the evaluation study. Perhaps most importantly, they can make informed and justifiable decisions about:

- Whether to collect data from a sample rather than the population as a whole
- Which type of sampling procedure best meets the needs of a particular evaluation study
- The degree of confidence and error that are acceptable for a particular sample.

Evaluators should carefully consider specific types of sampling approaches and select the one(s) that best meet the needs of the evaluation study.

To some degree, decisions about samples are likely to be based on the amount of time and resources available for completion of the study. Studies done in many library settings simply lack adequate time and resources to accommodate a sophisticated sampling design. However, effective evaluations can still be conducted without the use of sophisticated sampling techniques. The key is that evaluators recognize the tradeoffs between low-count samples and high-count samples, and between lower-confidence level samples and higher-confidence level samples. Evaluators must justify the decisions taken for whatever type of sample they use.

DISCUSSION ITEMS

1. Select an article from library and information science that uses sampling, and critique the method of sampling. Does the author supply adequate information to evaluate the method?
2. Provide an example of cluster and quota sampling.
3. Suppose that you wanted to conduct a survey of Texas academic libraries and that you wanted the sample to reflect the population. Using this example, contrast random to stratified sampling.
4. Review the section on determining sample size and compute the sample size necessary for 95% confidence, ±2, for question 3.
5. The population is divided into parts, each of which has certain common characteristics. The evaluator then draws from each part every 25th name. What type of sampling procedure is this?

6. Returning to question 5, this time all members of the population have an equal and independent chance of being selected. What type of sampling is this?
7. Again, returning to question 5, this time we are studying the elderly. Those included in the study will be selected by randomly taking nursing homes from a published list. What type of sampling procedure is this?
8. Is the most important characteristic of a sample its size or representativeness?
9. To select the sample, an evaluator has defined the population, compiled a list of all members of that population, and chosen a sample of population members using a table of random numbers or the random number generator of a microcomputer software package. What kind of sampling procedure was used?
10. Do all members of a well-defined group of people, events, or objects constitute a population or sample?

Chapter Seven
Improving the Evaluation Process with a Library Management Information System*

Libraries are complex organizations whose directors and staff must constantly evaluate a broad range of services and activities. Librarians often need timely and accurate information about services and activities in order to address managerial questions, and, at times, to determine if there is a potential problem that requires formal evaluation research (see Chapter 4). With careful planning, knowledge of microcomputers, and the use of appropriate software, they can develop a computer-based management information system (MIS) for monitoring a program or service and assessing its impact.

A MIS is a system providing managers with ongoing data collection and analysis. The focus of the MIS is to capture, organize, analyze, compare, and report a range of data describing library activities, services, and management. Typical functional categories included in a library MIS are:

- Budgeting
- Collections
- Physical facilities
- Services
- Staffing
- Community or service area characteristics.

Each of these functional categories comprise "modules" within the MIS. Data within these modules can be analyzed and related to data in other modules to assist decision makers in assessing library performance. Figure 7-1 graphically depicts this concept.

An effective MIS supplies decision makers with accurate and timely information in the form of carefully designed reports tailored to meet their information needs and preferences. A MIS supports different types of decision making, including:

---

* Portions of this chapter are drawn from McClure et al. (1989b), and were authored by Pat England, Lindsay Ruth, and Liz Hagerty-Roach. The chapter also draws upon Charles R. McClure, Liz Hagerty-Roach, Lindsay Ruth, and Pat England, "Design of a Public Library Management Information System," *Library Administration & Management*, 3 (Fall 1989): 192–198.

Figure 7-1.   Proposed Components of the Management Information System

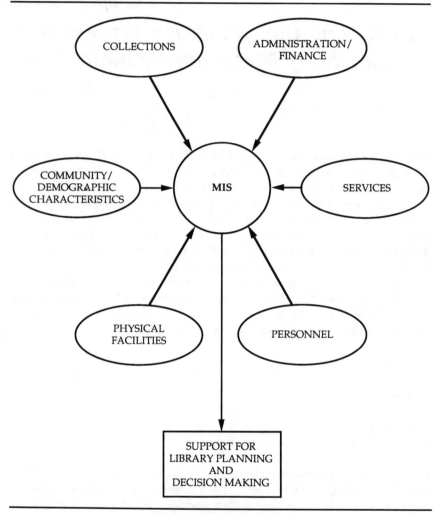

- Operational decisions (day-to-day decision making)
- Strategic planning decisions (determining appropriate objectives and accomplishing them)
- "What if" questions (if we increase expenditures on a particular service, what would be the impact on another service?)
- Exceptions (why has in-house use of periodicals increased drastically during the last month?)
- Resource control (ensuring that resources are expended on appropriate activities or items).

A MIS can significantly improve evaluation activities and, thus, library decision making for reasons such as the following:

- Decision makers obtain current responses from the system rather than having to wait for someone to collect and analyze the needed information
- "What if" computations and a wide range of alternatives allow the decision maker to revise and refine the data as needed
- Library management data are systematically collected and the reliability of the data can be increased
- Project activities, resource allocations, and service provisions can be regularly monitored
- A range of library staff can have access to the MIS and, thus, make decisions based on the same sources of information.

Typically, medium to large libraries collect and retain a broad range of management data relating to both internal and external activities. Indeed, many different individuals throughout the library may have or produce such data. Yet, not everyone may know what data are available, existing data may be unreliable, and little thought may be given to determining *which* data to collect and how often. Furthermore, the degree to which the data are easily available, and the amount of time and effort required to obtain that data, may be considerable.

Unfortunately, in the area of management information, libraries frequently are unable to:

- Comprehensively capture, organize, analyze, and report information that describe the library's environment and library-related activities and services
- Identify community information needs and respond to those needs in day-to-day decision making and strategic planning
- Demonstrate the overall effectiveness and efficiency of library activities
- Simplify and standardize the library data-gathering and reporting activities to ensure the collection of reliable and valid data.

Clearly, there is a significant need to design and implement a comprehensive, easy-to-use, computer-based library MIS. Such a system encourages libraries to be "evaluation minded" and to relate their activities and services to the planning process. Besides, a MIS can provide evidence, at any moment, regarding organizational accountability, effectiveness, and efficiency.

CONCEPTUAL FRAMEWORKS

While much of the automated data currently being collected in libraries follow functional or departmental lines, the literature reveals only a few examples of a systems view of library management information. Boland (1983) favors concentration on the library's relationship with its environment in designing a MIS. Management information, he noted, should be directed toward decisions related to a specified number of important factors that mean the difference between success and organizational survival.

These success factors encompass specific activities of the library and its relationship with its environment. The tendency in library MIS development has been to compile and aggregate internal operating data without integrating external factors affecting the library (Bommer and Chorba, 1982). The importance of environmental factors (such as community demographics, target market preferences, and competitive factors) for the success and survival of the library argues against the usefulness of purely internal data for managerial decision making.

McClure (1984) differentiates among types of models for management information systems and describes the evolution of MIS models proposed for library settings. The automation of data along functional lines has been replaced by models that attempt to integrate environmental inputs with library processing and output information. McClure notes a trend toward the development of models intended to support decision making at various levels of library management. This trend has implications for the traditional centralization of management control prevailing in libraries. Structural barriers to MIS development in libraries, discussed in a later section, may explain why there is so little evidence on the implementation of these models.

The data collected for library planning (which, by definition, includes information about the library's environment) and for inclusion in performance measures for evaluating the degree to which library objectives are met can be integrated with a management decision-support system. McClure (1978) provides a model that describes various components of evaluation and performance measures for the provision of management information useful for decision making and ongoing planning. He emphasizes *data utility* since the data represent activities and external factors identified in the planning process as critical to the success of the library in meeting its mission and goals.

In a British Library Research Paper, Thomas and Waghorn (1986) provide a preliminary outline of requirements for MIS in public libraries. They address the need for developing several models intended to address variations in information needs of differing library organizations and management styles. They discuss library inputs, such as cost allocation, staffing, facilities planning, and operations of public libraries, but they give little consideration to the integration of library functions or of environmental factors. Thomas and Waghorn treat each unit's activities independently rather than in the context of the contributions of various units to providing services or achieving library objectives. Their model, furthermore, does not include environmental responses to library outputs (services).

It is disappointing that there are so few examples of conceptual approaches to library MIS in the literature. There is little evidence to indicate the models proposed have been validated through a research process. Furthermore, the literature does not report actual applications of specific conceptual frameworks for integrating MIS in libraries.

AUTOMATED SYSTEMS FOR LIBRARY MIS

Several writers have taken a pragmatic approach and proposed designing library management information and decision support systems using existing automated data collection systems. Suggestions for configuring these data range from simple aggregation and exception reports to creating online integrated information systems with modeling capabilities. Lynch (1985) points out the lack of discussion and attention given to writings identifying library statistics that provide management information.

Numerous proposals for using MIS data have been advanced, but there has been little or no implementation of these proposals in actual library settings. Some of the more promising suggestions in the literature include:

- Enhancing OCLC data to provide microcomputer-based capability to capture, manipulate, and use the data for management decisions (Lynch, 1985; Dillon, Stephens, Flash, and Crook, 1988)
- Reconfiguring GEAC and NOTIS data to support management decisions relating to collection development and acquisitions (Hawks, 1988)
- Applying EXECUCOM's Interactive Financial Planning Systems model by using "a compilation of statistics furnished by a medium-sized library" for management decision support in financial resource allocation (Heindel and Napier, 1981)
- Using the statistics from the National Center for Educational Statistics (NCES) *Library Data Collection Handbook* for a generic "off-the-shelf MIS" for any size and type of library (Runyon, 1981).

The emphasis in these and other library MIS efforts is on compiling and reporting statistical data with little apparent consideration given to the relevance of the information for a range of managerial decisions. The sources mentioned above are oriented to either *inputs* (such as financial resource allocation) or *outputs* (such as circulation statistics). Data from specific activities and functions of the library do not appear to be integrated with each other to give decision makers a view of the system implications of management information.

Many of the vendor-designed management information systems are inflexible. They produce standardized status reports that do not address the concerns of managers above the day-to-day operational level (Lantz, 1986). These systems also have an unattractive appearance and produce awkward and confusing formats. The use of graphics and customized output design might enhance the appeal, and consequently the use, of management reports produced from vendor-supplied data.

Management information, as a by-product of automated operational control systems, appears unlikely to result in the strategic information needed for the semi-structured and unstructured decisions faced by middle and top management. Such decisions, by definition, require *relational* information that suggest possible impacts resulting from changes made in one library area or unit on the overall organization.

ORGANIZATIONAL FACTORS

The slow progress of MIS development in libraries is often attributed to a tendency toward traditional—and more conservative—organizational structures and managerial styles. Olsgaard (1983) discusses the impacts of an internally-oriented hierarchical chain of command and formal communication patterns as reasons why library managers fail to recognize the need for management information systems. He points out several characteristics of library managers that result in the nonuse of MIS data, including:

- Information overload
- Difficulty in dealing with numeric data
- A cultural bias against automation.

In addition, many managers simply have not received adequate education regarding library management or the use of data for decision making.

Shank (1983), who provides a useful practitioner point of view on the issue of managerial resistance to MIS, enumerates reasons for rejecting the use of empirical information. Among the more important reasons he cites are that the data are inconclusive, irrelevant, ambiguous, unrelated to objectives, and too numerous, as well as that they ignore political realities or managerial biases. Shank (p. 7) concludes that "What we need to do now is to build models of library operations. And the data to be inserted in them must be specific to the library being analyzed."

McClure (1986a) suggests the following strategies for preparing the organization for effective use of automated management information:

- Recognition of and support for organizational information resources management
- Analysis of organizational climate and adjustments, if necessary, to support the introduction of MIS
- Development of management styles that encourage the involvement of individuals at all levels

- Redesign of job structures based on the impact of technology on work flows
- Re-education and training of staff in computer-based systems.

An organization-wide understanding of the concepts of information resource management (IRM) and the purposes for which automated information systems are to be developed must exist prior to, or be introduced during, the implementation of a MIS (McClure, 1986a).

STRUCTURAL BARRIERS TO MIS IMPLEMENTATION

Traditional hierarchical reporting structures, division of labor, and centralization of authority common in libraries create barriers. The departmentalization of activities has produced "information systems centered on the needs of a single library department . . . with no perceived need and little attempt by any one department to produce data specifically designed for senior managers or for other departments" (Homer, 1986, p. 143).

Homer blames an organizational culture that perceives computerized systems as the exclusive domain of specialists for the inability of most libraries to carry automation beyond the level of reporting operating statistics. He suggests several prerequisites for achieving an integrated MIS capable of supporting management decisions, and he emphasizes the need for senior management support for and participation in MIS development. In order to eliminate the "mystique" attached to more sophisticated automated systems, Homer recommends wider participation by library staff. Their participation may necessitate a great deal of effort in the more traditionally managed hierarchical forms of library organization.

Heim (1983) explores the impact of organizational and individual variables on the implementation of a library MIS. While her analysis provides useful background information on the effects of MIS on (1) the degree of centralization of information, (2) management authority shifts, and (3) individual responses to organizational change, it offers few concrete recommendations for managing these impacts.

When they design and prepare the library for MIS-based decision making, as well as prior to implementation of an automated management information system, managers should review the following factors:

- Relevance of the management information to be generated
- Simplicity and ease of use of the system
- Senior management understanding of and support for MIS
- The ability of the organizational structure to accommodate communication of decision-making needs and priorities
- Integration of departmental data into a system that crosses functional lines and incorporates environmental inputs

- Individual sensitivity to sharing control and decision making
- Willingness to view decisions within the context of overall organizational goals.

Consideration of these factors is essential if a MIS is to be used successfully as a tool supporting the conduct of ongoing evaluation.

MIS OBJECTIVES

One of the persistent problems in MIS research and development has been the difficulty in defining objectives to be served by MIS and in measuring the degree to which an organization meets its objectives. Much of the research has focused on attempts to measure user satisfaction or the impact of information system use on the quality of decisions. However, there is little agreement on appropriate methodologies for empirical testing of these outcomes (Cooper, 1988).

The management literature cites instances of MIS implementation and use in both public and private sector organizations (other than libraries). "Success" has been measured in terms of frequency of use. Decision quality is a more difficult outcome to define and measure, and most of the research in this area is methodologically suspect or inconclusive (Ives and Olson, 1984).

There are likely to be competing objectives for MIS design and implementation in library settings. Some of the possible objectives might be to:

- Assist users in resolving their information needs
- Maintain better accountability and control over library resources
- Monitor and control resource allocations
- Improve overall library effectiveness
- Report legally-mandated information to local, state, regional, national, or accrediting institutions
- Assist library managers in making better operational decisions
- Improve the basis for long-range planning.

One information system cannot effectively be all things to all people. The organization must clarify and specify the objectives for which a MIS is to be designed and implemented in order to provide a focus for determination of information needs and output design to support management decisions.

DETERMINING INFORMATION NEEDS

The management (as opposed to library) literature over the past decade has focused on the primary importance of determining managers' information needs as a prerequisite to MIS design and development. Munro (1978) identified two methods of determining information needs: "data analysis" focuses on analyzing and improving existing information flows, and "decision analysis" begins with the decisions made by managers and attempts to determine the information required at each step.

In analyzing the strengths and weaknesses of each method, Munro concludes that data analysis has advantages in situations where an organization will use the system for the more structured decisions. Decision analysis is more appropriate for systems intended to serve unstructured or semi-structured decision making because such analysis is top-down oriented, i.e., the analysis begins with managers defining their decision processes.

Management scientists and managers have partially accepted the critical success factors (CSF) approach, which Rockart (1979) introduced as a means of imposing a structure on the decision analysis process. Boynton and Zmud (1984) reported on the results of two case studies using CSF and found that, although there were numerous benefits to be obtained through its use, the utility of CSF as a means of identifying managers' information needs was limited. Only the most senior managers could articulate their decision-making processes or their information requirements at various stages of information gathering.

Prototyping is another method to determine information needs for MIS development. A prototype is a system that represents a pattern or archetypal model encompassing the basic features of a later system (Naumann and Jenkins, 1982). The model is intended to be manipulated and modified or augmented by users as a means of refining the final system design. Prototyping can be effective in situations where experience with MIS applications is limited; however, there is a high cost associated with developing prototypes that represent realistic data elements and information systems (Cooper, 1988, p. 82). Although case studies and argument by analogy have been used to validate the benefits of prototyping, Cooper found limited empirical evidence to support the effectiveness of this approach in determining managers' information needs.

USER INVOLVEMENT IN SYSTEMS DESIGN

It has become almost axiomatic that user involvement leads to more successful management information systems (Cooper, 1988). Hirschheim (1985) found that user involvement is essential for the determination of information needs and that such involvement results in higher acceptance of the systems. Evidence from the literature of participatory management applied to system design also supports a higher level of acceptance and commitment to systems use by those involved in the design and implementation of information systems (Ives and Olson, 1984).

The drawbacks to user involvement include the time required for obtaining user input and resolving conflicts among groups of users. The political impact of multiple constituencies within an organization can lead to user resistance and counterproductive maneuvers by those who perceive a loss of power resulting from MIS implementation. User involvement alone does not resolve these conflicts. An assessment of the impact on the various constituencies must be undertaken in order to involve users effectively in system design.

Empirical evidence for the positive impact of user involvement is inconclusive, largely because of the problems in producing valid and reliable measures of system success. However, as Ives and Olson (1984) note, it is difficult to ignore the intuitive appeal of user involvement. An opportunity to raise and resolve conflict, better identify information needs, and obtain commitment to the system requires some degree of user participation in the design stages.

DESIGN OF A MIS

This section of the chapter provides a brief overview of a project intended to develop a MIS for a large public library. McClure et al. (1989a, b) provide detailed information about the project. The intent here, however, is simply to show how one MIS project evolved and to describe some of the key activities that occurred. Readers wishing to develop a MIS in support of their library's evaluation activities may find useful suggestions and lessons from this overview.

Project Goals and Method

The purpose of the project was to assist decision makers in improving both the timeliness and quality of their decisions and, more specifically, to:

- Capture, organize, analyze, and report *selected* information describing the library environment, activities, collections, and services
- Assist branch managers and administrative librarians in providing services and developing collections that better meet the community's information needs
- Assist branch managers and administrative librarians in demonstrating the overall effectiveness and efficiency of selected library activities
- Simplify and standardize the data gathering and reporting activities of the library.

In addition, the project was a logical continuation of the Public Library Development Project which resulted in the publication of two manuals: *Planning and Roles Setting for Public Libraries* (McClure et al., 1987) and *Output Measures for Public Libraries*, (Van House et al., 1987). A MIS would significantly improve the library staff's ability to plan and evaluate library performance along the techniques outlined in these two manuals.

Data Collection

The method for investigating existing MIS activities at the library and obtaining data regarding library MIS was multi-faceted and relied on a range of sources:

- Literature review
- Telephone interviews with librarians who had experience in the design or implementation of a MIS
- Focus group interviews of library branch managers and administrative librarians
- Follow-up interviews with various library staff and County Data Processing Department staff
- Forms/procedures analysis of various library data collection forms, and especially the library's "Monthly Activities Report"
- Software review and analysis.

Data collection activities focused on the following research questions:

- What are the information needs of branch managers?
- What are the information needs of administrative librarians?
- To what degree can available NOTIS[1] data and NOTIS extract files be integrated into a MIS?
- What are the existing MIS data collection/reporting activities in the system?
- What types of microcomputer-based MIS software would best meet the MIS needs of librarians?

The multiple data collection strategy allowed the study team to consider the design of the MIS from different perspectives. Furthermore, the team sequenced data collection in such a way that the initial focus group interviews could refine and direct later data collection activities.

Overview of Project Activities

Competing objectives for a MIS, the difficulty of determining information needs, the value of user involvement, and the need for a supportive organizational climate were all factors that affected the completion of activities during the project. Indeed, the focus of the project changed due to two factors identified during the data collection activities.

---

[1] NOTIS is an integrated computer-based library system intended to automate a number of library processes and functions, including cataloging, authority control, acquisitions, serials, circulation, and an online public catalog. Additional information about the NOTIS system can be obtained from NOTIS Systems, Inc., 2nd Floor, 1007 Church Street, Evanston, IL, 60201–3622.

First, it became apparent from the review of existing data collection activities and in the focus group interviews that there was an immediate need for a higher quality of current information collected by branch librarians. Furthermore, there is no justification for entering "dirty" data into the MIS. For these reasons, the study team decided to direct its efforts toward upgrading the "Monthly Activities Report" in order to provide the branch librarians with useful and timely information for decisions made at the branch level. Second, NOTIS data required for the MIS could not be extracted for use within the time frame of the project.

Within this context, the following activities were completed during the project:

- *A review and assessment of the literature*: The study team reviewed the existing literature describing library MIS and conducted telephone interviews with libraries that had engaged in MIS design or development
- *Identification of information needs of library decision makers*: Library decision makers identified specific types of decisions for which they needed data, and listed the type of data currently being collected
- *An audit of existing data collection activities*: The team reviewed various, existing data collection and reporting forms, collated and reviewed specific data elements being collected, and analyzed the procedures for collecting the data
- *Determination of the feasibility of obtaining NOTIS extract files as input to the MIS*: The team identified data elements generated by NOTIS that the librarians considered to be important components for the MIS. The team also outlined procedures necessary for importing those data elements from the various NOTIS files
- *Determination of the management information system requirements*: A part of the overall design process, the team produced and discussed, with library staff, a preliminary statement of the MIS requirements; that document is appended to McClure et al. (1989b)
- *The redesign of data collection reporting forms and procedures*: The team redesigned the "Monthly Activities Report" submitted to library administrative offices from branch libraries and rewrote the procedures for collecting and submitting the data. The purpose was to focus on the most important management data and to increase the likelihood of obtaining higher quality data; these forms and procedures are appended to McClure et al. (1989b)
- *Selection of appropriate data elements for inclusion in the database*: Based on the literature review and the above activities, the team identified candidate lists of data elements for inclusion in the database
- *Selection of appropriate hardware and software for the MIS*: Based on the completed systems requirements statement, the team determined that Paradox

3.0 database manager (produced by Borland), operating in a PC-based, IBM-DOS environment, would best meet the library's MIS requirements[2]

- *The design and configuration of one module of the database*: The team developed the design for a services module (based on the "Monthly Activities Report" and other data) and had to design and configure the software to match the data being collected and the needs of library decision makers
- *Production of a MIS user manual*: The team developed a short training manual, demonstration diskette, and database templates to assist library staff in inputting data into the Paradox software, manipulate the data, and generate reports; this manual is appended to McClure et al. (1989b)
- *Staff training*: The study team conducted formal and informal training sessions with library staff on data collection, using data for decision making, and operating the database management software.

Throughout the project, library staff participated in a number of data collection activities, reviewed project material, and provided direct input and assessment of the MIS design. Again, this direct involvement of the *users* in the design of the proposed MIS is an important component of the project.

Database Design

The database design evolved out of a careful analysis of the system requirements, the data to be manipulated, and the needs of the decision makers. Figure 7-1 graphically depicts the MIS envisioned as a collection of data entry and report modules. The data elements are related to each other, thereby producing a broad range of information describing the library.

Data were to be collected through three basic sources: NOTIS, the branch libraries, or by library administration. Reports covering specific decision areas would be generated for a number of different purposes. Figure 7-2 describes the relationship between data collection and data reporting, while Figure 7-3 depicts the data flow for the MIS.

After a review and testing of a number of software packages, including spreadsheets, relational and nonrelational databases, wordprocessing and graphic packages, as well as integrated software, the study team determined that a relational database would provide the basis for the MIS. Relational databases differ from other database structures in that the data are stored in tables and

---

[2] Recent reviews of Paradox appeared in the April 10, 1989 issue of *InfoWorld* and the March 28, 1989 issue of *PC Magazine*. Both reviews found Paradox to be the best overall DOS relational database currently on the market. Additional information about Paradox software can be obtained from Borland, 1800 Green Hills Road, P.O. Box 660001, Scotts Valley, CA 95066–0001.

Figure 7-2. Relating Data Elements to Decision Areas

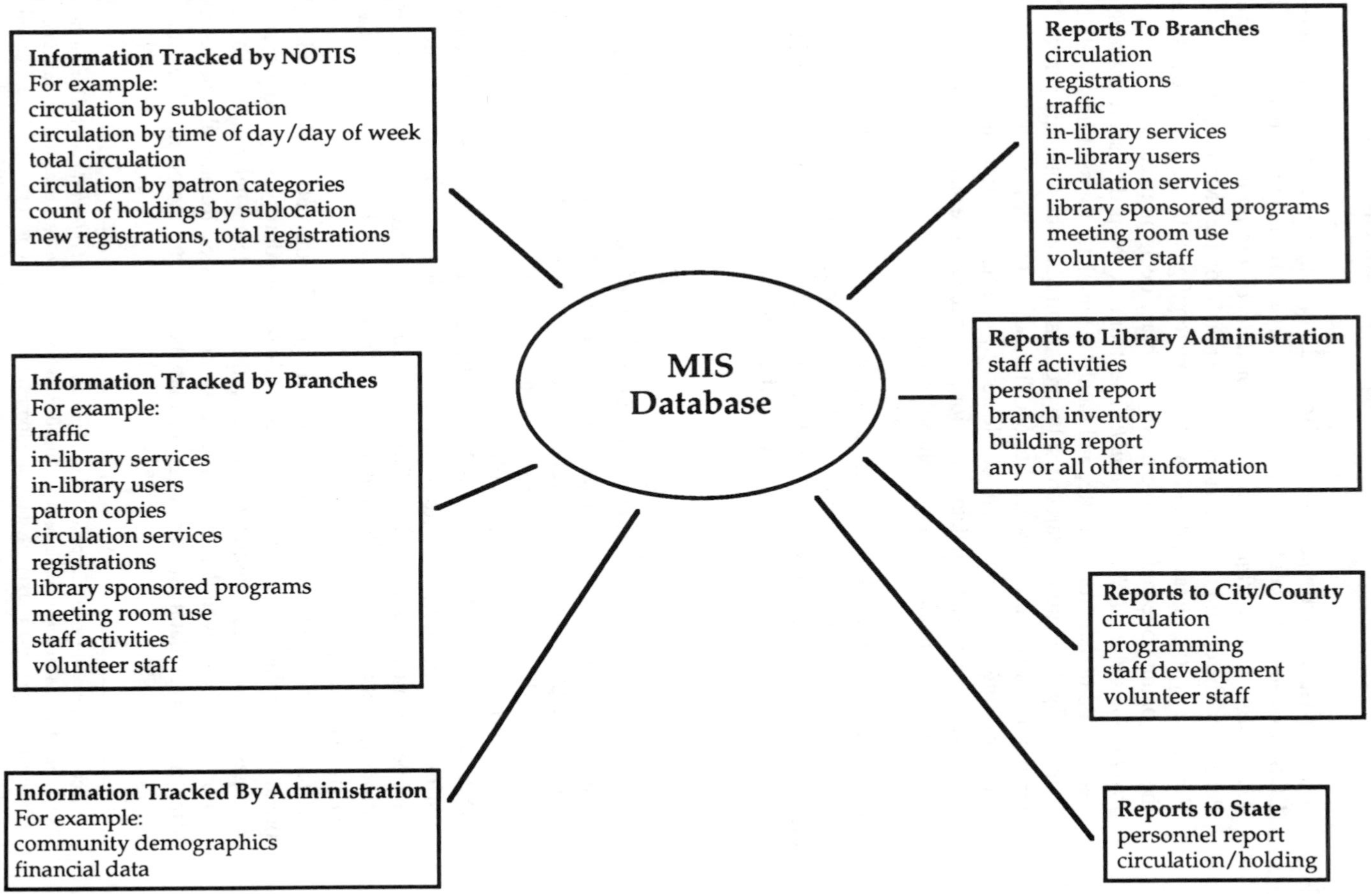

Reports To Branches
circulation
registrations
traffic
in-library services
in-library users
circulation services
library sponsored programs
meeting room use
volunteer staff

Reports to Library Administration
staff activities
personnel report
branch inventory
building report
any or all other information

Reports to City/County
circulation
programming
staff development
volunteer staff

Reports to State
personnel report
circulation/holding

MIS
Database

Information Tracked by NOTIS
For example:
circulation by sublocation
circulation by time of day/day of week
total circulation
circulation by patron categories
count of holdings by sublocation
new registrations, total registrations

Information Tracked by Branches
For example:
traffic
in-library services
in-library users
patron copies
circulation services
registrations
library sponsored programs
meeting room use
staff activities
volunteer staff

Information Tracked By Administration
For example:
community demographics
financial data

Figure 7-3. Data Flow for Management Information System

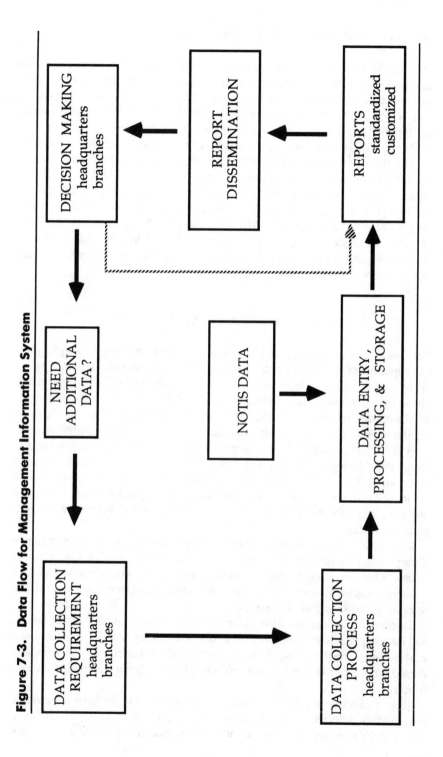

133

subjected to a set of rules that are transparent to the users but ensure structural quality and data integrity. Tables can be "joined" to other tables, with specific pieces of data that were previously unrelated. Once linked together, they provide analyses that previously were unavailable. Tables can also be updated, queried, and reported either separately or while joined to other tables.

Paradox 3.0 offered not only the aspects of a relationally structured database, but also the added features of graphics capabilities and uploading and downloading of data from a variety of other software packages (e.g., LOTUS and dBase). Paradox 3.0 also has the capability to structure the data centrally within the MIS and to report the data from within different modules. The codebook portion of the *User Manual*, an appendix to McClure et al. (1989b), includes a complete list of data elements contained in the database. Clark (1989) provides additional suggestions for hardware and software in the design of a computer-based information system to support library decision making and evaluation.

DEVELOPING A SUCCESSFUL MIS

Relevance of information, simplicity of design, and user understanding of possible applications and uses of the data are key issues in initiating MIS in any organization that has little or no prior experience with MIS. Clearly, one critical phase is determining the information needs of the MIS users. Another is the administrative integration of the MIS into library operations as a normal and regular means of assisting library managers in decision-making activities.

A library MIS should be an integrated system that incorporates a range of community/demographic data and draws on data from the various functional areas within the library as they relate to specific decisions. The current use of automated systems for many clerical and data-gathering functions in libraries can provide a basis for the next step in information systems development—a comprehensive MIS.

Currently, there is limited research into the design and implementation of library MIS. Few libraries are involved in MIS activities, and few library administrations have invested the time and resources necessary to implement a management information system. Because so few systems are operational, it is difficult to evaluate MIS success in libraries.

Despite the limited attention given to library MIS, a number of suggestions and issues appear to be especially important in the design and implementation of a MIS. Interestingly, most of these concerns do not focus on the computer-related aspects of MIS design, but rather emphasize planning and organizational concerns.

First, much of the effort involved in MIS design must be spent on ensuring that the data collected are reliable and valid. All areas within a particular library must use the same data element definitions and collection procedures in order to ensure consistency. Existing data collection procedures and reporting forms almost certainly must be reviewed, revised, and standardized[3] across units or branches. There is no point in designing a sophisticated MIS to analyze and report "dirty data."

Second, data elements to be collected and reported should be carefully chosen. Implementation of a MIS provides the opportunity to collect an abundance of information, but all data should be evaluated to ascertain their usefulness in decision making. Data that have been traditionally collected should not be included solely for tradition's sake. Avoiding information overload is essential. It is better to collect fewer data elements of higher quality.

Third, in order to make the system valuable to managers at all levels, there must be a balance between tracking data to (1) evaluate the total library system; (2) meet the individual information needs of specific libraries, units, or branches; and (3) report to local, state, or Federal agencies. Each unit may have unique characteristics that should be taken into consideration in order to enhance the usefulness of the MIS at that level.

Fourth, intended uses and applications of the system should be clearly stated to avoid unrealistic expectations. For example, if the primary purpose of the system is to facilitate external reporting processes, then the system may not provide much assistance to branch managers needing to make daily operational decisions. A MIS is limited by the data available to it; a MIS cannot analyze decision situations for which data are unavailable.

Fifth, the design of the MIS must be based on the information needs of library decision makers. Once again, there is no point in designing and implementing a MIS that decision makers will not use. Involving library decision makers directly in the design, obtaining their input into MIS data elements and reporting procedures, and providing them with training on the use of data for decision making are factors critical to the success of the MIS *after* it is implemented.

Sixth, obtaining the necessary MIS data from automated library systems, such as NOTIS, tends to be a significant effort. Unfortunately, various automated library systems have poorly considered the production and reporting of management data from these systems (Lynch, 1985). Thus, the design of the MIS has to account for some original programming, develop extract files from the automated library systems, analyze these files with appropriate statistical analysis software, and download the results from such analyses into the MIS.

Finally, and most importantly, in order for an MIS to be successful, the library should have a history of active involvement in planning activities and already recognize the need and importance of having access to reliable empirical data for decision-making purposes. Designing a MIS that can generate intricate

---

[3] Three sources provide useful guidance and suggestions for the standardization of public library data elements: *Library Data Collection Handbook* (1981); *PLDS Statistical Report '88* (1988); and *An Action Plan for a Federal-State Cooperative System for Public Library Data* (1989).

reports and assessments serves no practical purpose if the library administration and staff are not committed to improving services and planning for the future.

MIS AND EVALUATION

The development of an MIS is not an end in and of itself. The major concern for library managers is not the computer-related aspects of system design, but rather the need to ensure that the end product of the MIS is reliable information that meets the needs of library decision makers for a range of evaluation processes.

As the library becomes more involved in ongoing evaluation, collects and analyzes a range of evaluation data, and attempts to organize and better utilize those data, the need for a MIS increases. The MIS is best seen as a *tool* that can significantly improve the evaluation process by:

- Organizing and storing evaluation data in a centralized information system
- Allowing evaluators to analyze data easily across a range of library activities and services
- Promoting the use of basic statistical analyses on the data and presenting the data with high-impact graphics
- Encouraging evaluators to relate evaluation results from one area of library services to another (e.g., impact of increased library visits on particular types of services)
- Monitoring the effectiveness and efficiency of various library services and activities over time, and thereby producing trend data
- Assisting evaluators to identify and develop a range of performance measures.

Clearly, a MIS can provide a broad range of support to specific components of the evaluation process as it is depicted in Figure 2-1.

Although the thrust of this book is not on the design and implementation of library MIS, it is useful for readers to appreciate the potential role and importance of a MIS as a direct support for the evaluation process. Those libraries that regularly collect statistics (either for internal reasons or for external agencies) and/or are otherwise engaged in the regular evaluation of library services would do well to consider the development and implementation of a MIS to support that data collection and analysis process.

DISCUSSION ITEMS

---

1. Why is a management information system an important tool for library decision makers?

2. Consider a library situation with which you are familiar. Describe typical types of evaluations that might be made and identify the data elements necessary to include in a MIS.
3. What factors contribute to the successful design and implementation of a MIS?
4. Why are there so few library MISs currently in operation?
5. What kind of training activities might be necessary to assist library staff in using a MIS effectively?
6. Which of the specific components within the planning/evaluation process (see Figure 2-1) could a MIS improve? Why?
7. What steps can be taken to ensure that only accurate, reliable, and valid data be included in the MIS?
8. What criteria might be used to determine which library staff should have access to specific data in the MIS?
9. Discuss possible MIS output formats, e.g., reports and graphics, that would be especially useful in conducting evaluations.
10. What are the benefits and limitations of having a MIS on a relational database rather than a spreadsheet?

Chapter Eight

Importance of Performance Measures in the Evaluation Process*

Performance measures represent a broad managerial concept that encompasses both *input* (indicators of those resources essential to library services) and *output* (indicators of the services resulting from library activities) measures. Performance measures can assess the extent, effectiveness, and efficiency of library operations, services, and programs. Perhaps with the exception of those measures that only indicate extensiveness or the amount of service provided, the purpose of performance measures is to direct the attention of librarians to the question: "How well is the library doing what it claims to be doing?"

Before librarians draw conclusions and inferences from such measures they need to develop quantifiable and measurable objectives that place performance in proper context. In some instances, librarians collect data and compute performance measures, but do not exploit the potential usefulness of these measures for decision making, problem identification, planning (McClure, 1986a), and the identification of the services they want to provide and improve. Performance measures can assist librarians in determining the degree to which the organization accomplishes goals and objectives, in setting priorities for resource allocation, in justifying services, and in demonstrating library effectiveness to external agencies (Van House, Weil, and McClure, 1990, p. 9).

The primary utility of a performance measure is for "internal self-diagnosis of library services and activities" (McClure, Zweizig, Van House, and Lynch, 1986, p. 51). Managers must select and use measures having value to their libraries and the information needs of their clientele. They should not consider a particular score derived from calculating a measure as "inherently 'good' or 'bad'" (Ibid.). Rather, managers must place a score in the context of their expectations and their libraries' goals and objectives.

When people compare the performance of one library to that of another, they may be distorting the mission, goals, and objectives of each library. They must also recognize the strengths and weaknesses of the sampling frame, self-reporting questionnaires, circulation records, and other methods of data collection. Furthermore, they might question the extent to which evaluators collected reliable and valid data. Consequently (Van House, Weil, and McClure, 1990, p. ii),

---

* This chapter updates and expands upon Peter Hernon, "Utility Measures, Not Performance Measures, for Library Reference Service?," *RQ*, 26 (Summer 1987): 449–459.

Specific local decisions about measurement methods may make data noncomparable across libraries, so external comparisons can only be made with extreme caution and with a detailed understanding of how each library implemented these measures.

PLANNING AND EVALUATION

Library managers can benefit from the use of performance measures that capture the quantity and, more importantly, the quality of services provided. Furthermore, these managers should relate any measure that they utilize to other available information and to the planning process.

Performance measures encourage library managers to re-examine their priorities and the extent of their commitment to the provision of services that meet the information needs of clientele. Without such priorities and commitments, clearly stated and examined on an ongoing basis, many libraries will not be future- (or change-) oriented: they will not improve the quality of their information services. Libraries should meet patrons' information needs effectively and efficiently while meeting their mission, goals, and objectives. Without data collection, libraries will either make decisions based upon intuition or avoid making them. Consequently, they may fail to recognize service areas that require immediate attention and improvement.

When librarians select possible performance measures for local use, they should consider the appropriateness, validity, reproductibility, comparability, and practicality of the measures (see Orr, 1973). Appropriateness refers to whether the measures accomplish what decision makers want, and validity questions whether the measures mean what decision makers think they do. Reproducibility refers to whether someone else would get the same answer, while comparability questions whether others using the same procedures and definitions would discover similar findings. Practicality questions whether the library can afford the time, money, and effort to gather data for these measures.

By setting goals and stating specific performance measures that they wish to evaluate, libraries identify areas in which additional planning and decision making is necessary. For instance, by stating that they want to increase *title fill rate* by 10% per year as an objective, the area of planning is related to collection development and management, especially if managers view the fill rate within a subject context (e.g., for history). Upon the collection of pertinent data, library staff can initiate specific activities to increase the fill rate for a particular subject.

Managers can use performance measures for either formative (ongoing) or summative (at the end of an activity) evaluation. However, there may be tradeoff relationships between specific performance measures. In other words, increasing the score on one measure may decrease that on another. Figure 8-1, which graphically represents the importance of this relationship, suggests that the rela-

Figure 8-1.   Relating Effectiveness to Efficiency*

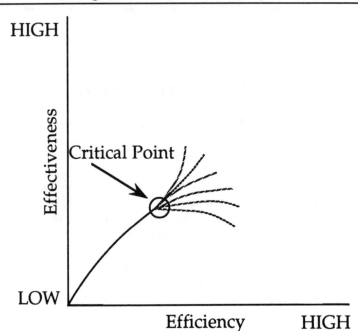

* While initially there may be a direct relationship between efficiency and effectiveness of a particular library activity, a "tradeoff" is likely to occur, and while one measure is increased, the other may begin to decrease.

tionship between efficiency and effectiveness may be one in which there is a "critical point," e.g., increasing the performance of either the effectiveness or efficiency of a service diminishes the performance on the other. This concept of a "critical point" underscores that there might be a relationship between/among various performance measures. Because performance measures examine differ-ent components of the same system, they are interdependent; that is, changing one component of the system (such as retention policy) may affect another component of the system (such as collection turnover).[1]

In addition to this tradeoff relationship, a number of other factors must be remembered when using performance measures:

- Each measure only emphasizes one facet of library activity; measures are best used in conjunction with each other information about the library
- Conditions can be manipulated to improve the performance on a particular

---

[1] Van House et al. (1987) discuss the tradeoffs for each measure.

measure without always improving the quality of the service or operation, e.g., increase the *turnover rate* simply by heavily weeding the collection
- There are no "right" or "wrong" scores on a performance measure; the scores are tied to specific library goals and objectives, and provide "benchmarks" to assess the effectiveness of library activities
- A primary use of a performance measure is to identify areas where change is desired, to determine if change has occurred, and to identify areas where additional research is required
- Performance measures should suggest not only what is happening in the library, but also the quality of what is occurring, "without going into the details of how those outputs were produced." Performance measures "do not in themselves diagnose the causes of inadequate performance" (Van House, Weil, and McClure, 1990, p. 8)
- "Output measures reflect services delivered, uses made of the library. The archival function of the library's collection is not fully reflected. In some libraries, this is a major consideration" (Ibid.)
- Measures "reflect user success in the library, not simply library performance. The final outcome is a function of the library, the user, and the library's success in anticipating user needs and assisting in the user's search" (Ibid.)
- Measures "reflect the interaction of users and library resources, constrained by the environment in which they operate. The meaning of a specific score on any measure depends on a broad range of factors including the library's goals, the current circumstances of the library and its environment, the users, the manner in which the measure was constructed, and how the data were collected" (Ibid.).

PERFORMANCE MEASURE CONTROVERSIES

The literature of librarianship has discussed the use of performance measures in academic, corporate, and public libraries (e.g., Van House et al., 1987; Kantor, 1984; Cronin, 1985; McClure and Reifsnyder, 1984; and Van House, Weil, and McClure, 1990). Authors have tended to either encourage librarians to adopt these "imperfect" but "practical and useful" measures (Van House, 1985, p. 105), or to conclude that fill rates and user satisfaction measures are questionable indicators of library effectiveness (e.g., Lee, 1987). Some authors contend that these measures do not adequately assess the reactions and experiences of library patrons (Goldhor, 1983), but that they necessitate the collection of more reliable and valid data than many libraries have gathered, and that data collection should be based on larger sample sizes (D'Elia, 1985). Ballard (1989) discusses egalitarian issues if access to state financial aid is tied to performance measures. Curran and Clark (1989) also examine the implications of tying state aid to such measures.

According to Childers and Van House (1989b, p. 44),

the development of the output measures was done without an empirical base; there was no systematically laid foundation for choosing which measures to adopt. Nor is there a systematically laid foundation for selecting output measures over other kinds of measures to describe library effectiveness.

Clearly, managers have choices and must match measures to their need for information in making decisions.

In the debate between D'Elia and Van House in *Public Libraries* over the utility of fill rates as a type of performance measure, Van House (1988) discusses the limitations of the chi-square test and encourages the application of higher-powered statistical analyses. However, as D'Elia (1988, p. 29) observes, "given the nature of the fill rate data . . . , the chi-square test is the only appropriate test for differences." He concludes that "the problem is not the statistical test but rather the inherent weaknesses of fill rate data that mandated the chi-square test." Clearly, fill rate data involve the use of a lower level of measurement—nominal and perhaps ordinal levels. They do not involve the use of interval or ratio data (see Hernon et al., 1989, pp. 37–40).

In response to such criticisms, McClure, Zweizig, Van House, and Lynch (1986) note that the collection of data having value to management need not be evaluated from a research perspective. Managers must recognize both the constraints under which their staff collect data (e.g., the extent to which they have the necessary research skills and competencies) and the impact of these constraints on the utility of the data collected. Library staff may have neither the financial resources nor the time to collect more accurate and valid data. When data portray only one aspect of a service, and do so in a general manner, they may still provide useful impressions to aid decision making, especially when they are used with other information concerning the service. The assumption is that collecting general data that demonstrate extensiveness, effectiveness, or efficiency only in a general manner is better than having no available data on a program or service.

Clearly, over time, there have been advancements in the conceptualization, development, and implementation of performance measures. Van House, Weil, and McClure (1990) summarize these advancements; together with Van House et al. (1987), they provide information essential for any library wanting to gather performance measures. Of course, more remains to be accomplished. Still, the foundation is present and becoming increasingly more solid.

PURPOSE OF CHAPTER

This chapter encourages the linkage of performance measures to evaluation and planning. As discussed in Chapter 4, the research process includes a component of reflective inquiry called *study objectives*. These objectives differ from library objectives. The former are statements that guide the collection of research or evaluation data, while the latter are concrete expressions of library tasking, and they explain the extent to which the library meets formal goals (see McClure et al., 1987). It should be noted that research studies need not focus on performance measures. Rather, these measures provide one means of producing data useful for planning and decision making. Chapters 10 and 11 illustrate studies that do not involve the computation of performance measures. Performance measures may serve as a substitute for formulation of evaluation objectives, hypotheses, and research questions.

This chapter encourages the development of performance measures, discusses a conceptual gap in part of the literature on performance measures, and modifies certain measures to maximize their utility for decision making. Clearly, individual managers must decide on those measures for which they want data collected.

Any measures used should have utility, internal validity (measure what they purport to measure), reliability, and the fewest conceptual and practical weaknesses. Utility encourages library managers to review formal goals and objectives, to identify information needs, and to ask (Paisley, 1969):

- What use will be made of the data collected?
- What decisions will these data impact?
- What can be learned from data collection—what are the benefits to the library?

Utility deals with applications, impacts, and usefulness of the data, and presupposes that a primary purpose of data collection is to influence library policies and decision making.

Library managers should select those measures that have the most utility for local planning and decision making. Utility refers to the information needs of local managers and encourages managers to prioritize those needs. They must also remember the interrelationships between inputs and outputs and determine that a measure adequately reflects what it purports.

Van House, Weil, and McClure (1990) view the library as a system consisting of inputs, processes (activities transforming resources into a product, e.g., cataloging), outputs, outcomes (the effect of the outputs from the library on the larger environment), environment, and feedback (information from both the system and the larger environment that helps the organization to improve its processes and outputs, and to obtain resources). An effective library becomes one that achieves its goals and objectives. The purposes for judging the quantity and quality of services provided to library clientele include (p. 4):

- "Assessing current levels of library services
- Comparing past, current, and desired levels of performance
- Diagnosing a particular *problem* area or service

- Monitoring progress toward specific objectives
- Justifying resource allocations
- Demonstrating accountability to the library's parent organization."

In determining effectiveness, librarians need to compare indicators of current performance to library objectives or previous performance. Only with extreme caution can the library make comparisons system-wide, to other libraries, or to predetermined standards. These external comparisons "must be made in the context of the libraries' mission and goals and individual constraints and environmental factors" (Van House, Weil, and McClure, 1990, p. 7).

AN APPROPRIATE TERM

The term performance measure is broader and more generic than the term output measures. Output measures, a type of performance measure, concentrate on the extensiveness, effectiveness, or quality of the services or products that a library offers its clientele. Output measures are user-based and have a specific focus—the result or end product of a service/activity, or the impact of that service/activity on a user.

In contrast, input measures examine the allocation of library resources. Interrelationships between inputs and outputs exist (Chapter 9 expands on this point). Where clear distinctions between them are not easily made, evaluators might examine inputs in relationship to outputs. Therefore, a key issue becomes which term—input, output, or performance measures—to use. Complicating matters even more, some authors are introducing the term *productivity measures*, which compare unit input to unit output, and which encourage an organization to examine both effectiveness and efficiency (see Kast and Rosenzweig, 1985, p. 644). Williams (1988) offers examples of productivity measures for special libraries.

When input measures have a direct impact on output measures, the term *performance measures* is perhaps preferable; performance measures encourage evaluators to examine interrelationships. However, some librarians might mistakenly assume that such measures represent a type of personnel evaluation—the examination of an individual's performance for the purpose of rendering a decision regarding retention or a salary increase.

According to Lynch (1983, p. 393), "it seems very possible that 'output measures' are much less threatening to library staff than 'performance measures'." Furthermore, "'performance measures' implies that what is being observed or counted is the person who is doing something." In contrast, output measures "implies a focus on . . . the result of the activity, not the person doing it" (Ibid.).

The term *productivity measures* may be more beneficial (Williams, 1988).

Although the term avoids the unfortunate connotation of performance measures, some librarians will resist efforts to link their activities and performance to productivity—they will question whether a measure adequately reflects an organization's and their own productivity. For example, does a determination of the number of reference questions answered, in comparison to the number of questions asked, truly suggest productivity? Perhaps the number of questions answered *correctly* is a better base for determining productivity. Productivity obviously may not adequately characterize effectiveness. Effectiveness consists of more than just productivity.

Clearly, future research should review key terms and analyze the concept of productivity measures in actual library settings. This chapter does not resolve the differences in terminology. Rather, it underscores that some librarians use the terms "output measures" and "performance measures" interchangeably, while others treat them differently. Perhaps, it is more important to discuss what library managers want to measure than the label to be applied to a measure.

EXAMPLES OF MEASURES

A performance measure provides only one indicator of library service and does not encompass *all* potential areas. Library decision makers should decide which activities have the highest priority and evaluate the effectiveness and/or efficiency of programs and services in priority areas (see Childers and Van House, 1989a, b). If appropriate, they should identify the measures that best reflect these activities. Nonetheless, performance measures may represent an oversimplified means of evaluation if they fail to address complex interrelationships between input and output measures.

Librarians can link specific measures to collection development policy statements and priorities, reference services, and so forth. Figure 8-2 identifies five measures commonly presented in the literature. The first three are general indicators of collection development, user success, and title availability. These measures of extensiveness become a type of indicator of effectiveness when they are linked to a library's goals and objectives.

Both *title fill rate* and *collection turnover rate* lack a specific context for providing a maximum benefit to decision making. The literature on collection development and management emphasizes the importance of imposing a structure of literature or subject context on selection and deselection decision making (Baughman, 1977). Viewing *title fill rate* within a subject context acknowledges the conceptual base and maximizes the decision-making utility of the measure. Library managers can compare fill rates by subject and determine the extent of their satisfaction with the documented use of parts of the collection. Obviously, libraries collect more extensively in some subject areas than in others, and imposing a subject context on a measure recognizes this fact. A potential limita-

Figure 8-2. Examples of General Measures Discussed in the Literature

TITLE FILL RATE

$$\frac{\text{Titles Found (1)}}{\text{Titles Sought (2)}} \times 100 \qquad = \underline{\hspace{1cm}} \text{ \% of Titles Found}$$

SUBJECT FILL RATE

$$\frac{\text{Subjects Found (3)}}{\text{Subjects Sought (4)}} \times 100 \qquad = \underline{\hspace{1cm}} \text{ \% of Subjects Found}$$

COLLECTION TURNOVER RATE

$$\frac{\text{Annual Circulation (5)}}{\text{Holdings (6)}} \times 100 \qquad = \underline{\hspace{1cm}} \text{ Circulations per Item in One Year}$$

REFERENCE QUESTIONS PER CAPITA

$$\frac{\text{Reference Questions Asked (7)}}{\text{Jurisdiction Population (8)}} \qquad = \underline{\hspace{1cm}} \text{ Reference Questions Asked of Library Staff per Person in One Year}$$

REFERENCE FILL RATE

$$\frac{\text{Reference Questions Answered (9)}}{\text{Reference Questions Asked (10)}} \qquad = \underline{\hspace{1cm}} \text{ \% of Reference Questions Asked of Library Staff That They Answered}$$

EXPLANATION OF DATA ELEMENTS

1. The number of titles that library users both sought and found on the same visit.
2. The number of titles they sought during that visit.
3. The number of subjects for which users both sought and found information during the same visit.
4. The number of subjects on which they sought information during a library visit.
5. Annual circulation.
6. The number of items (titles or volumes) the library holds.
7. The actual or estimated number of reference questions asked during the previous year.
8. Jurisdiction population is the number of people in the community the library serves.
9. The number of reference questions asked during the sampling period that the reference staff believe they also answered that same day.
10. The number of reference questions asked during the sampling period.

tion of *title fill rate*, however, might be that it does not adequately reflect the information needs of clientele and the extent of their sophistication in using the library.

Collection turnover rate compares annual circulation to the library's holdings. In libraries with sizable noncirculating collections, such a comparison may not adequately reflect collection use. To standardize the measure and to maximize its benefit for decision making, librarians should calculate the number of library holdings eligible for circulation. Otherwise, the equation is not comparing like objects.

Subject fill rate indicates the percentage of sought subjects found. Because the measure always tends to be high, it may not produce useful insights. Linking such a measure to information-gathering situations or subject areas would not enhance its value. A final observation about *subject fill rate* is in order; the measure does not recognize the degree of importance of a subject to the library's collection profile.

As this brief discussion of title and subject fill rates and *collection turnover rate* illustrates, staff must review measures before employing them, ensure that they measure what they purport to measure (i.e., both the numerator and denominator examine like objects), and maximize the benefit of the collected data to decision making.

Figure 8-3 modifies these measures and addresses the points raised. Extensiveness measures, either by themselves or when linked to effectiveness, benefit from having a context, which might be subject or information-gathering situations. Nonetheless, extensiveness measures, even when viewed in the context of a library's goals and objectives, represent one type of indicator of effectiveness. They provide library managers with data that they might not otherwise have.

Reference Service

The other two examples depicted in Figure 8-1 portray aspects of reference service. They reflect the types of measures shown in the literature that a library could develop and employ. Still, a library could modify these measures and compare, for example,

- The amount of time spent answering questions to the number of questions asked during a time period
- Telephone service to in-person service
- The extent of staff referrals and the source of referral
- The fill rate for a type of reference question (e.g., factual or ready-reference) and a type of information service/resource (e.g., database services or audiovisual resources).

Figure 8-3.   Modification of Selected Measures Depicted in the Previous Figure

TITLE FILL RATE

$$\frac{\text{Titles Found}}{\text{Titles Sought}} \text{ (by Subject)} \times 100 = \underline{\hspace{2cm}} \text{ \% of Titles Found per Subject}$$

COLLECTION TURNOVER RATE

$$\frac{\text{Annual Circulation}}{\text{Holdings Eligible for Circulation}} \text{ (by Subject)} = \underline{\hspace{2cm}} \text{ Circulations per Item by Subject (for Specified Time Period)}$$

REFERENCE TRANSACTIONS PER POPULATION SERVED

$$\frac{\text{Reference Transactions Completed (Number)}}{\text{Population Served (Strictly Defined)}} \text{ (by Subject or Type of Question)} = \underline{\hspace{2cm}} \text{ Reference Transactions Completed (for Specified Time Period)}$$

REFERENCE FILL RATE

$$\frac{\text{Reference Questions Answered}}{\text{Reference Questions Asked}} \text{ (by Subject)} = \underline{\hspace{2cm}} \text{ \% of Reference Questions Asked (by Subject) That Staff Answered}$$

Managers have choices and can collect diverse but interrelated pieces of information. (Chapter 9 provides additional suggestions concerning the use of performance measures that characterize library reference services.)

Both *reference questions per capita* and *reference fill rate* are indicators of extensiveness and efficiency. Although measures emphasize a certain aspect of measurement (e.g., extensiveness), they can still deal simultaneously with other dimensions. Decision makers might want to investigate the extent to which staff members answer questions correctly. Furthermore, they may not want to base their estimate on staff perceptions. In such cases, *correct answer fill rate* becomes an appropriate measure. Either unobtrusive testing or direct input from library users provides insights into staff accuracy in answering questions and into user satisfaction (Murfin and Gugelchuk, 1987). Even *correct answer fill rate* might benefit from having a context—type of question or subject area. For example, decision makers might want to examine the ability of reference staff members to field social science questions requiring the use of U.S. government statistical publications.

Correct answer fill rate. The effective use of performance measures is linked to the development of a formal planning process and an indication of service roles. Librarians must decide on the service roles they want to fill. While planning is likely to be most effective when instituted throughout the library, it can also be used effectively on a department or individual basis. For example, if members of a reference department in a medium-sized academic library want to improve the rate by which they provide correct answers to reference questions, they must first establish objectives that are measurable, time limited, challenging, concise, and single purpose.

Olson (1984) suggests a scheme of reference goals and objectives dealing with evaluation. Some of the objectives in her model are not time limited and do not suggest specific measures to determine when they are accomplished. Nonetheless, they are useful examples of areas in which evaluation goals and objectives for reference services can be established.

The staff might want to:

• Increase the percentage of correct answers that the department gives to telephone requests, from 45% to 60%, by December 1990.

An individual might also establish a similar objective. The objective assumes that the staff (or individual) have or can obtain data that describe the current level of performance at 45%.

The next step is to make certain that measures exist to determine the degree to which the objective is, or is not, accomplished. In this case, the staff can use *correct answer fill rate*.

Correct answer fill rate, a type of effectiveness measure, examines the percentage of correct answers to a predetermined set of reference questions (Hernon and McClure, 1987b). The rate represents a broad measure that might compare the number of correct answers to staffing patterns (professional and paraprofessional), the number of hours the reference desk is staffed, duration of service (average time spent in providing a correct answer), or efficiency (staff salary) (see also McClure, 1984b, pp. 219–221).

Managers can compare the direct costs for providing reference service to the number of questions that the reference staff answer correctly on the same day. By doing so (for a specified time period), they can determine the cost of reference service for questions correctly answered. The measure, *cost per correct answer*, therefore examines cost-effectiveness. Both *correct answer fill rate* and *cost per correct answer* could be studied within a subject context or by type of question.

Libraries can also examine *correct answer fill rate* for either telephone or in-person questions, or they can compare staff responses to in-person and telephone questions or *focused* and *unfocused* questions. *Focused* questions examine staff responses to factual and bibliographic queries on specified subjects or types of materials. The more focused the set of test questions is (e.g., concentrated on a subject area or type of information source), the more useful the data become for staff development. Once managers identify general (not individual) staff weaknesses, they can initiate corrective action (see Hernon and McClure, 1987b).

Correct answer fill rate provides insights into the accuracy of staff responses to test questions. The performance measure might be modified to probe staff search strategies, question-negotiation skills, and the amount of time staff spend on reference transactions. An examination of responses to test questions would disclose the extent to which staff members engage in referral, either internal or external to the department or library. Further checking would determine the appropriateness of a referral and whether the referral resulted in the receipt of a correct answer.

Viewed in a research context, *correct answer fill rate* may fluctuate depending on the sample size (number of libraries tested), thoroughness of testing (number of staff tested per library), and number of questions asked. How many questions are necessary for an accurate portrayal of staff performance to emerge? Obviously, the greater the number of questions asked, the more complete the picture of a library's fill rate that emerges. Librarians wanting to use *correct answer fill rate* will need to examine the constraints under which they operate and set the number realistically.

Where libraries develop a set of test questions that unintentionally reflects different levels of difficulty, the utility of the fill rate is compromised. If library managers want questions reflecting a range of difficulty levels, they must determine each level of difficulty and select a random sample of questions from each level (see Hernon and McClure, 1987b). The purpose is to have the *correct answer fill rate*, or any other measure, reflect the phenomenon under investigation (validity) and be useful for decision making.

For *correct answer fill rate* to be a valid indicator of staff performance, evaluators would need to examine the performance of all the reference-desk staff of a department or library, in proportion to their actual involvement in reference service. The *correct answer fill rate*, like any other measure, indicates the quality or quantity of a service or program at one point in time. A regular program of evaluation provides trend data and a means of comparison over time.

It is important for evaluators to recognize that *correct answer fill rate* neither explores all the factors affecting reference service nor considers factors that might impact patron satisfaction. For example, it does not compare the importance of a correct answer to the understandability of the information provided and to the ease of access to that information. Murfin and Gugelchuk (1987), and Van House, Weil, and McClure (1990) exploded patron satisfaction,[2] while Chen and

---

[2] Van House, Weil, and McClure (1990) discuss a reference satisfaction survey in which users evaluate the relevance of information provided, amount of information provided, completeness of the answers received, helpfulness of staff, quality of service provided, and overall level of satisfaction. The survey provides data indicating the patron's level of satisfaction with aspects of the information services used.

Hernon (1982) examined the relative importance that users of public libraries attach to the receipt of a correct answer. By combining insights gained from determination of the *correct answer fill rate* with other internal assessments, the library can gain a more complete understanding of the impact of reference service upon library patrons. Similar to other measures, *correct answer fill rate* is multidimensional, has different uses, and is subject to modification.

Measures, such as *correct answer fill rate*, document current levels of performance. The primary purpose of this measure, however, is to improve the *quality* of reference services. Thus, it is critical that once the results of the measures are known, managers develop specific treatments or interventions that attempt to improve services and staff competencies (see Hernon and McClure, 1987b, Chapter 4). In addition, those activities or staff skills that have the greatest impact on the quality of services, that have the greatest chance for improvement, or that cost the least should be attacked first. The overriding emphasis should be on attempting to improve the service *outputs* delivered to library clientele.

1987 MANUAL ON OUTPUT MEASURES
AND 1990 ACRL MANUAL

Output Measures for Public Libraries (Van House et al., 1987) standardized a core set of measures for public library use. To be expected, the manual is highly selective in the measures that it covers and recommends for public library use. Of course, one library can only collect so much data. A similar manual covering academic and research library performance has recently been published (Van House, Weil, and McClure, 1990). This manual shows diverse areas subject to measurement (overall user success, materials availability and use, facilities and equipment availability and use, and information services). It also explains that (Ibid., p. ii):

> The basic question to be asked in choosing measures to be implemented is: What difference will it make for us to have this information? Which data will be most useful for the decisions that face us? Some libraries will want to go into greater depth in specific areas: for these, each measure is followed by "Further Suggestions. . . ."

The 1987 public library manual defines terms and offers step-by-step, standardized procedures to guide data collection. Nonetheless, it encourages the collection of management, as opposed to research, data. Clearly, the manual, together with the more recent manual for academic and research libraries, makes a major advancement in the literature and in the application of performance measures. Still, as the authors caution, neither one should be regarded as all-inclusive or definitive. Libraries should decide which measures to use, adopt standardized procedures so that trend data emerge, and review the sampling frame. The larger the sampling period, the more likely that the data have wider external validity (generalizability).

AREAS MERITING FURTHER RESEARCH

Existing performance measures can provide library managers with useful, and at times vital, information, and thereby improve the quality of their decision making. However, these measures are far from ideal or perfect. Library use of performance measures must keep pace with the development of a theoretical and applied research base—sufficient insights into the conceptual base of different measures and their application to decision making and corresponding theory. Refining measures, such as those suggested in Figure 8-3, underscore this observation.

Topics requiring additional research include:

- Examining the conceptual base for measures, such as those depicted in Figures 8-2 and 8-3
- Identifying other measures and data collection procedures
- Refining the validity of measures and the extent to which they adequately describe the phenomenon under investigation
- Specifying key terms—output, performance, and productivity measures
- Probing different types of indicators of effectiveness
- Identifying areas not amenable to the development of measures
- Identifying the impact of existing measures on the evaluation of library services
- Developing models that investigate relationships among input measures and other types of measures
- Examining the relationship among library performance, productivity, use, and information-gathering behavior
- Identifying the similarities and differences between/among measures; comparing measures to effectiveness, efficiency, and extensiveness criteria; and developing the framework for assessing and applying measures (performance, output, or productivity)
- Comparing the application of measures in different library settings.

In brief, this chapter encourages the use and further examination of performance measures. Others can build on the foundation provided here and in the two recent manuals, and offer more detailed analyses.

Continued reliance on "input" data, e.g., the number of reference transactions, circulations, or materials added to the collection per year, rather than "outputs," provides little assistance in making decisions to better meet clientele information needs and increasing access to resources within the collection. Performance measures provide: (1) a yardstick to interpret the extent to which goals and objectives are met, and (2) a means to hold libraries "accountable for the effectiveness of their services" (Powell, 1988, p. 34). However, "user-oriented performance measures" (Ibid.) are most meaningful when the types of issues addressed in this chapter have been resolved. Performance measures can signal the existence of potential problems related to library reference service, collection development, etc.

Having access to such information, managers can pinpoint areas requiring more in-depth study and analysis—the type of research discussed in Chapter 4. Performance measures represent an appropriate evaluation tool, in part because they encourage managers to be "evaluation-oriented or minded."

DISCUSSION ITEMS

1. Assess the measure, *library visits per capita*, which is the number of library visits during the year per person in the community served. The measure is calculated by dividing the annual number of library visits by the population of the legal service area. Population of legal service area is the "number of people in the geographical area for which a public library has been established to offer services and from which (or on behalf of which) the library derives income, plus any area served under contract for which this library is the primary service provider" (Van House et al., 1987, p. 93). Van House et al. (1987) recommend data collection by a turnstile counter, or count of people entering the building during one week.

2. Assess *in-house materials use per capita*, which is the number of materials used in the library per persons served. The measure divides the annual in-house materials use by population of legal service area. For one week, staff ask users not to reshelve materials and then the staff count all materials *used*.

3. Assess *program attendance per capita*, which is program attendance per person in the population served. The measure divides the annual program attendance by the population of the legal service area. For data collection, the staff count the audience at all programs offered during the year.

4. For one hour, take one of the measures depicted in Figure 8-1 and collect data. Assess the outcome and value of the data for library decision making.

5. Now, take one of the measures depicted in Figure 8-2 and do the same as in the previous question.

6. How can a library ensure that baseline data would be incorporated into library decision making?

7. "Very high *fill rates* could indicate an underutilized collection" (Van House et al., 1987, p. 51). Discuss. How might a library reduce fill rates?

8. What specific use might library managers make of performance measures, such as those depicted in Figures 8-1 and 8-2, or Van House et al. (1987)?
9. Identify an evaluation topic that does not readily lend itself to the use of performance measures.
10. Do you prefer the term performance, productivity, or output measures? Why?

Chapter Nine

Evaluation of Library Reference Services

There is increasing pressure on libraries to assess the degree to which their services demonstrate criteria of "quality." Perhaps the most important development in this area is the national attention accorded to the use of performance measures as indicators of effectiveness (see Chapter 8). The emphasis on these measures and services provided to library clientele requires librarians to view "quality" of reference services from the patron's perspective and not to equate "quality" merely with collection size, diversity, and comprehensiveness.

Ironically, libraries frequently have little knowledge or empirical evidence about the overall quality of the reference services that they provide. They often do not engage in an ongoing program of assessment, training, and program development for reference services. As a consequence, published research on reference and referral services must still encourage library managers to ask:

- What is the quality of reference service in our library? Is this level acceptable to us? Why do we believe the level is either acceptable or unacceptable?
- What ongoing evaluation and educational programs do we employ to improve the quality of reference service? How successful are these programs?
- Does the library have a clear sense of the reference service objectives that the staff are trying to accomplish? How do these objectives relate to goals and to other library objectives.

Answers to these questions are critical especially since research has challenged the claim that a number of reference staff members regularly provide effective and efficient reference and referral services. Complicating matters, Bourne (1965) suggests that the initiation of efforts to make services more effective may require more resources that many libraries have or are willing to commit.

As Kantor (1980, p. 132) notes,

> Reference services pose considerable problems for those who seek to develop quantitative measures of library performance [in that] the road from [information] need to [patron] satisfaction is often complicated, and it is not in general possible to define either the need itself or the nature of the satisfaction.

Part of the problem is that reference services are multifaceted and the study of these facets may require knowledge of research strategies used in psychology, education, sociology, anthropology, history, public policy, public administration, as well as library and information science. Nonetheless, many facets of reference service have been explored, but some only superficially.

Library staff have evaluated both the *direct* (personal assistance, the effectiveness and efficiency of online database searching, bibliographic instruction, etc.) and *indirect* (collection development and management, preparation of guides and other supporting documentation, etc.) aspects of reference service. Both aspects are interrelated. For example, the development of collections containing resources needed by client groups may have a direct relationship on the accuracy of the assistance that staff members provide. Or, response to studies observing traffic patterns might influence the location of public service microcomputers and a reference desk, the staffing of that desk, and the placement of guides alerting patrons to particular reference sources.

Various factors impact the provision of quality reference services. Examples of these factors include:

- Staff skills and competences
- Willingness of patrons to seek assistance
- Collection size and holdings
- Physical organization and location of materials
- The information needs of clientele
- The extent of bibliographic control that the library exercises over its holdings
- Organizational climate and management style
- Technical support, e.g., online and CD-ROM services, offered by the library.

Because these factors may interact with each other, library managers must explore the implications of attacking one factor but not another. For example, the degree and type of bibliographic control that a library provides for its collections relate to the size, type, and complexity of these collections. Technical support may improve bibliographic access but may necessitate that the staff obtain basic technological skills and competencies. Technical support and bibliographic control are important for libraries with complex physical organizations and a decentralized placement of resources.

Research has not explored all the facets of reference service and the interrelationships among all the factors. Management decision making for reference service frequently operates within a knowledge void, and managers often make decisions based on intuition or incomplete data. Library managers need to obtain as much usable data as possible from evaluation studies. Those data might tend to be impressionistic or more accurately reflect what they are intended to portray (research data). At the same time, managers should probe and challenge presumptions, intuition, and traditional approaches to reference services.

This chapter provides an overview of selected aspects of reference services amenable to evaluation, sample methodologies for data collection, and selected performance measures. Library managers will have to decide which activity areas have the highest priority and evaluate the effectiveness and/or efficiency of programs and services in priority areas. No library can simultaneously collect data on all facets of reference service. To attempt such an endeavor would necessitate the commitment of significant resources and a willingness of staff to do nothing else but collect and interpret data.

AREAS AMENABLE TO EVALUATION

Typically, evaluation activities relating to reference services focus on the following:

- A count of the reference requests received
- The currentness and *adequacy* of the titles in the reference collection
- Ascertaining the information needs of clientele
- Development of written polices, goals, and objectives (Bundy and Bridgman, 1984, pp. 164–165).

Both this section and the chapter on performance measures suggest many more areas where staff might initiate formal evaluation.

Evaluators might examine the staff itself, the clientele, the library's capability to provide service, the reference questions asked, the resources needed to answer questions, or the answers given. Library staff might be evaluated in the context of factors such as personnel classification, departmental organization, duties, educational background, experience, financial support, and range of work activities (professional versus nonprofessional). In such instances, evaluators might examine:

- Staff attitudes toward patrons
- Effectiveness and efficiency of staff, by personnel classification, in answering questions
- Patterns in the search strategies of staff and the information sources they consult
- Speed with which staff members answer questions (e.g., the amount of time spent answering questions in relation to the total time spent at the reference desk)
- Staff's success rate in negotiating incomplete and faulty information questions and in making appropriate referrals
- Interview skills of staff
- Staff willingness to assist library users
- Extent of staff burnout and ways to cope with burnout.

In relation to library clientele, their characteristics and information needs, evaluators might examine:

- Extent of patron awareness of library services and programs
- Frequency of library use
- Perceptions of the appropriateness and completeness of the information received
- Perceptions of the roles, duties, and functions of reference staff
- Information-gathering patterns and preferences
- Preferences in types and formats of information
- Reasons for library use and nonuse
- Extent of satisfaction with information sources and services
- Hesitancy or extent of willingness to ask questions (e.g., how long must they wait to receive service, are staff available when they approach a reference desk, and will patrons approach the same staff member again for further assistance?).

The library's capacity to provide reference service, another area of potential evaluation, might focus, for example, on the level of bibliographic control over the resources in the collection, financial support, organizational climate/managerial style, composition of reference desk staff (professional versus support), opportunities for (and quality of) staff training, and staff duties. For example, it would be a useful exercise for staff members to maintain a log of daily activities and to compare the logs to departmental goals and objectives. Within such contexts, evaluators might assess the:

- Cost and effectiveness of reference desk service and departmental programs and services
- Extent of user communities served
- Impact of traffic patterns on staffing of the reference desk and placement of reference aids.

Information on the number of questions asked becomes useful for decision making when compared to the information needs of clientele, subject, or types of questions asked. Additional insights emerge by determining:

- Accuracy of staff in answering questions
- Amount of time staff spend on a transaction
- Cost of question answering (e.g., the number of questions fielded in comparison to the salaries for reference staff or the cost in time of having staff answer reference questions)
- Staff response to a question (e.g., how often they respond with "don't know" and terminate the interview or search)
- Number of internal and external referrals made in the department or library
- Number of and types of steps that staff/users take to answer questions
- Search locations (by types of questions)

- Situational factors, e.g., problems that staff members have with interpersonal skills and communication
- Type and number of sources that staff members consult
- User perceptions about whether a reference transaction was completed.

The ability to answer questions may depend, in part, on the budget; the organization, physical location, and types of materials held; the staff; and the quantity and quality of the collection.

Receipt of an answer, the final general area of discussion, might be considered within the context of, for example, the extent of bibliographic control for sources in the collection; financial support; staffing (availability of staff to assist clientele, how busy staff are, etc.); number and complexity of the questions that staff members receive; information needs of the clientele; organizational and physical location of materials; organizational climate/managerial style; and the quantity and quality of the collection. Within these contexts, evaluators might analyze:

- Search failures
- *Correct-answer fill rate*—accuracy of performance, comparing the rate to staffing decisions, departmental policies and budget, hours of operation, amount of time taken to answer questions, etc.
- Reasons for poor performance, e.g., lack of subject knowledge or time.

They might also enumerate and classify questions by categories—subject, type or source of question, and search location. They might also investigate the impact, if any, of special subject strengths of the collection and staff on the receipt of a correct answer.

SAMPLE METHODOLOGIES

The evaluation of reference services tends to rely on self-reporting assessments that represent a one-time examination of a particular problem. Although the studies rarely collect data by drawing repeated measures over long periods of time, the research has employed a variety of methods for data collection.

Evaluators have used questionnaires administered by mail or telephone; interviews administered in-person or by telephone; observation of users and staff; logs completed by staff or users; obtrusive testing (having staff members knowingly participate in a study and answer test questions within a specified time period); unobtrusive testing (testing staff unaware that they are study subjects); and costing analysis (cost-effectiveness and cost-benefit). Evaluators might also administer a standardized inventory (e.g., to measure burnout) or conduct an activity analysis of the tasks performed by public service staff (see Reeves,

Figure 9-1. Reference Question Tabulation Form

Month	Day	Time		Form of Request		Question Answered	
Jan. ☐		AM		In-Person	☐	Yes	☐
Feb. ☐				Phone	☐	No	☐
March ☐		8–10	☐	Mail	☐	Unsure	☐
April ☐		10–12	☐				
May ☐							
June ☐		PM					
July ☐							
Aug. ☐		12–2	☐				
Sept. ☐		2–4	☐				
Oct. ☐		4–6	☐				
Nov. ☐		6–8	☐				
Dec. ☐		8–10	☐				

Duration		Type of Request		Search Location	
Under 1 min.	☐	Directional:		No Search	☐
1–3 min.	☐	1) Location of	☐	Card Catalog	☐
3–5 min.	☐	Specific	☐	Reference Coll	☐
Over 5 min.	☐	Reference Title	☐	Periodicals Coll	☐
		2) Change	☐	Gov. Documents	☐
		3) Location of Part	☐	Microform Coll	☐
		of Building	☐	Circulation Desk	☐
		4) Non-library	☐	Stacks	☐
		Related	☐	Technical Serv	☐
		Card Catalog	☐	Combination	☐
		Periodical Holding	☐	(of areas)	☐
		Dissertation Holding	☐	Other	☐
		ILL Request	☐		
		Research Problem	☐		
		Other	☐		

General Subject Area		Record Difficult to Answer Questions Verbatim
Health Sciences	☐	
Humanities	☐	
Physical Sciences	☐	
Social Sciences	☐	
No Subject	☐	

Howell, and Van Willigen, 1977). They might also evaluate the reference collection or have staff keep tallies of the reference questions asked, queuing patterns, etc.

Figure 9-1 offers a sample reference question tabulation form, which could be optically scanned, input onto disk, and analyzed using microcomputer statistical analysis software. Of course, staff would have to agree on the fields and the interpretation of each category. For example, under "general subject area," would they mark history as part of the humanities or social sciences?

Robbins and Zweizig (1988, p. 77) maintain that "keeping counts of reference transactions throughout the year is a tedious task and has been repeatedly described as prone to wide margins of error." Furthermore (Ibid.),

> the definition of reference transactions used will begin to blur over time, and different staff will come to use differing definitions. Also, it is quite typical for staff during a particularly busy period to forget to record transactions handled.

As a consequence, Robbins and Zweizig recommend the tabulation of reference transactions based on "a sample period, such as a week, and multiplied to produce an annual estimate" (Ibid.). Such data collection produces impressionistic findings. One week is not an adequate sampling frame. How can one week represent fully and accurately periods of heavy, moderate, and light use, as well as the full range of questions asked? In addition, it becomes important to monitor the percentage of questions asked but not recorded, during the sample week.

Obtrusive and unobtrusive testing does not examine the same factors related to reference services and question answering. Obtrusive testing looks at the accuracy of responses and the amount of time it took to answer questions in comparison to status (professional or nonprofessional), and demographic and socioeconomic variables. In contrast, unobtrusive testing probes the accuracy of answers to questions. It might also examine staff willingness to engage in referral, staff ability to negotiate questions correctly, the amount of time spent in answering questions, and patron willingness to request assistance again. Neither methodology places the accuracy of responses in the context of such variables as patron reading and comprehension level, understandability of the information supplied, and patron need for information within a very short time frame. Nonetheless, "few would dispute that the purpose of reference services is to provide *accurate* answers to users' questions" (Robbins and Zweizig, 1988, p. 79).

Unobtrusive testing has found that reference staff provide "half-right" answers to factual and bibliographic questions. The staff may be unfamiliar with the contents of basic publications in their collections, spend minimal time in conducting reference interviews and in searching for answers, and conduct superficial reference interviews and fail to identify the actual information need. They may also respond with "don't know" and terminate the reference interview/search process, without providing a correct answer or a referral. They infrequently engage in referral, either internal or external to the department. Studies using different methodologies have substantiated the findings of unobtrusive testing (see, for example, Murfin and Gugelchuk, 1987, and Benham and Powell, 1987). Murfin and Gugelchuk (1987) provide a data collection instrument that provides input from users and offers a measure of user satisfaction.

Van House, Weil, and McClure (1990) provide other data collection instruments, ones, for example, addressing user success, ease of use, and user satisfaction.

Robbins and Zweizig (1988, p. 80) identify one method by which libraries might engage in unobtrusive testing. Prior to the adoption of their approach, evaluators should consult Hernon and McClure (1987a, 1987b) and McClure and Hernon (1983) for additional insights into the application of such testing. Unobtrusive evaluation should not be linked to salary, promotion, and tenure decisions. Rather, the purpose is to identify strengths and weaknesses in the service provided by reference staff, as a whole, and to develop general training programs as necessary.

PERFORMANCE MEASURES

If libraries focus on both *inputs* (what goes into the library) and *outputs* (the result or end product of a service activity or the actual service/activity received by a user), managers have many choices about which reference activities they might examine. Library personnel might look at inputs, outputs, outcomes, or products (see Chapter 8), or interrelationships among these components. Primary concentration on performance measures is a reminder that the library has as its primary goal meeting the information needs of clientele.

For illustrative purposes, suppose that library X finds that it had 770 reference transactions during the month of August. Of these transactions, 43% were quick fact, 34% were directional, and 23% were bibliographic. Further, suppose that the number of transactions is up 7% over the previous August and that the breakdown of transaction types remains approximately the same. Having such data, one still does not know the:

- Degree to which reference services meet stated objectives and service priorities—should the library concentrate on providing quick-fact reference service or other types of service
- Degree of accuracy with which staff members respond to the questions—what percentage of all the quick-fact reference questions answered correctly is acceptable?
- Relationship between the number of staff hours at the reference desk and services provided—how many staff hours per reference transactions were needed? For example, if 185 staff hours this month were dedicated to reference services but 260 were used for the same month a year ago, are reference staff now more productive?
- Amount of time necessary for the receipt of a correct versus incorrect response, or to produce a satisfied versus dissatisfied client—for instance, how much time is acceptable as a response time for a correct answer to a quick-fact question?

These and other key issues must be addressed if, in fact, there is to be a reliable and valid assessment of reference services. Furthermore, the evaluation of reference services in terms of *outputs* is essential for a valid assessment of the degree to which information services actually resolve clientele information needs.

Assessing reference services in terms of outputs and outcomes encourages a planning environment where written goals and objectives are developed, performance measures are linked to objectives, and the degree to which objectives are accomplished is measured. Identifying the factors that contribute or detract from *high-quality* reference service forces agreement about which services or activities the library will emphasize or give priority. Regular monitoring of the factors provides trend data showing how various indicators of reference service change over time.

Output Measures for Public Libraries (Van House et al., 1987) only discusses the computation of two reference-related output measures, *reference transactions per capita* and *reference completion rate*. However, a review of Van House, Weil, and McClure (1990) and Figure 9-2 suggest additional areas of reference service amenable to evaluation.[1] McClure (1984b) offers additional examples of effectiveness and efficiency measures, ones that can be gathered using unobtrusive testing of reference services. Clearly, libraries must decide which measures to use. The two recommended in the output measures manual may not have the highest priority for all libraries.

Those libraries collecting *reference transactions per capita*, the number of reference transactions per person in the community served, ascertain the percentage of questions indeed asked by members of the community. Managers using this measure should remember that not everyone in the community may be a library user, and for those who are, their use may vary from occasional to frequent. The measure does not distinguish among subjects, information-gathering situations, and types of questions asked.

Reference completion rate is "the proportion of reference transactions successfully completed on the same day that the question is asked, in the judgment of the librarian" (Van House et al., 1987, p. 69). A reference transaction includes (Ibid., p. 65):

* Requests for help with the catalog, other than mechanical questions, e.g., how to operate a microfilm catalog
* Questions of fact
* General requests for help
* Requests for information and referral
* Database searches
* Directional transactions
* Questions of rules and policies
* Telephone requests for specific library material.

---

[1] Powell (1984, pp. 14–16) offers examples of studies that have used a combination of measures.

Figure 9-2. Input and Output Measures for Reference Service*

LIBRARY CLIENTELE

A. INPUT MEASURES
- Characteristics of clientele
- Information needs of clientele

B. OUTPUT MEASURES
- Extent of awareness of library services and programs
- Frequency of library use
- Perception of the appropriateness and completeness of the information received
- Perceptions of reference staff—their roles, duties, and functions
- Preferences for types and formats of information
- Reasons for library use and nonuse
- Satisfaction with information sources and services
- Sources used to answer questions
- Their hesitancy or willingness to ask questions (e.g., how long must they wait to receive service, and are staff available when patrons approach a reference desk?)
- Their information-gathering patterns and preferences

LIBRARY STAFF

A. INPUT MEASURES
- Classification
- Departmental organization
- Duties
- Educational background
- Experience
- Financial support
- Range of their work activities (professional versus nonprofessional)

B. OUTPUT MEASURES
- Attitudes toward patrons
- Effectiveness and efficiency in answering questions by personnel classification
- Extent of burnout
- Patterns in their search strategies and the information sources consulted
- Sources used to answer questions
- The speed by which staff answer the questions (e.g., the amount of time that a staff member spends in answering questions in relation to the total time spent at the desk)

Figure 9-2.—(*Continued*)

- Success rate in resolving indirect and faulty information questions and in making appropriate referrals
- Their reference interview skills
- Willingness to assist library users

C. COMBINED INPUT/OUTPUT MEASURES
- Examine the input measures in the context of whether or not staff correctly answer questions

LIBRARY MANAGEMENT

A. INPUT MEASURES
- Availability of staff to assist clientele
- Extent of bibliographic control the library provides to source material in its collection
- Composition of public service staff (professional versus support)
- Financial support
- How busy are the staff
- Organizational climate/management style
- Staff duties (the range of staff work activities, including how much time is spent on activities other than servicing the public)
- Staff training and continuing education opportunities

B. OUTPUT MEASURES
- The cost and effectiveness of reference desk service and departmental programs and services
- The extent of staff burnout
- The extent of the user communities served
- The impact of traffic patterns on the staffing of the reference desk and the placement of reference aids

REFERENCE QUESTIONS

A. INPUT MEASURES
- Information needs of clientele
- Number of questions received
- Subject of questions
- Types of questions asked (e.g., directional and bibliographic)

B. OUTPUT MEASURES
- The accuracy of staff in answering questions
- Amount of time that staff spend on a transaction
- The cost of question answering (e.g., the number of questions fielded in comparison to the salaries for reference staff, or the cost of time devoted to reference transactions)

continued

Figure 9-2.—(*Continued*)

- Librarian response to a question
- The number of referrals internal and external to the library
- The number of steps staff/users take to answer questions
- *Reference fill rate*—the number of reference transactions completed in proportion to the total number of such transactions
- *Reference transactions per capita*
- Search locations
- Situational factors, e.g., problems in communication
- Type and number of sources staff consult
- User perceptions about whether a reference transaction was completed

C. COMBINED INPUT/OUTPUT MEASURES
- The relationship between questions asked and the use of the catalog

RESOURCES NEEDED TO ANSWER THE QUESTION

A. INPUT MEASURES
- Budget
- Organization and physical location of materials
- Quantity and quality of the collection
- Types of materials

RECEIPT OF ANSWER

A. INPUT MEASURES
- Availability of staff to assist clientele
- Extent of bibliographic control the library provides to source material in its collection
- Composition of public service staff (professional versus support)
- Financial support
- How busy are the staff
- Information needs of clientele
- Number of questions received
- Organization and physical location of materials
- Organizational climate/management style
- Quantity and quality of the collection
- Staff duties (the range of staff work activities, including how much time is spent on activities other than servicing the public)
- Staff training and continuing education opportunities
- Subject of questions
- Types of questions asked (e.g., directional and bibliographic)

Figure 9-2.—(Continued)

B. OUTPUT MEASURES
- Analysis of search failures
- Correct answer fill rate—accuracy of performance and a comparison of the rate to staffing decisions, policies, budget, hours of operation, the amount of time it takes to answer questions, etc.)
- Enumeration and classification of categories by subject, type of questions, source of question, and search locations
- Reasons for poor performance (e.g., lack of subject knowledge or a lack of time)

C. COMBINED INPUT/OUTPUT MEASURES
- Impact of special subject strengths on the receipt of a correct answer
- Size of the library collection in contrast to the receipt of a correct answer

* This figure was adapted from Ronald R. Powell, "Reference Effectiveness: A Review of Research," Library & Information Science Research, 6 (1984): 3–19.

Some libraries may want to omit database searching from this general category.

Reference completion rate reflects the perceptions of library staff about "users immediate success in getting their questions answered" (Ibid.), but does not address user satisfaction, other than in an indirect way. The measure assumes that staff members have no motive other than the supplying of truthful and objective assessments. *Reference completion rate* could provide a subject context and identify the number of questions asked and answered in science, history, political science, literature, psychology, law, etc. Taking the subject into account would produce data more meaningful for collection development and decision making. However, the data collection process would become more complex and time-consuming.

Both of these measures represent extensiveness measures, or the number of questions answered. Such measures might be interpreted in the context of library goals and objectives, and thereby become a type of effectiveness measure. *Reference transactions per capita* estimates the number of questions asked and the community served. In contrast, *reference completion rate* may "overestimate reference service quality. On the other hand, sometimes staff have higher expectations than do users, so the measure may underestimate service quality" (Ibid., p. 69). This measure also assumes that patrons clearly, fully, and accurately articulated their information need.

Computation of a performance or output measure produces a result that should be interpreted within the context of library policy, collection, librarian, question-related, and user factors (Lancaster, 1988, pp. 118–119). For example, library policy may suggest how much time staff should devote to questions. In addition, *reference completion rate* might be calculated during an extremely busy week, when staff members lack sufficient time to spend with particular questions. Furthermore, staff members might spend more time answering questions of those individuals perceived as more important—e.g., faculty members. The dangers of libraries using performance measures are that staff might treat management data as research data, read too much into their interpretation of a measure, and either ignore or downplay the type of factors identified by Lancaster. However, as discussed in Chapter 8, the benefits outweigh the disadvantages of using performance measures.

TAKING ACTION

Many libraries must cope with limited resources and a tight budget. In addition, libraries may have few opportunities to obtain supplemental resources. The ability of the larger institutions to support various library/information services may be decreasing. At the same time, libraries may encounter increased demands to provide "better," "more accurate," or "more timely" information services to their clientele. Services, however, cannot be improved until they are assessed and decision support systems (i.e., information systems that assist staff in decision making by providing specially structured and easily accessible data) are established to assist in decision making (Heindel and Napier, 1981).

As pointed out by Bommer and Chorba in the context of establishing decision support systems, "critical to any evaluation of a program is the availability of measures of performance by which the output of a system can be assessed according to some stated criterion" (1982, p. 23). Thus, for the immediate foreseeable future, a primary objective for many libraries will be to demonstrate accountability and increase organizational productivity, i.e., increase the services or outputs and keep costs from increasing, or maintain current levels of services and decrease costs.

Key areas of library services to which significant resources are allocated, and from which key services result, are especially likely to come under review concerning their overall effectiveness and efficiency. Reference services surely demand attention, review, and possible changes. Librarians would be better advised to initiate a careful assessment of reference services themselves, first, rather than wait for external pressures either from higher-level administrators or clientele themselves.

Libraries may indicate a desire to evaluate reference services and to determine the effectiveness and efficiency of programs and services. However, they might justify the status quo by stating that "at present we can barely keep up with our desk work and the reference collection's maintenance and development" (Bundy and Bridgman, 1984, p. 165). Clearly, libraries must re-examine the duties and responsibilities of staff and question the effectiveness of what they are doing.

Libraries need to set priorities and not attempt to do everything or be all things to all people.

Should the status quo be maintained where staff members suffer from burnout and cannot cope with their work on a daily basis? "Burned-out" staff members may inadvertently convert library users into nonusers and severe critics of the library and its role as an information provider and disseminator. Furthermore, what is the purpose of staffing the reference desk with individuals who experience numerous problems in answering reference questions, display discourteous service, fail to negotiate the actual information need, and respond to questions with "I don't know" and terminate the reference interview without making referral either internal or external to the library?

The research reported in the literature of library and information science focuses on extensiveness (how much) and, to some extent, efficiency (the allocation of resources) and effectiveness (the meeting of formal goals and objectives). Some studies examining effectiveness have probed cost-effectiveness. As Powell (1984, p. 16) correctly observes,

> The research that has been done on reference effectiveness seems to represent a small percentage of all research on library effectiveness and the opinion pieces far outnumber the true research reports. But the reference-related research does represent a substantial building block for future research that hopefully will follow. What does appear to be needed is greater coordination of research on reference effectiveness in order to reduce duplication of effort and to promote more efficient and effective research.

Clearly, the literature of reference service evaluation is increasing and provides numerous examples of high-quality studies, and appropriate research designs and methodologies, that evaluators might replicate.

Until libraries assess their reference services, library managers will not know the quality of the services provided.[2] The key point is less which evaluation assessment design and methodology library managers prefer and actually use, than that they employ some regular assessment technique to document and improve, as necessary, the quality of library reference services.

---

[2] A management study of the Brigham Young University library reference service examined the quality of assistance provided by student and department assistants, the adequacy of the training program, and the effectiveness of the referral process to subject specialists. The library was dissatisfied with the status quo, but wanted to obtain a better understanding of the current situation prior to introducing change. Christensen et al. (1989) report on the internal assessment of the department and provide important insights for other libraries wanting to conduct a similar review.

DISCUSSION ITEMS

1. Write a goal and three objectives covering aspects of reference service.
2. Monitor reference desk service for two hours, one of which is a busy time and the other is not. Complete a form (see Figure 9-1) for *every* question asked. Assess the form, the experience, and the value of such information to decision making.
3. Do you believe library users really care if they receive accurate and complete answers to their reference questions?
4. Assess the strengths and weaknesses of obtrusive and unobtrusive testing of reference desk service.
5. Name three priority areas in which libraries might evaluate their reference services. Justify your selection of the three.
6. For each of the three areas identified in the previous question, offer an appropriate performance measure.
7. How might evaluators investigate the degree to which reference staff at a medium-sized academic library suffer from burnout?
8. If that study revealed that the staff did suffer from burnout, how might library managers cope with the problem?
9. How could managers ascertain that the corrective remedies, in fact, reduced or eliminated burnout?

Chapter Ten
Sample Topic: Interlibrary Loan Analysis as a Collection Development Tool

By Barbara Klein*

BACKGROUND

Tjoumas and Horne (1986) reviewed collection evaluation techniques in libraries associated with graduate schools of library and information science (GSLIS). They reported that few of these libraries evaluate their collection due to insufficient staff, lack of time, or inadequate funds. However, when they do engage in evaluation, librarians make a significant commitment in time and effort, and use a number of methods, often in tandem, to gather information.

The analysis of interlibrary loan (ILL) requests is one of the techniques that GSLIS staff have used. As all libraries generally use interlibrary loan, completed request forms comprise a useful, readily available source of data. Review of the requests logically provides a broad indication of the need for materials that the present collection does not meet. Evaluators can analyze the requests by subject, type of material requested, and date across all user classes depending on the inclusion of these fields on the request form. An analysis of patterns among the requests for materials suggests areas in the collection that may require attention. The value of such analyses increases if evaluators review requests over time and indicate trends.

ILL request demand may indicate specific titles for purchase. The *National and Model Interlibrary Loan Codes* (1980) suggest that purchase is recommended when materials requested through ILL conform to the library's collection development policy or when there is recurring demand. Libraries should comply with the copyright law, which limits copying of articles and other works through ILL. To repeat, requests for monographs that fall within the desired collection level, and repetitive requests for serial titles may indicate a possible purchase decision (Intner, 1985, p. 417).[1]

---

* This chapter is a condensed version of a paper that Ms. Klein wrote for the course "Evaluation of Library/Information Services" taught at Simmons College in the spring of 1988. Ms. Klein is now Manager, Marlboro Market Research Center, Digital Equipment Corporation, Marlboro, Massachusetts 01752–9102.

[1] The copyright law places the primary responsibility for compliance on the library requesting the item, and not on the library fulfilling the request (Boucher, 1984). Repetitive title requests should be monitored in any case.

PROBLEM STATEMENT

The college has not yet conducted a comprehensive evaluation of its library collection. The extent to which the present collection meets the needs of its user community is unknown. The GSLIS librarian has, in the past, periodically reviewed ILL statistics and request forms to track usage and identify titles for purchase. However, a statistical review of all requests has not been conducted since fiscal year 1983/1984. The GSLIS librarian has proposed a detailed analysis of more recent ILL requests as one tool to discern whether gaps in the collection exist, and whether specific titles merit purchasing.

For the purpose of this study, gaps are defined as multiple requests by users for titles not found but falling within the areas designated by the GSLIS librarian as collection strengths (collected at research/study levels as defined in Perkins, 1979). This study takes on particular significance in light of the library's goals to provide materials that support the curriculum, professional growth, and research during a period where libraries face the contradictory pressures of expanded published output and increased fiscal restraint.

LITERATURE REVIEW

Research focusing on the collections of library school libraries has been extremely limited. The few studies reported in the literature have relied on surveys of opinion regarding collection content, or the compilation of statistics concerning collection size, budget, etc. (Kaser, 1964; Kiewitt, 1978). No study analyzes ILL requests in a GSLIS setting. A more general search for the application of this method in all types of libraries was more fruitful, but while there is some precedence in the literature for the use of ILL statistics in the manner proposed, the number of studies is not substantial.

Roberts and Cameron (1984) surveyed book and periodical ILLs at Drexel University library by subject, class, and date of publication, among other factors. They discovered that a significant portion of the requests "consisted of recent, inexpensive, in-print items, rarely outside the immediate subject interest of the requesting faculty, and [they added] a new dimension to the borrow or buy dilemma" (p. 31). New and Ott (1974) analyzed ILL book requests, for the California State University Library at Fullerton, by Library of Congress (LC) class, and periodical titles by number of requests. They found weaknesses in specific subject areas of the book collection, and suggested further research to discern whether weaknesses in the periodical collection were due to the need for backfiles or for increased current subscriptions. Their article stimulated discussion regarding their research methodology and mathematical errors. They responded to the criticisms by reaffirming their original premise, "interlibrary loan is one way of communicating inadequacies in the collection to those responsible for its development" (Drott and Griffith, 1976, p. 98).

Research conducted in the 1960s applied ILL statistics in order to determine which serial backfiles to acquire. Over a three-year period, Graziano (1962) reviewed serial requests by user class, number of requests/titles, and date of publication for the science library at Southern Illinois University. He found that the majority of requests were for newer material and that requests were not significantly repetitive. He therefore recommended that the library emphasize current subscriptions. Graziano concluded that ILL records were of limited value in selecting specific titles for backfile purchase in the scientific fields. However, in remarks made after duplication of his research, he suggested that such records might be more useful in the humanities (see Wilson, 1962).

Wender (1969) confirmed Graziano's suggestion by finding ILL statistics to be a useful tool in another subject field. She analyzed serial requests by number of requests/titles and date of publication, and identified major gaps in the collection at the University of Oklahoma Medical Center, which had introduced a new doctoral program in biological psychology. Wender recommended serial titles for purchase and backfile acquisition. She concluded that materials in the behavioral sciences have a slower "decay rate" than those studied by Graziano and Wilson, and therefore better lent themselves to analysis of ILL requests. Indeed, in contrast to the infrequency of repetitive requests discovered in the latter studies, Wender found that several titles were requested numerous times over a one-year period. Her findings clearly identified titles for purchase.

Finally, Pritchard (1980) investigated ILL requests as a predictor of future use after the libraries had purchased the monographs identified through an analysis of these requests. He noted circulation frequency over a three-year period for purchased titles that were:

- New editions of titles already held
- Titles originally requested through ILL
- Titles selected by library staff
- Titles recommended by academic staff.

Though the sample chosen was small, the study found that the selection of monographs originally requested through ILL was the second best predictor of future use; the first choice was selecting newer editions of titles already held. He concluded that "requests for books on ILL might in fact represent a continuing need for access to those books presumably from other library members in addition to the requester," and that "more weight [should] be given in the future to this category of request in the library's acquisitions policy" (p. 135).

In summary, the studies have largely focused on analyzing ILL statistics by format (book/serials), subject class, date of publication, and number of requests per title. While some controversy has been raised concerning the methodologies chosen, the evaluators have generally found the analyses to provide them with information useful for decision making. The value of the results has been enhanced by gathering data over an extended period of time (greater than one year), and in disciplines other than the hard sciences, where the time-sensitivity of material is greatest. Also, while the majority of the studies emphasized the importance of repetitive requests/titles, the Pritchard study (1980) suggests that even unique ILL requests warrant review as a predictor of future demand.

OBJECTIVES AND RESEARCH QUESTIONS

The objectives of the evaluation, with corresponding research questions, are as follows:

- To identify patterns in ILL requests for GSLIS holdings:
  - Monographs
    - Are some subjects more heavily requested than others?
    - Are there any repeat title requests over one year? Over two years?
    - Are requested titles within areas designated for collection strengths? If yes, should these titles be acquired?
    - What is the range for the age of materials requested?
  - Periodicals
    - Are periodical title requests repeated over one year? Over two years?
    - Are repeat periodical titles within areas designated for collection strengths? If yes, should these titles be acquired?
    - Are specific article requests repeated over one year?
    - What is the range for the age of materials requested?
- To compare patterns within user categories
  - Monographs and periodicals
    - Does one user category make heavier use of one form?
    - Does one user category request newer material?
    - Do a small number of users generate the majority of requests?
  - Monographs only
    - Does one user category request different subjects than another?
- To compare patterns across forms (monographs and periodicals)
  - Is the number of requests per year higher for periodicals or monographs?
  - Does the age range of material change for different forms? (Do monographs have a wider range of ages than periodicals?)
- To compare patterns across fiscal years
  - Have the above patterns changed across fiscal years?

RESEARCH DESIGN AND METHODOLOGY

Overview of the Evalaution

This study analyzes ILL requests as one method for gaining insight into possible gaps in the collection. Because the collection is primarily composed of monographs and periodicals, the study investigates requests for both forms, although it treats the forms somewhat differently. The evaluator reviewed all forms in order to establish request patterns by user category and age of material, and across fiscal years. In addition, she analyzed monographic requests by subject classification to determine whether *clusters* of requests fell within the collection guidelines, and thereby indicated the need for selection. Similarly, repetitive title requests served as the criterion for indicating possible gaps in the periodical collection.

Although it would have been useful, the evaluator did not perform subject analyses for the periodical requests because the current ILL form does not include this information. Looking up LC classification numbers for periodicals would have increased the data preparation efforts and overall study duration. In any case, evidence of repetitive user requests over time may be the most useful criterion for justifying purchase of a serial, which by definition is a continuing publication.

Data Preparation and Definition of Categories

The raw data for this study were collected from interlibrary loan forms completed for monographs and periodicals from July 1985 through June 1987. This time period corresponds to the college's fiscal year periods (July-June), and includes the majority of available request forms. The time period is a logical one for gathering information toward assisting purchase decisions for the academic year that begins each September. Two fiscal years were included for comparative purposes and to indicate trends.

The ILL librarian initially sorted 584 request forms completed by students, faculty, and staff from the pool of all ILL requests generated for the period. Only requests from within the Graduate School of Library and Information Science (GSLIS) were included in this sort; requests for materials by other students, faculty, or staff that may have fallen within GSLIS collection guidelines were excluded. The librarian then reviewed all the slips to verify that the requests should indeed be included in the GSLIS count, and that each form accurately indicated the user category.

The following decisions guided the classification of users:

- Interns were designated as students
- Staff requests made specifically for faculty were designated as faculty requests
- The problem of staff members who were also students was resolved by querying staff about the reason for their request. If the request related to coursework, it was allocated to the student category.

Twenty-two slips were deleted from the total count due to this second review of requests; these requests consisted of forms that had originally been incorrectly designated as relating to the GSLIS collection. The remaining 562 slips were divided into two groups—the first and second fiscal year—and separated by form (monographs and periodicals).[2]

The slips were then reviewed for completeness of information. Only several periodical requests needed checking to find information about a missing date. All of the requests for monographs were searched via OCLC to assign LC subject classifications and to verify publication dates. In cases where an edition different from the original request may have been used to fill the user's request, the publication date of the original request was utilized for tallying purposes. Conflicting or incomplete dates were, however, corrected from online information. Where LC classification information was lacking or conflicting, the librarian assigned a classification number. At the end of this data preparation phase, 276 completed periodical requests and 286 monograph requests were available for data collection and analysis.

Data Collection

The evaluator designed logs for collecting data by user category for subject classification and age of the material.[3,4] To determine repetitive titles, articles, or users, the evaluator alphabetized request slips by title and user respectively, for comparisons within and across fiscal years.

RELIABILITY AND VALIDITY

To ensure the reliability of scoring each request, the ILL and GSLIS librarians reviewed all requests to verify the categories checked on the request form. For monographs, the evaluator verified subject headings and publication dates via OCLC. The GSLIS librarian also reviewed the verification decisions and assigned LC subject headings when there was any potential confusion in the logging of a specific request. Totals on all logs were cross-checked to verify the inclusion of all 562 request forms. The study therefore reflects the extent and pattern of ILL use by GSLIS faculty, students, and staff during the study period.

---

[2] Six dissertations were included in the monograph category, and six newspaper requests were included in the periodical category. Annual proceedings were included in the periodical category, and irregular proceedings were placed in the monograph category.

[3] Some preliminary data collection had been completed prior to designing the logs in order to determine appropriate subject and date divisions. Date divisions were chosen to more graphically indicate the predominance of requests for recent material. Previous studies reported in the literature used similar divisions.

[4] This chapter selectively reports findings related to staff. Rather, the chapter concentrates more on faculty and students.

RESULTS[5]

Patterns within Forms

Periodicals. The evaluator reviewed 139 periodical requests for the first fiscal year and 137 for the next fiscal year (see Table 10-1). The age of the material requested ranged from the 19th century to 1987, though the majority of requests were for material published during the 1980s. Less than 20 periodical titles were requested more than once during each fiscal year. An additional seven titles were requested at least once in both fiscal years. Several repeat titles within and across fiscal years fall within the areas deemed as collection strengths.

Monographs. The evaluator reviewed 164 monograph requests for the first fiscal year and 122 for the next one (see Table 10-2). The age of material requested again ranged from the 19th century to 1987, with the majority of requests for material published since 1959. LC classes most heavily requested included B, H, P, and Z, with the Z class heading the list for both fiscal years combined (see Table 10-3). Of these classes, H, P, and Z titles fall within the areas deemed as collection strengths. There was only one repeat title request within one year. (This was a student request to retrieve a book that had just been returned to the lending library.)

Patterns across Forms

Number of requests. It would be difficult to state that requests for periodicals generally outstripped those for monographs, or vice-versa, by examining the data recorded for both fiscal years. Adding requests by form for both years yields similar findings (requests for 276 periodicals and 286 monographs).

Age of material. The age of material distribution was wider for monographic than for periodical requests across all user groups. Percentages calculated for periodical articles published since 1980 were similar to requests for monographic material published since 1959.

Patterns across User Categories

Number of requests. For both monographs and periodicals, faculty are heavier users of ILL than are students or staff. Some 29% of the faculty versus 10% of the student body use ILL for periodicals, while 43% of the faculty and 14% of the students use ILL for monographs. However, student requests represent a

---

[5] This section of the chapter highlights selected findings of the actual study. In addition to summarizing study findings, a results section answers each research question or hypothesis. Such a summary figure, however, has been excluded from this chapter.

Table 10-1. Periodicals (Number of Requests by Age of Material and User Category, with Average Requests/Users)

	Faculty		Students		Staff		Totals	
Year*	85/86	86/87	85/86	86/87	85/86	86/87	85/86	86/87
1899		3						3
1909			1				1	
1929		4						4
1939		1						1
1949	2		3	2	1		6	2
1969	1	1	1	3			2	4
1974	1	1	1	3			2	4
1979	3	1	6	10	1		10	11
1980	1		1	5			2	5
1981			5	13			5	13
1982			19	16	2	2	21	18
1983	2	1	25	11	3		30	12
1984		1	34	10	2		36	11
1985	4		16	19	1		21	19
1986		10	3	16			3	26
1987		4						4
Totals:	14	27	115	108	10	2	139	137
#Users Making Requests	5	5	29	37	3	2	37	28
# Requests/ # Users	2.80	5.40	3.97	5.14	3.33	1.00	3.76	4.89

*Note: No requests fell into the age categories of 1910–1919 and 1950–1959.

> General Findings:
> ○ Recent material was generally requested
> ○ Faculty requested older material than did students
> ○ Faculty requested proportionately more material for their numbers than did students.

wider distribution of their user group than do faculty requests. To illustrate this point, for both fiscal years, one faculty member accounted for more than half of the monograph ILL requests for faculty.

Age of material. Faculty generally request older material than students in both periodical and monographic forms.

Subjects. Students and faculty most generally requested monographs in the P or Z class. Faculty requested more publications in the Ps than did students. Faculty requested more publications in the B class for the first year, but students made more requests in the second fiscal year.

Table 10-2. Monographs (Number of Requests by Age of Material and User Category, with Average Requests/Users)

Year	Faculty 85/86	Faculty 86/87	Students 85/86	Students 86/87	Staff 85/86	Staff 86/87	Totals 85/86	Totals 86/87
1899	1						1	
1909	2			1			2	1
1919				3				3
1929	4	4					4	4
1939	7	8		2			7	10
1949	12	1	9	2			21	3
1959	2	4	8	2			10	6
1969	6	1	11	3			17	4
1974	2	2	15	6	2	2	19	10
1979	3	1	10	9	2	1	15	11
1980		1	7	7	1		8	8
1981	1	1	6	4			7	5
1982	6	2	9	8			16	10
1983	5	2	5	11			10	13
1984	6	2	8	14	1		15	16
1985	5		7	8			12	8
1986		3		6				9
1987		1						1
Totals:	62	33	95	86	7	3	164	122
# Users Making Requests	9	8	39	25	5	1	53	34
# Requests/ # Users	6.89	4.13	2.44	3.44	1.40	3.00	3.09	3.59

> General Findings:
> O Faculty requested older materials than did students
> O Faculty requested proportionately more material for their number than did students
> O In 1986/1987, the percentage of requests for monographs and periodicals for each user category was about the same. In contrast, for 1985/1986, faculty requested a higher percentage of monographs than periodicals, and students requested a higher percentage of periodicals than monographs.

Patterns across Fiscal Years

Periodicals. There appeared to be relative stability across fiscal years in the number of total requests and duplicate titles, as well as the distribution of requests and the age of the material requested across all user categories.

Monographs. The number of requests for monographs dropped from 164 to 122 from the first to second fiscal year. This appears to be at least in part due to

Table 10-3. Monographs (Number of Requests by LC Classification and User Category)

Class	Faculty 85/86	Faculty 86/87	Students 85/86	Students 86/87	Staff 85/86	Staff 86/87	Totals 85/86	Totals 86/87
A	1						1	
B	6	2	3	11	1		10	13
C	2	1		1			2	2
D	3		4	5			7	5
E	3	1		1			3	2
F		2		1				3
G	1		3	2			4	2
H	8	7	4	9	1		13	16
J	1	1					1	1
K	3	1	1	1			4	2
L	1	3	7	2			8	5
M			2				2	
N	1	1	6		1		8	1
P	18	4	30	7	3		51	11
Q	1		2	4			3	4
R	1		3	1			4	1
S				1				1
T	3	1	6	8			9	9
Z	9	9	24	32	1	3	34	44
Totals	62	33	95	86	7	3	164	122

General Findings:
- Both students and faculty most frequently requested P or Z titles
- Z requests from students increased from the first to second fiscal year
- Faculty made more requests for titles in the H class for the first but not the second fiscal year
- In the first fiscal year, faculty made most of the requests for titles in the B class. In the second fiscal year, students made more requests
- Both students and faculty made fewer requests for titles in the P class in 1986/1987 than they did in the previous fiscal year (1985/1986).

the sharp decrease in requests for titles in the P class. Requests for Ps decreased for both students and faculty in 1986–1987, with the student category posting the sharpest decline. Table 10-3 illustrates the trends across classes and indicates a constant number of Z requests by faculty for both fiscal years. The number of student requests for Z titles increased the second year. In addition, there was a sharp reversal in requests among faculty and students for B class titles from one fiscal year to the other. The distribution of the number of requests and the age of materials requested were relatively stable across fiscal years for all user categories.

SUMMARY

Periodicals

There was not a high number of repeat requests for specific titles over the two fiscal years covered in the study. No individual title, or group of titles, would therefore be immediately identified for purchase by the analytical methods employed. However, eight duplicate title requests fell within the areas designated by the GSLIS librarian as collection strengths, and these were examined more closely to determine whether or not purchase was desirable. Of the eight titles:

*   Three were already in the collection, but specific issues were either missing or otherwise unavailable at the time of the request. The library already subscribed to two of the three in multiple copies
*   Two titles were rejected for purchase due to their narrow scope and lack of indexing
*   Three titles will be purchased as a result of the ILL review.

Monographs

The requests within the H, P, and Z classes bear further examination. (B is omitted here as the class is not designated as a collection strength.) Both students and faculty have requested Hs and Zs with some consistency. Because the collection development policy indicates that the library collects parts of these classes at research/study levels, the requests merit formal review for potential acquisitions.[6]

Of the 34 Z title requests for fiscal year 1985–1986, the GSLIS librarian selected 14 for purchase (41%). Seven of these had been in the collection but had been noted as missing. Of the 44 Z titles requested for 1986–1987, one is a duplicate and 32 titles were earmarked for purchase (73%).

CONCLUSION AND RECOMMENDATIONS

The analysis of GSLIS ILL requests has indicated subject areas for which users made multiple requests for both periodicals and monographs. Inspection of "clusters" among the requests can result in the selection of titles for purchase. The study disclosed collection gaps and provided a context for the review of specific titles to fill those gaps. The study also provided GSLIS management with summary data regarding the overall use of ILL services. Findings that were an outgrowth of the study, with corresponding recommendations, are as follows:

---

[6] This chapter only reviewed the requests for the Z class.

ILL Use

ILL use concentrated among a relatively small number of faculty and students. Further research regarding the following questions is needed:

- Is the student population generally aware of ILL procedures and the benefits of ILL? Do students rely on sources within the collection rather than using ILL? (One corollary may be the preference to not wait for the typical two-week turnaround time for ILL, and to substitute instead sources more readily available.)
- Are students and faculty making heavy use of materials outside the collection by other means (e.g., visiting other libraries in the area or self-purchase)?

ILL Form Design

The current ILL form does not include fields for LC classification number, even though this information is readily retrievable during the OCLC search for lending libraries. Adding this field to the form would make continuing analysis of ILL a much quicker process. In addition, thought should be given to the following:

- Adding a field to capture the reasons behind the requests—personal, research paper, etc. The check-off could also indicate whether the item is in the collection but missing, damaged, checked out, etc. This field would provide more information to library management regarding why individuals make requests. It would also assist in the assignment of user categories. Wording of the field could be devised so that there is no infringement on the patron's privacy (Stone, 1983, p. 24).

Use of ILL Form

Fifteen percent of the ILL forms had incomplete or faulty information regarding titles, publication or request dates, etc. Not only did this lengthen the data preparation time for the study, but also this must have contributed to increased staff time to process and record the initial request. Patrons should be reminded to complete the form as fully as possible, and be instructed where necessary. The library staff should review the forms for correct category assignments (periodical/monograph, and user categories) and correct completion of all other fields.

Methodology for ILL Analysis

Subject Classification. Due to the low number of repeat periodical and book title requests, the LC classification method appeared to be a more successful indicator of areas of concern and of the need for further investigation. Periodical requests might also be analyzed by subject, thus allowing groups of titles within similar classes to be reviewed together. Completion of the title review for monographs in the H and P classes is also recommended.

If the forms included LC classification numbers, paraprofessional staff could accomplish most of the data gathering. The GSLIS librarian could then receive a list of titles by class for purchase review.

Repetitive titles. The requesting of repetitive titles might be tracked not only within the GSLIS, but also across all Simmons College libraries, to monitor copyright compliance and indicate possible additions for the general collections.

Library planning. At this time, the GSLIS librarian is developing planning documents. The completion of these documents is highly recommended. Periodic evaluation should be incorporated within these plans as one strategy to ensure that goals and objectives are met, and to provide information to management for future plan revision. The continuing use of ILL analysis will:

- Identify subject areas of interest for faculty and students, and provide indicators for current and retrospective purchases
- Identify serial titles that may need claiming
- Identify missing materials
- Indicate titles that may require purchase of additional copies.

COMMENTS

This chapter provides an example for conducting an evaluation of interlibrary loan activity. As such, it serves as a model for how similar evaluations might be conducted. It is especially important to notice that the basic steps in any evaluation were included:

- Literature review and analysis
- Problem statement
- Evaluation objectives and research questions
- Methodology and data collection techniques
- Techniques to ensure the collection of reliable and valid data
- Findings
- Recommendations.

In evaluation studies, it is especially important that recommendations for how management can use the data are included. In addition, such evaluations can have greater impact if *specific* steps for implementing the recommendations can also be offered.

This example demonstrates the importance of taking time to conduct such a study, assess "what is really happening" with the interlibrary loan process, and determine what can be done to improve overall collection development and management. Without such a study, gaps and problems with the collection could not have been identified, and recommendations for improving the collection (and better meeting user needs) could not have been made.

DISCUSSION ITEMS

---

1. Examine the recent issues of *Library Literature* and *Resources in Education*. Are there any studies that complement the literature review?
2. Display some of the findings in one of the tables in graphic form, e.g., bar, line, or pie chart.
3. Produce a visual diagram of the study—a logical structure—that identifies key steps in setting up and completing the study.
4. Rewrite one of the research questions as an hypothesis.
5. Could any further precautions be taken to ensure reliability and validity? If so, explain what these are.
6. Identify a follow-up study to the one reported in the chapter.
7. Instead of using interlibrary loan records, how else might an evaluator have gained insights into possible titles meriting purchase?

Chapter Eleven
Sample Topic: Student Nonuse of Library Literature *on* CD-ROM

By Elizabeth H. Murray*

BACKGROUND

Libraries, such as the one at Simmons College, include CD-ROM (compact disc-read only memory) products as part of their reference collections and services. CD-ROM products typically include indexing and abstracting services and, in some cases, numerical datasets from the U.S. Bureau of the Census and other sources. Now an increasing number of handbooks (e.g., *The World Factbook*), reports, space and geographical imagery, geological data, etc., are available in CD-ROM format.[1]

Many libraries view technology as a means to improve their services and better meet the information needs of their clientele in an efficient manner. Reference personnel must evaluate the utility of CD-ROM, as they do any other information product. They base their assessment on many factors, e.g., relevance to stated goals and collection priorities, cost, amount of duplication with sources already in the collection, ability to use the product on equipment already in place, and the extent of perceived use.

Once libraries have integrated CD-ROM products into their reference services, staff members have noticed long lines of students waiting their turn to use a workstation that provides access to one or more of these products. Ironically, the students might be standing next to the print counterpart, but, for whatever reason(s), they do not examine that source while patiently waiting their turn for the next available workstation.

Because we live in an information age and information-handling technologies have greatly expanded access to a diverse array of information and data, library staff might assume that their clientele are becoming more technologically oriented and that *most* users prefer to use CD-ROM than a print counterpart. The assumption is that the number of nonusers of CD-ROM is declining.

---

* This chapter was written by Elizabeth H. Murray, a Master's student at the Graduate School of Library and Information Science, Simmons College, Boston, Massachusetts 02115.

[1] Approximately 1,500 floppy discs can be stored on one CD-ROM, a 4.71-inch disc whose pits and grooves can be read by a laser. A CD-ROM disc contains the equivalent of 250,000 typewritten pages.

PROBLEM STATEMENT

Published research, as well as in-house investigations conducted at Simmons College library, have concentrated on users of selected CD-ROM products. That research has probed who these individuals are as well as their search patterns. Absent from these studies is an analysis of nonusers and their reasons for nonuse. Questions central to nonuse that need examination are:

- How many nonusers are there?
- Who are the nonusers?
- What segments of the population comprise nonusers?
- Why do they not use CD-ROM?

Identification of nonusers, and exploration of their reasons for nonuse, will provide the library with insights about the composition of this group and its receptivity to the use of CD-ROM. At the same time, the staff can review library policies and procedures that might adversely affect student willingness to use CD-ROM. Nonuse of CD-ROM may raise questions of access: Are there enough microcomputers to meet student needs? Is enough computer time allotted for a patron to use CD-ROM effectively and efficiently? Should the scheduling of computer time be changed? Nonuse might also impact on collection development and management. If the user community does not broadly use CD-ROM, how extensively should the library acquire new and additional CD-ROM products?

A final advantage of investigating nonusers is that staff members can explore strategies to entice these students to become part of the user population. Knowing the reasons for nonuse, librarians involved in the conduct of bibliographic instruction can specifically address these reasons as they attempt to make students, and other groups, more sophisticated library users in an information age.

LITERATURE REVIEW

Writings continually reaffirm that CD-ROM has become an integral part of the reference budget and services in many libraries. The literature abounds with reports documenting the frequency with which clientele use CD-ROM, their satisfaction with the products used, and their reasons for use. The existing research indicates that library clientele like to use CD-ROM and that they require little, if any, training in its use.[2] These studies typically use a survey, either completed by the users or administered orally to them.

No studies published in library literature have concentrated on nonusers and

---

[2] Allen (1989) offers an excellent review of published studies that show patron response to the use of CD-ROM.

the reasons for their nonuse of CD-ROM in general or of a specific product. Of course, numerous studies have investigated nonusers and nonuses of libraries and particular services and collections. To be expected, these studies have relied on a variety of data collection techniques, including, for instance, questionnaires, systematic observation, and structured interviews.[3]

LOGICAL STRUCTURE

Because the study was intended to provide information useful to the library and the library school librarian at one college library, the evaluation comprised a case study (see Yin, 1989). The population then became the student body of the Graduate School of Library and Information Science, at Simmons College. As such, the study can also provide useful feedback to the faculty as to whether or not students enrolled in their courses use CD-ROM, specifically *Library Literature* on CD-ROM.

CD-ROM in Print, 1988–1989 (1988) estimates that there are approximately 239 CD-ROM products on the market. Undoubtedly, the number has increased since the publication of this guide. *Library Literature* is one example of an index available in this format. Produced by H.W. Wilson and Co., this index includes current books, pamphlets, periodical literature, films, microforms, and theses relating to librarianship. *Library Literature* indexes over 200 journals, and can be a source that students in the program consult when conducting research. They can use either the print or CD-ROM version of the index. Three copies of the printed index are kept near the office of the library science librarian, while the CD-ROM version (Wilsondisc) remains at the reserve desk and must be used in the Technology Laboratory.

OBJECTIVES, HYPOTHESES, AND RESEARCH QUESTIONS

The objectives and corresponding hypotheses and research questions for this study are as follows:

Objectives	Hypotheses and Research Questions
To determine the number of nonusers of CD-ROM products held in the collection	How many students in the program are nonusers?

---

[3] Char (1987) discusses nonuser studies in academic, public, and school libraries.

Objectives	Hypotheses and Research Questions
To determine the number of nonusers of *Library Literature* on CD-ROM	How many students in the program are nonusers of *Library Literature* on CD-ROM?
To identify any past use of *Library Literature* on CD-ROM	How many students in the program were nonusers of *Library Literature* on CD-ROM in past semesters?
To identify the reasons for nonuse of *Library Literature* on CD-ROM	What are the reasons for nonuse?
To compare the reasons for nonuse of *Library Literature* on CD-ROM to the following variables: • Class status (master's, doctoral, or other) • Number of courses in the program completed • Courses currently being taken.	There is no statistically significant difference (at the .05 level) between the reasons and class level, number of courses completed, and the courses currently being taken.

For this study, a *nonuser* was defined as a student who had not used CD-ROM in the library and information science collection during the present school term.

RESEARCH DESIGN

The study population comprises 418 students enrolled in one graduate program at Simmons College, during the Fall 1989 term. This total includes full and part-time master's, doctoral, and auditing students. Each student has a mail folder located adjacent to the lounge and reserve collection. Library staff and the evaluator obtained a complete list of students from the admission's office and verified that, indeed, each one had a mail folder.

Faculty, the administration, and classmates place written communications in student folders. Because the admission's office inserts registration information for the upcoming school term in students' mail folders in November, the evaluator believed that students would more likely examine their folders on a regular basis during this period. For this reason, she included a copy of the questionnaire in every mail folder in early November. Data collection took place for the two and one-half weeks prior to Thanksgiving vacation.

As insurance that students would examine their mail folders during the data collection period, the evaluator placed signs throughout the library and the student lounge calling attention to the survey. In addition, many faculty members announced the study in their classes and invited student participation. The evaluator changed the signs each week in an attempt to attract student attention and remind them that the library would appreciate their participation.

One poster explaining CD-ROM and showing a copy of one product was placed directly over the mail folders. Another sign was positioned next to the box at the reserve desk, where students were to return their completed forms. In case students misplaced their form and wanted another one to complete, reserve desk staff supplied a copy upon request. However, the staff, the signs, and class announcement discouraged the completion of more than one form per student.

METHODOLOGY

Because the library staff only wanted to gather self-reporting data that provide an overview of student nonuse, data collection centered on the use of a questionnaire placed in student mail folders.

The questionnaire was developed in stages. First, the evaluator set up a panel consisting of two faculty members from the Graduate School of Library and Information Science who teach courses related to information-handling technologies, the library science librarian, the Technology Laboratory teaching assistant, and two library staff members. The panel developed a set of initial questions that conformed to the study's objectives, hypotheses, and research questions. The evaluator took the preliminary set of questions and devised a short questionnaire. The panel reviewed the questionnaire and offered suggestions to guide its revision.

Next, the evaluator revised the questionnaire and pretested it on three graduate students. After making minor adjustments to the form, the evaluator pretested the questionnaire on five other students.

Once finalized, the questionnaire was word processed and placed on a one-half sheet of fluorescent green paper. This color was chosen so that the form would stand out in the mail folders. Figure 11-1 reprints the questionnaire. The actual one used contained the logo of the school and the signed signature of the library science librarian. The purpose was to make the questionnaire both official and personal.

In summary, the evaluation considered the quality of the data to be collected. Reliability and validity build upon each other. "If data are not reliable, the degree to which they are valid is likely to decline; if the findings are not valid, the

Figure 11-1. Data Collection Instrument

Please complete this survey and return it to the box at the Reserve Desk.
COMPLETE ONE FORM ONLY.

FOR EACH QUESTION, PLEASE MARK THE APPROPRIATE SPACE

1. Use of CD-ROM at Simmons College GSLIS Library—do not indicate work at other libraries, including the 2nd floor at Simmons College library.

    I have used this semester: Yes _____   No _____

2. Use of CD-ROM at Simmons College GSLIS Library—do not indicate work at other libraries, including the 2nd floor at Simmons College library.

    I have used in past semesters: Yes _____   No _____

3. Use of *Library Literature* index on CD-ROM at Simmons College GSLIS Library—do not indicate work at other libraries or with other CD-ROM products.

    I have used this semester: Yes _____   No _____

4. Use of *Library Literature* index on CD-ROM at Simmons College GSLIS Library—do not indicate work at other libraries or with other CD-ROM products.

    I have used in past semesters: Yes _____   No _____

5. If you have not used *Library Literature* on CD-ROM at Simmons College GSLIS Library this semester, mark the reasons why not
                        (MARK ALL THAT APPLY)

		YES	NO
a.	Difficulty using equipment in Technology Lab		
b.	Do not know how to use CD-ROM		
c.	Do not know how to use *Library Literature*		
d.	Prefer other indexes to *Library Literature*		
e.	Prefer print version of *Library Literature*		
f.	Unable to get computer time in the Lab		
g.	Unaware that GSLIS Library has *Library Literature* on CD-ROM		
h.	Use *Library Literature* on CD-ROM at another location		
i.	Other (Please explain): _____		

6. Are you a:

    Master's student _____   Doctoral student _____   Other _____

7. Name course(s) currently taking:

8. Number of courses completed, *before this* semester:

    0–2 _____   3–5 _____   6–8 _____   9 or more _____

Thank you for your participation in this survey. Your answers are important.

degree to which the study has utility is injured" (Hernon and McClure, 1987a, p. 79). The study was intended to have external validity—reflect the reporting of the student body. At the same time, the need to demonstrate reliability and internal validity guided the development of the questionnaire and the conduct of the pretest.

DATA ANALYSIS

Of the 418 questionnaires distributed, 293 (or 70.1%) were returned.

Upon conclusion of data collection, the evaluator checked student folders and discovered 35 questionnaires that had not been completed. A comparison of the names of the students to office records indicated that these students fell into three groups: doctoral students having continued status (registered but not taking courses this term), students taking independent study, and students enrolled in the school library practicum. Each group only visits the school on an irregular basis.

Data from the completed questionnaires were entered into StatPac, a micro-computer statistical analysis software package. The evaluator compared the actual data entered to the responses marked on each questionnaire and verified that the data had been correctly entered.

A chi-square analysis compared the number of respondents per week as to whether or not they used *Library Literature* on CD-ROM. There was no statistically significant difference (at the .05 level), lending further support to the premise that findings reflect use and nonuse by the population. In addition, the evaluator identified four nonrespondents. Subsequent interviewing of them showed that two were users and two were not. Clearly, not all nonrespondents comprise nonusers.

FINDINGS

The Number of Nonusers of CD-ROM and *Library Literature* on CD-ROM

As shown in Figure 11-2, 102 (34.8%) of the 293 respondents do not use CD-ROM in the collection, while 138 (47.1%) of them do not use *Library Literature* on CD-ROM.

The figure also summarizes nonusers for past semesters. A chi-square analysis was not performed because nonusers in past semesters include students who had just started the program—Fall 1989. The figure therefore only provides benchmark data for making comparisons to findings from future studies.

Most interesting is the comparison of the ratio of *Library Literature* CD-ROM

Figure 11-2. Nonuse of CD-ROM

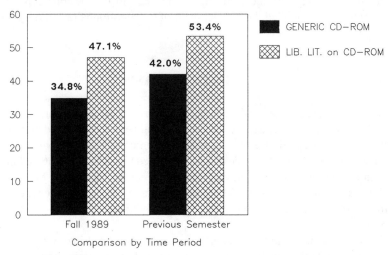

nonusers to generic CD-ROM nonusers for both time periods. A total of 26% of the *Library Literature* nonusers in the Fall 1989 also do not use any other CD-ROM product. In previous semesters, 22% of the *Library Literature* nonusers did not use any other CD-ROM. These percentages suggest a similarity in nonuse patterns of *Library Literature* and generic CD-ROM products over time. However, it merits mentioning that the library has not always maintained a high commitment to the collection, promotion, and use of CD-ROM.

Reasons for Nonuse

Of the 138 nonusers of *Library Literature* on CD-ROM, 136 provided reasons for their nonuse. Figure 11-3 summarizes their reasons and the percentage of nonusers who checked each reason; respondents could check as many reasons as were applicable.

The reasons for nonuse can be divided into two categories: those that the library might address, and those independent of library actions. The library might deal with problems relating to:

- Unawareness that the library has *Library Literature* on CD-ROM (23.5%)
- Lack of knowledge about how to use CD-ROM (18.4%)
- Use of equipment in the Technology Lab (14.0%)
- Inability to get computer time in the Lab (10.3%).

Figure 11-3. Reasons for Nonuse as Reflected by % of Nonuser Response

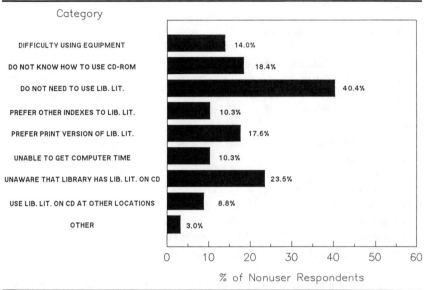

The second category of reasons include:

- Do not need to use *Library Literature* (40.4%)
- Prefer print version of *Library Literature* (17.6%)
- Prefer other indexes to *Library Literature* (10.3%)
- Use *Library Literature* on CD-ROM at other locations (8.8%).

In summary, not all students needing to use *Library Literature*, presumably for the completion of class assignments, consult the CD-ROM version of that index. Nonusers most likely do not know (1) about that version, or (2) how to use CD-ROM.

CHARACTERISTICS OF NONUSERS

Class Level

Not surprisingly, given the composition of the student population, respondents were overwhelmingly master's students (95.2%). Eleven doctoral students (3.8%) and three "other" students (1.0%) responded. There was no statistically significant difference between class level and whether or not students used CD-

ROM. Perhaps the key finding is that not all doctoral students use *Library Literature* on CD-ROM.

Course(s) Currently Taking

As already indicated, the three most frequently mentioned reasons for nonuse were: "Do not need to use *Library Literature*," "unaware that the library has *Library Literature* on CD-ROM," and "do not know how to use CD-ROM." Each of these reasons was compared to the courses that the respondents currently take.

Respondents mentioning that they "do not need to use *Library Literature*" most likely take:

- Organization of Knowledge in Libraries (38.8%)
- Reference/Information Services (27.7%)
- Introduction to Archival Methods and Services (14.8%)
- Collection Development and Management (11.1%)
- Photographic Archives and Visual Information (9.2%).

Students checking "unaware that the library has *Library Literature* on CD-ROM" most likely take:

- Organization of Knowledge in Libraries (34.4%)
- Reference/Information Services (24.1%)
- Principles of Management (20.7%)
- Technical Services (13.6%)
- Introduction to Archival Methods and Services (10.3%)
- Literature of Science and Technology (10.3%).

The third reason, "do not know how to use CD-ROM," most likely corresponds with students taking:

- Reference/Information Services (40.0%)
- Organization of Knowledge in Libraries (20.0%)
- Principles of Management (15.0%)
- Children's Literature and Media Collections (15.0%).

Common to all three lists were two required courses, Reference/ Information Services, and Organization of Knowledge in Libraries. Another required course, Principles of Management, appeared on two of the three lists. However, there was no statistically significant difference between the reasons for nonuse and the courses taken.

Figure 11-4. Reasons for Nonuse vs Courses Completed

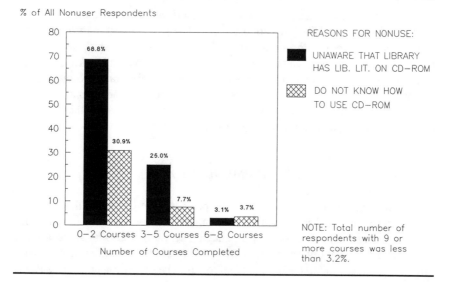

An interesting contrast relates to the number of courses taken and the reason "unable to get computer time in the Technology Lab." Newer students tended not to check this reason; only 7.1% did so. Half of the respondents mentioning this reason had already completed 3–5 courses.

Number of Courses Completed before Present School Term

Almost half of the respondents (44.7%) have completed no more than two courses. Almost one-third (30.0%) have completed 3–5 courses. Of the remaining respondents, 22.9% have completed 6–8 courses and 2.4% have finished 9 or more courses.

Excluding "do not need to use *Library Literature*," the two most frequently mentioned reasons provide useful comparisons to the number of courses completed. Concerning, "unaware that the library has *Library Literature* on CD-ROM," Figure 11-4 shows that 68.8% of the nonusers were newer students, those having completed no more than two courses. The number of students checking this reason sharply decreases as the number of courses completed increases.

There is a similar trend for the reason "do not know how to use CD-ROM." Newer students were more likely to check this reason.

An interesting contrast relates to the number of courses taken and the reason "unable to get computer time in the Technology Lab." Newer students tended not to check this reason; only 7.1% did so. Half of the respondents mentioning this reason had already completed 3–5 courses.

In summary, the null hypothesis is rejected. There was a significant difference between the reasons cited and the number of courses completed. This finding suggests that the library needs to target special services toward newer students.

Summary

Some 47.1% of the students were nonusers of *Library Literature* on CD-ROM. Additionally, almost 35% have not used any CD-ROM product in the collection. The typical nonuser of *Library Literature* on CD-ROM is a master's student who has completed no more than two courses. This person is probably taking required courses, Reference/Information Services, and/or Organization of Knowledge in Libraries. Most likely, the student is a nonuser because he or she does not perceive a need to use this index, is unaware that the library had this index on CD-ROM, and/or does not know how to use CD-ROM.

RECOMMENDATIONS

The recommendations focus on two areas: promotion of CD-ROM holdings and subsequent research. Library staff might inform faculty members on a regular basis of newly acquired CD-ROM products. There might also be an occasional workshop for the faculty, the purpose of which would be to familiarize them with different products and to encourage them to base class assignments on CD-ROM products.

There might also be periodic workshops conducted throughout the semester for students. These workshops would review the use of the equipment and how to search specific products. To publicize CD-ROM for new students, the library might devote a part of the new student orientation to an explanation of CD-ROM technology and products.

Library staff might also place signs near the print *Library Literature* noting that the same index is available in the Technology Lab on CD-ROM. Signage in the Lab might remind students of various CD-ROM titles that the library owns. Additional signage might explain how students can receive assistance during those times in which the Lab staff assistant was not present.

Because this study only produced baseline data, the library should decide how often to replicate this study. Any replication should be linked to planning and the establishment of performance measures aimed at reducing the number of nonusers (see Chapter 8). The library can set goals and attempt to reduce the number of students who do not use CD-ROM, either *Library Literature*, or in general, by a certain percentage each school term.

Any replication of this investigation might consider the replacement of questions 6 (class status), 7 (courses taking), and 8 (number of courses completed) with questions relating to full or part-time status and whether or not this is the person's first semester in the program (see Figure 11-1).

The library might also consider the initiation of another study examining *users* of CD-ROM products. This study, however, might probe how students learned about CD-ROM. Such an investigation would complement the nonuser study and, it is hoped, provide additional information useful for library planning.

Any subsequent study relying on a written survey of students could adopt the same procedure as used in this study—placement of surveys in all mail folders. However, such a procedure requires extensive promotion of the survey, including signs that capture student attention and remind them of the importance of their participation in library planning.

COMMENTS

This chapter complements the previous one by providing another example of a typical evaluation study. Similar to Chapter 10, the basic evaluation steps are included here as well. In addition, however, this study provides an opportunity for subsequent studies to develop performance measures and to link study findings more directly to the planning process. In short, the basic steps for evaluation (outlined in Chapters 2 and 4) provide a model for conducting many types of library evaluations.

Another key point is that the study did not produce any startling findings. The lack of present knowledge or insights into a key service and collection priority provides a sufficient rationale for the conduct of an evaluation study. Regardless of the particular findings, a well-executed evaluation study provides library managers with important information useful in making decisions and allocating resources.

The examples of evaluation studies reported in Chapters 10 and 11 stress the importance of producing recommendations and findings that library decision makers can utilize. Simply making the recommendations, however, does not ensure that decision makers will adequately consider them. Thus, it is essential that evaluators effectively communicate findings and recommendations to decision makers. The next chapter offers strategies for encouraging successful communication of evaluation findings and recommendations.

DISCUSSION ITEMS

---

1. Diagram the logical structure (see Chapter 4) for the study.
2. Check *Library Literature*. Can you find any studies to add to the literature review section of this chapter?
3. Graph some of the percentages given in the text of the chapter. Make either a bar graph or pie chart.
4. Revise the data collection instrument contained in Figure 11-1, taking into account the comments raised in the "Recommendations" section of the chapter.
5. Should the library replicate the study or investigate another topical area?

6.   Set up an investigation of both users and nonusers of a particular CD-ROM service at a library familiar to you. Provide all the components of reflective inquiry, research design, and methodology (consult Chapters 2, 4, and 5 as necessary).

Chapter Twelve
Communication of Study Findings

Upon completion of a study, evaluators often communicate their data-gathering strategies, findings, and recommendations orally and in written form. The presentation might be aimed at library managers and staff, an oversight group (library board, city officials, etc.), community groups, fellow evaluators/researchers, other organizations interested in the subject or approach to problem solving, the professional at large, or others. The presentation may address political agendas or other considerations. The purpose of a written report might be to summarize findings, persuade the library to take action, support a planned action or recently made decision, alert others to potential problems and strategies for problem resolution, or seek publication. Publication might take the form of a monograph, scholarly article or chapter, poster paper or research note, conference paper, or report contained in the database of the federally-sponsored Educational Resources Information Center (ERIC).

Morris, Fitz-Gibbon, and Freeman (1987, p. 22) provide excellent coverage on how to communicate evaluation findings, and include a number of practical techniques. In addition, the authors show how to match possible communication forms to different audiences. To be expected, the popular article has the broadest appeal and is aimed at program administrators; board members, trustees, and other management staff; political bodies; community groups; current clientele; and organizations and individuals interested in the content of an evaluation study. Potential clients, as well, might see the article and decide to use the services of the evaluator.

Regardless of the form in which evaluators communicate study findings, these individuals must consider both the message and the receiver of that message. In effect, they address questions such as:

- Who is the target audience for the message and what are the needs and expectations of that audience?
- What message do evaluators want to convey?
- Is the message applicable to decision making?
- Is the message credible and understandable to its receiver?
- How can they create and maintain an environment in which decision makers take the message and translate it into action—organizational change?

Evaluators should present their message clearly, succinctly, and simply.
Illustrations attract attention and enable evaluators to present messages quick-

ly, concisely, clearly, and visually. They stimulate reader and audience interest. Nonetheless, they should not be overused or inappropriately used (Wurman, 1989, pp. 260–290).

This chapter briefly highlights the communication of study findings. However, the chapter is not a substitute for examination of the literature on scholarly report writing, interpersonal communication skills, or enrollment in formal courses on technical writing. One excellent guide is Bradley and Bradley's *Improving Written Communication in Libraries* (1988). This work discusses communications theory and the stages of planning, drafting, revising, editing, and producing documents. The authors analyze the writing of memos, policies, procedures, monthly and annual reports, and minutes of meetings. Furthermore, they present common problems of grammar, sentence structure, and word usage. Finally, they offer checklists to assist in the evaluation and revision of one's work.

This chapter also illustrates the contributions that microcomputer software make in the written and visual communication of a message (information content). In particular, when using such software, evaluators must address:

* Legibility—the ease of recognition of letters, numbers, and words in the text
* Readability—the lay out of the text so that the audience can clearly and easily scan the message
* Comprehensibility—the intended audience understands the message.

Careful consideration about how to *best* present evaluation study findings and recommendations is essential if evaluators want to affect organizational decision making.

ORAL PRESENTATIONS

Ideally, speakers attempt to create the impression that they are communicating with each member of the audience. This means that the speaker maintains eye contact with the audience and is mobile (not stationary during the entire presentation). However, their movement is not abrupt and does not detract from the message. In addition, the speaker ("Guidelines for Speakers," n.d.):

* Emphasizes the significance of the findings but [does] not dwell on detail
* Uses short sentences and pause[s] often so that listeners can absorb the ideas
* Speaks slowly, clearly, and audibly in a conversational manner. Listeners quickly lose interest if the paper is read
* Should not mumble
* Faces the audience, not a screen
* Repeats questions from the audience before answering them.

To this list, we might add:

- Determine the audience for the presentation and its current level of understanding of evaluation, research, and statistics
- Know the key points that will be of interest and value to the particular audience.

The speaker should attempt to say something memorable and to answer questions directly and succinctly. The former is most important when speaking at a conference session in which the evaluator is one of several speakers, or when the audience has already read the written report.

According to the "Guidelines for Speakers" (n.d.), speakers benefit from the use of *good* visual materials. Proper preparation of these materials:

> is crucial to the success of . . . [a] presentation. Poorly prepared, cluttered visuals will mar an otherwise interesting presentation.
>
> Legibility is the most important factor for visuals. Everyone in the audience, including those in the rear of the room, must be able to read easily what is projected on the screen.
>
> Letters and numbers must appear more than one inch high on the screen to be seen from 30 feet away. This will be the case for a slide made from material on an ordinary 8 1/2 x 11 inch page if the letters on the original are about 1/4 inch high. (An orator type element provides 1/4" letters.) Slides showing light information on a dark background are much easier to read than dark information on a light background. A good check on the potential legibility of your projected material is the ability to read the slide with your unaided eye.
>
> Your presentation will be more effective if you:
> - Do not clutter your slides with too much information. Use more slides with less information on each, rather than fewer slides with more information
> - Use graphs instead of tables. It is important that both graphs and tables be easy to understand
> - Use each slide only once. Make duplicates if you need to refer to a slide more than once
> - Mark all your slides on the bottom lefthand corner to indicate correct loading position. Also number all slides in the order in which they are to be shown
> - Organize your materials before the start of the session
> - Bring your slides in preloaded slide trays.

The final point to note is that the presentation should not exceed the time allotted and should allow time for questions and discussion. It is important to involve the audience in the presentation and, where feasible, demonstrate humor.

Evaluators might use microcomputer software for the production of visual material to support the oral presentations. For example, some spreadsheet, database management, statistical analysis, and other software generate graphs. *Harvard Graphics* (Software Publishing Corp., 1901 Landings Drive, Mountain

View, CA 94039–7210) is one example of special software that produces pie charts, bar and line graphs, etc. Hernon et al. (1989) contain numerous examples of graphs made with such software that would aid the understanding, comparison, and application of study findings.

Bar graphs and pie charts portray descriptive information and should be easy to understand. A line graph displays the results from two or more groups over time. Regardless of the type of graph used, evaluators should make each figure self-explanatory. They should use a short title reflecting content, labels, footnotes (if needed), etc. Furthermore, they should highlight the major findings in the text or speech.

Evaluators can use numerous types of software, such as MAC DRAW or *Showtext* (MicroPro International Corporation, 33 San Pablo Ave., San Rafael, CA 94903), to produce visuals and text charts for a presentation before an audience. Using such software, they can create tables, bulleted lists, signs, outlines, quotations, and brief text. They can print individual items on a laserjet printer. With the printed output, they can produce transparencies, perhaps with colored lettering, that an audience can clearly see, even from the back of a large room. Evaluators might even make slides of the illustrative matter produced.

Libraries in many different locations have access to firms that produce slides and graphics commercially, e.g., Autographix Inc. (Waltham, MA, 617–890–8558). Evaluators can make graphs using *Harvard Graphics*, and send them to the Massachusetts company via disk or modem. For a moderate cost of $5.00 (for one color overhead) and $12.00 (for one slide), they can have presentation graphics generated for next-day delivery.

Flip charts and even chalkboards might be useful tools. Flip charts provide an opportunity to summarize and stimulate audience comments. The purpose is to direct group interaction toward a common or desired end.

REPORT WRITING

Analyzing the data, stating results, and developing recommendations are not the same as reporting those findings and alternative recommendations. Specific techniques to communicate and disseminate the findings of an evaluation study are essential if evaluators want to have the recommendations implemented. This reporting process is ongoing, in that library management and staff should be kept informed throughout the evaluation process of its progress. Nonetheless, a written report on the evaluation is essential.

In short, the report should be concise and well-written. It should also include summary graphics and data results, and be written with an easy-to-read style. Clearly, every effort should be made to write and present the report in a manner that encourages action—the making of decisions and the development of strategies to implement one or more of the recommendations.

Figure 12-1.   Organization of a Typical Report

Preliminary Materials

- Title Page
- Table of Contents
- List of Figures and Tables
- Abstract or Executive Summary

Body of the Report

- Chapter 1: Introduction (Background, Key Terms and Concepts, Statement of the Problem)
- Chapter 2: Review of the Literature (Places the Problem in Context and Draws upon Findings and Experiences of Previous Research)
- Chapter 3: Setting up the Study (Logical Structure—the Conceptual Framework, Objectives, Hypotheses and/or Research Questions, Procedures—Research Design, Methodology, Reliability and Validity Indicators, and Study Limitations)
- Chapter 4: Findings
- Chapter 5: Summary, Conclusions, and Recommendations

Reference Materials

- Bibliography
- Appendix (Includes a copy of the Data Collection Instrument and Other Items as Appropriate)
- Index (Optional)

Figure 12-1 illustrates the components of a report. A journal article, for instance, might present all the chapter components, but in an abbreviated form. The report is written primarily to satisfy the needs of a specific and well-defined reading audience. It focuses on what that particular audience needs/wants to know, and what the evaluators consider to be most important for the audience to learn.

The executive summary explains what was evaluated, why it was evaluated, and how the evaluation was conducted. It also outlines the major findings and recommendations of the study. The summary, which is designed for those too busy to read the entire report, does not exceed several pages.

To produce the report, evaluators might use microcomputer software that performs wordprocessing, produces outlines, checks spelling, word choice, grammar, and writing style, or serves as a group writing tool. Wordprocessing software, such as *WordPerfect 5.0* and *WordStar Professional 5.0*, contains a spelling checker, thesaurus, and outliner (the composition of a report in outline form). Such software also imports graphics and enables their users to engage in desktop publishing and to lay out a visually pleasing report.

Lake and Rodarmor (1989) identify examples of software that serve as writing tools. Under the heading of "Spelling, Grammar, and Style Checkers," they discuss, among other packages:

- *Grammatik III* (Reference Software, Inc., 330 Townsend St., Suite 123, San Francisco, CA 94107)
- *Readability Plus* (Scandinavian PC Systems, 51 Monroe St., #1101, Rockville, MD 20850)
- *RightWriter* (RightSoft Inc., 4545 Samuel St., Sarasota, FL 34233).

Evaluators produce a word processed file of their report and use one or more of these packages to obtain tips for stylistic and/or grammatical improvements. (See Hernon et al., Chapter 11, 1989, for an example of report writing using *RightWriter* 2.0 and 3.0, and *Grammatik III*.)

Grammatik III checks grammar, stylistic, phrase, and mechanical errors. For example, it diagnoses incomplete sentences, disagreement between subject and verb, improper use of infinitives, overused and wordy phrases, paragraph and capitalization errors, and incomplete sentences.

Readability Plus analyzes a file and makes suggestions based on nine different models: general purpose writing, magazine feature stories, advertising copy, children's books, technical writing, government reports, and "bureaucratic gobbledygook." It also includes four widely accepted measures of readability: the Flesch Reading Ease Index, the Flesch-Kincaid Index, Gunning's Fog Index, and LIX (the Fog Index's European counterpart). The software compares the mix of short and long sentences, the percentage of sentences containing only short words, and the ratio of difficult to more common words. *Readability Plus* does not analyze sentences word-by-word. Rather, it assesses the overall writing style and its appropriateness to a particular audience. The software identifies weak sentences and indicates what is wrong with them, but leaves the solution to the writer.

*RightWriter** checks a word processed file for grammar, usage, punctuation, and stylistic errors. It points out the use of cliches, wordy phrases, passive voice, repetitive words, and split infinitives. The software rates the document's reading level, use of jargon, and strength of presentation. As do other packages, it also counts the number of words in a document.

Although Lake and Rodarmor (1989) do not discuss it, *Correct Grammar*

---

* The latest edition of *RightWriter* is 3.1.

Figure 12-2. Part of a Hypothetical Proposal

Background

Unobtrusive testing is the process of asking reference questions (for which answers have been predetermined) of of library staff members who are unaware that they are being evaluated. The advantages of unobtrusive testing include: observation of staff members under operating conditions assumed to be normal, measurement of the success with which staff members answer questions, and conjecturing why they might not be answering certain types of questions correctly. Other advantages include the viewing of reference desk service from a user's perspective and from the context of organizational goals and objectives.

The body of unobtrusive research studies conducted over a 20-year period challenge librarians' blind faith that reference desk service for factual and bibliographic questions is necessarily fine and of high quality. These studies numbering 30 to date have tended to reach similar conclusions (ones supported by research employing other research methodologies). The staff members tested tend to conform to the 55% Rule—they answer slightly more than half of the factual and bibliographic questions correctly; they infrequently engage in referral, either internal or external to the library; the length of the search process does not increase the likelihood that a correct answer will be received; the interpersonal communications skills of some library personnel are limited and these people can be abrasive in there dealings with the public; and staff may fail to fully negotiate questions.

Statement of the Problem

Unobtrusive research has exclusively concentrated on the staff of academic and public libraries assigned to general reference and/or government documents departments. Such research has not probed the reference desk service provided by state library staff and related the findings to fill rate measures such as *correct answer fill rate* and *referral fill rate*.

Four primary benefits would result for the proposed study: (1) the effectiveness with which state libraries answer short-answer type questions, (2) recommendations and strategies could be offered for improving the effectiveness of their reference desk service, (3) the linking of findings to performance measures should have great appeal to those state libraries adopting or planning to adopt such measures, and (4) reference desk service provided by state libraries can be placed in the context of the larger literature on the evaluation of reference service. The information that results from the testing can by incorporated by library managers into their decision making and the planning process.

Figure 12-3. Marked up Copy of Previous Figure Using RightWriter 3.0

Background
Unobtrusive testing is the process of asking reference questions (for which answers have been predetermined) of of
<<* PASSIVE VOICE: been predetermined *>>^
<<* REPEATED WORD *>>
library staff members who are unaware that they are being evaluated. The advantages of unobtrusive testing include:
^ <<* PASSIVE VOICE: being evaluated *>>
<<* REPLACE BY FORM OF SIMPLER check or test or rate? *>>
^ <<* SPLIT INTO 2 SENTENCES? *>>
^ <<* LONG SENTENCE: 28 WORDS *>>
observation of staff members under operating conditions assumed to be normal, measurement of the success with which staff members answer questions, and conjecturing why they might not be
<<* REPLACE conjecturing BY FORM OF SIMPLER guess? *>>
answering certain types of questions correctly. Other advantages
‹MDNM›<<* SPLIT INTO 2 SENTENCES? *>>^
<<* LONG SENTENCE: 40 WORDS *>>^
include the viewing of reference desk service from a user's perspective and from the context of organizational goals and objectives.
<<* REPLACE objectives BY FORM OF SIMPLER aim or goal? *>>

The body of unobtrusive research studies conducted over a 20-year period challenge librarians' blind faith that reference desk service for factual and bibliographic questions is necessarily fine and of high quality. These studies numbering 30
<<* SPLIT INTO 2 SENTENCES? *>>^
<<* S3. LONG SENTENCE: 31 WORDS *>>^
to date have tended to reach similar conclusions (ones supported by research employing other research methodologies). The staff members tested tend to conform to the 55% Rule—they answer slightly more than half of the factual and bibliographic questions correctly; they infrequently engage in referral, either internal or external to the library; the length of the search process does not increase the likelihood that a correct answer will be received; the interpersonal communications skills of some
^ <<* PASSIVE VOICE: be received *>>
library personnel are limited and these people can be abrasive in
<<* PASSIVE VOICE: are limited *>>
there dealings with the public; and staff may fail to fully
^ <<* SPLIT INTO 2 SENTENCES? *>>

Figure 12-3.—(Continued)

^ <<* LONG SENTENCE: 73 WORDS *>>
<<* SEMICOLONS SEPARATE INDEPENDENT CLAUSES *>>
negotiate questions.
^ <<* SPLIT INFINITIVE: to fully negotiate *>>

Statement of the Problem

Unobtrusive research has exclusively concentrated on the staff of academic and public libraries assigned to general reference and/or government documents departments. Such research
^ <<* LEGALESE: and/or *>>
has not probed the reference desk service provided by state library staff and related the findings to fill rate measures such as *correct answer fill rate* and *referral fill rate.*
<<* SPLIT INTO 2 SENTENCES? *>>^
<<* LONG SENTENCE: 32 WORDS *>>^
Four primary benefits would result for the proposed study: (1) the effectiveness with which state libraries answer short-answer type questions, (2) recommendations and strategies could be offered for improving the effectiveness of their reference
^ <<* PASSIVE VOICE: be offered *>>
desk service, (3) the linking of findings to performance measures should have great appeal to those state libraries adopting or
^ <<* IS THIS JUSTIFIED? great *>>
planning to adopt such measures, and (4) reference desk service provided by state libraries can be placed in the context of the
^ <<* SPLIT INTO 2 SENTENCES? *>>
^ <<* LONG SENTENCE: 63 WORDS *>>
<<* PASSIVE VOICE: be placed *>>^
larger literature on the evaluation of reference service. The information that results from the testing can by incorporated by library managers into their decision making and the planning process.
<<** SUMMARY **>>
READABILITY INDEX: 18.02
  Readers need a 18th grade level of education.
  The writing is complex and may be difficult to read.
SENTENCE STRUCTURE RECOMMENDATIONS:
  1. Most sentences contain multiple clauses.
      Try to use more simple sentences.
  3. Most sentences start with nouns.
      Try varying the sentence starts.

(Lifetree Software Inc., 33 New Montogmery St., Suite 1260, San Francisco, CA 94105) also analyzes sentence structure and highlights parts of speech, inflectional forms, and syntactic relationships. The software flags grammar, punctuation, and spelling errors, and identifies wordy prepositional phrases and cliches.

Figure 12-2 represents part of a hypothetical proposal that contains numerous stylistic and grammar mistakes. Figure 12-3 indicates the suggestions offered by *RightWriter 3.0*. The other software packages flagged additional potential problems. For example, *Grammatik III* marked the misuse of "there" and split infinitives. It labeled the term "and/or" as "clumsy, awkward, of," but made inappropriate suggestions as well. Because evaluators assign a specific meaning to *effectiveness*, the word should not be replaced with "success." Clearly, as it should be, writers must regard every diagnostic as a suggestion and decide for themselves which ones to accept or reject.

Figure 12-4 contains the rewritten passage from Figure 12-2. Part of the rewriting resulted from just reading the passage, and deleting unnecessary words and thoughts. Writing-aid software provides an additional review of the passage. Clearly, evaluators should not become overtly dependent on such software. The use of shorter and less complex sentences significantly lowers the reading level. For some audiences, a lower reading level, perhaps combined with the preparation of a report using desktop publishing software, would be appropriate.

Two other software packages merit mention. *ForComment 1.16* (Broderbund Software, 17 Paul St., San Rafael, CA 94903–2101) "lets up to 15 reviewers add comments to a file while allowing only the author or editor to alter it." The program "can retain 26 versions of a document and 15 comments on a given line of text" (Lake and Rodarmor, 1989, p. 182). *Red Pencil 1.21* (Capsule Codeworks, P.O. Box 3026, Renton, WA 98056) "enables users to proofread and mark text for eight common operations: move, delete, insert, change, paragraph, no paragraph, stet, and query" (Lake and Rodarmor, 1989).

Evaluators might ask selected members of a target audience to review a draft of the report and comment on both style and substance. Prior to completion of the written report, the evaluators should review the types of questions identified in Figure 12-5. The purpose is to ensure that the content is well written, factually accurate, and appealing to readers. In addition, the report should address the purposes for which data were collected and offer feasible recommendations.

PUBLICATION

Often evaluators make the decision to seek publication when they plan out the study—set the study's reflective inquiry and procedures (see Chapter 4). At that time, they may decide to produce research rather than management data, and to provide indicators of reliability and validity. The desire to collect publishable

Figure 12-4.   Rewritten Passages from the Hypothetical Proposal

Background

Unobtrusive testing is the process of asking reference questions (for which answers have been predetermined) of library staff members who are unaware that they are study subjects. Such testing observes staff members under normal working conditions, measures the success with which they answer questions, and provides insights into reasons for incorrect responses. Other advantages include the viewing of reference desk service from a user's perspective and in terms of stated goals and objectives.

The body of unobtrusive research studies conducted over a 20-year period challenge blind faith that libraries offer high quality reference desk service. These studies have generally found that libraries conform to the 55% Rule—their staff answer slightly more than half of the factual and bibliographic questions correctly. Furthermore, they infrequently engage in referral, either internal or external to the library; the length of the search process does not increase the likelihood that patrons will receive a correct answer; some staff members have limited interpersonal communications skills and are abrasive in their dealings with the public; and staff may fail to negotiate questions.

Statement of the Problem

Unobtrusive research has exclusively concentrated on the staff of academic and public libraries assigned to general reference and government documents departments. Such research has not probed the reference desk service provided by state library staff and cast the findings in terms of fill rate measures (correct answer fill rate, referral fill rate, etc.).

The proposed study would have three primary benefits. First, knowledge would be gained about the effectiveness with which state libraries answer short-answer type questions. Second, the linkage of findings to fill rates would be appropriate for those state libraries adopting, or planning to adopt, performance measures. Third, state librarians might incorporate the test results into their decision making and the planning process.

> Number of Words: 290
> Grade Level: 15

Figure 12-5.   Partial Checklist of Items for a Report

1. Are the study components (e.g., the problem statement and objectives) clearly and concisely stated?
2. Have the objectives, hypotheses, and/or research questions been adequately addressed?
3. Are the findings, conclusions, and recommendations clearly stated and do they match the objectives, hypotheses, and/or research questions? Do the findings, conclusions, and recommendations appeal to the intended audience?
4. Where necessary, are significant or potentially controversial statements supported by the literature?
5. Are there weaknesses in logic or mistakes in spelling or grammar?
6. Are concepts and technical words adequately explained?
7. Could a major point be better represented though a table or figure?
8. Are sentences repetitive, clearly expressed, and easy to read?
9. Is the report/article objective?
10. Does the report/article read well?
11. Does the title adequately describe the contents of the report?
12. Is the use of headings and subheadings consistent throughout the report?
13. Is each paragraph essential and in its proper place?
14. Does one paragraph flow naturally into the next?
15. Does the report/article contain contradictions?
16. Do sentences contain passive voice, wordy thoughts, and unnecessary words?
17. Is there consistent use of hyphens, spelling, and word capitalization?
18. Are references accurate and do the dates in the list of references match those presented in the text?
19. Are pages numbered correctly?
20. Are tables and figures correctly numbered?
21. Are quotations correct?
22. Is there any copyright problem associated with the quotation of text?
23. Are all references necessary?

data may require the permission of those commissioning, supporting, and participating in the study. Library managers and funding organizations may encourage the dissemination of study findings. However, the decision to publish signifies that they are willing to "live" with the findings and have the profession at large know what occurred. It also means that managers and evaluators are willing to have others critique the manner in which the evaluation was conducted.

Publication involves the making of choices—to seek journal or monograph

Figure 12-6. Partial Checklist of Items for a Paper Intended for Publication

---

1. Does the manuscript match the areas of interest for the journal or book series?
2. Have the stylistic and submission requirements of the journal or book series been met?
3. Is the manuscript well-written and does it include the most appropriate references?
4. Are sources in the footnotes or references complete and accurate?
5. In case of a monograph, have the proper copyright permissions been obtained?
6. Is only the most essential information quoted from other sources?

---

publication and to decide on the journal or book publisher. Those seeking publication should address the types of questions identified in both Figures 12-5 and 12-6. They should also compare the advantages and disadvantages of publication in either journal or monographic format.

Libraries are particularly concerned about maintaining their serials collection in times of severe financial constraints. They may accord the development and management of serials, especially those in the sciences, as one of the highest (if not the highest) collection priorities. "Paying for scientific journals takes an increasing percentage of the acquisitions budget, and the humanities and social sciences suffer" (Lynch, 1988, p. 89). Furthermore, "libraries are just beginning to confront this allocation problem and are looking carefully at the expenditures for serials and the reallocation of book funds to sustain the serial subscriptions" (Ibid.).

As a result of the decision to transfer funds from the monographic to serials budget, libraries become even more selective in the monographs acquired, especially those from library and information science. Limited demand, static library budgets, increasing production costs, and higher book prices directly impact the sales potential for many library and information science monographs. Many publishing houses have lowered their expectations concerning what is a "best seller." Clearly, many monographs in these times have a lesser opportunity to make a broader impact. A further complication is that *Library Literature* and other indexes in library and information science emphasize journal over monograph contents.

Despite the declining sales potential for many monographs, decreased coverage of book reviews in many journals, and insufficient coverage of monographs in appropriate indexes, many publishers maintain book series in library and information science. Some of these series add new titles each year and regularly sign a number of book contracts. Clearly, publishing opportunities exist despite the low sales potential of many titles and the pricing policies of some publishers.

Despite these limitations, monographs serve an important function. They provide in-depth coverage of an issue, an extensive literature review, and copies of data collection instruments. The findings and data collection instruments might also provide an opportunity for staff training. For example, studies reporting the results of unobtrusive testing (see Figure 12-4) may include the actual test questions as part of the appendix. The staff might practice with these questions and even engage in role playing (see Williams and Wedig, 1984).

Among the quantity of monographs published each year, it becomes important to identify the subset of those of quality. One component of quality might be the identification of noteworthy problems that merit the attention of staff. Library staff can trace the perceived value of older monographs from book reviews, the literature, and citation patterns. Important journal articles might be identified from related writings, coverage in textbooks, and citation patterns. These methods definitely favor works that have been in print for awhile. Newer titles lack a traceable record. Instead, the profession must depend on the author's proven research and writing record, publishers' brochures and catalogs, and inclusion in scholarly, refereed journals.

Despite the increasing volume of literature on library and information science, library managers frequently do not consult that literature when they make decisions (McClure, 1980). Evaluators need access to the literature when they set up a study or link findings to broader trends. For this reason, the research literature perhaps has the greatest utility to evaluators, although failures are infrequently reported. Library managers may regard the literature more as a promotional devise: the reporting of study findings that draws national visibility to their collections, services, and activities. They are probably more supportive of those studies that reflect positively on their library. Perhaps this is part of the reason that library literature tends to focus on action research deemed a success.

TAKING RESPONSIBILITY FOR
COMMUNICATING FINDINGS

A frequent complaint of many evaluators is that library decision makers failed to act on the study findings and recommendations. The reasons for such inaction may rest with the evaluators rather than the decision makers. Evaluators must recognize that simply designing and implementing the evaluation will not, in and of itself, affect library decision making. The evaluators have a responsibility to make certain that study findings and recommendations are carefully presented to decision makers for maximum impact and affect.

A primary reason for decision makers not taking action on evaluation findings is that evaluators failed to include specific recommendations for how decision makers might use the findings to improve library services or activities. Another reason for limited impact is that evaluators did not provide suggestions for

implementing the recommendations and comparing alternative means to implement those recommendations. They also probably did not discuss which implementation strategies might have the best chances for success.

Finally, a key reason for lack of action on evaluation findings is that evaluators did not provide decision makers with a coherent, well-organized, concise,
and readable report. And even with the writing of a high-quality report, chances
for action being taken on the evaluation findings will be enhanced if evaluators
make a short oral presentation to the decision makers. Such an oral presentation,
as a follow-up to the written report, provides an opportunity for evaluators to
discuss study findings, answer questions, and "sell" some of the recommendations and implementation strategies.

Taking responsibility to communicate evaluation findings effectively—both
in writing and orally—is essential if evaluators want to affect decision making
and ultimately organziational change. However, in communicating study findings, evaluators must also recognize the political realities within the organization. Recommendations that evaluators propose may appear to be straightforward
and easily implemented, but these recommendations may not address the "politics" within the organization. The following chapter discusses these political
considerations.

DISCUSSION ITEMS

1. Diagnose a passage of your own writing using *RightWriter* or one of the
    other software packages. Now rewrite the passage using the software's
    diagnostics and simpler sentences. Discuss the results.
2. Construct a table of study findings. Capture the same information as a bar or
    line graph, or pie chart. Discuss the value of the visual display of data.
3. Videotape yourself delivering a short presentation. Critique your delivery
    and ask others to do the same.
4. Find published examples of evaluation studies reported in either *Library
    Literature* or ERIC's *Resources in Education*. Critique the presentation of
    study findings, conclusions, and recommendations.
5. Compare *Grammatik III*, *Readability Plus*, *RightWriter*, and *Correct Gram-
    mar*. Which do you prefer? Why?

Chapter Thirteen
Barriers to Evaluation—
The Political Context

Library staff frequently gather data/information that they might use for political purposes. For instance, they record the number of reference questions asked, titles borrowed and waiting for reshelving, and titles cataloged. Such data have a political connotation when library directors use them to try to persuade university officials, mayors, etc., that the library does a high volume of business with inadequate resources, and therefore needs additional staff or resources to function more effectively. Data such as these reflect extensiveness or how much of an activity the library says it accomplishes. They do not convey effectiveness unless managers view extensiveness within the context of library goals and objectives. Nonetheless, even when linked to goals and objectives, extensiveness is a lower-order indicator of effectiveness and does not, in and of itself, suggest quality (see Chapters 8 and 9).

Regardless of whether the library collects data reflecting extensiveness, effectiveness, or efficiency, managers and others must anticipate the barriers that might be encountered in the completion of an evaluation study. For example, library staff may regard evaluation as a threat to the status quo (see Chapter 14). They may view study findings as disruptive and as a direct attack on current policies and practices that they support.

Contradictory expectations from a study may also be a barrier to conducting an evaluation study. For instance, the library director may believe that the evaluation study will be conducted superficially and not provide in-depth insights into a program, service, or operation. On the other hand, a department head and the evaluator may regard the study as providing the library with data necessary to make better decisions. "Conflicting values are common in any evaluation process, and they tend to generate far more questions than answers" (DeProspo, 1975, p. 305).

Information is a tool useful for acquiring and retaining power. Information may enable an organization to advance its image and role as dynamic and meeting its mission, goals, and objectives. Even in dynamic organizations, decision makers might want to monitor carefully any evaluation study that was contemplated and to determine the extent to which findings conform to that image and their expectations. Because of the inherent problems associated with attempting to *control* research and study findings, image protectors and inflators probably would prefer not to engage in evaluation. Rather, they would merely

rely on perceptions and subjective impressions. Evaluators would probably be reluctant to conduct studies in a repressive or restrictive environment. Evaluation is most conductive in an open organization truly interested in planning and self-improvement (see Chapters 1 and 2).

Evaluation involves compromises and a process of negotiation. Evaluation is more interested in attacking practical problems than in developing new knowledge. However, the emergence of new knowledge may be a by-product. Lincoln and Guba (1986) distinguish between research and evaluation. Each approach, they maintain, has different objectives, intended outcomes, and audiences. In contrast, this book views evaluation as a type of research activity. Both research and evaluation apply similar steps as outlined in Chapters 4 and 5. The purpose of evaluation studies is to help decision makers, while still presenting them with objectively gathered and factual information. The presentation of facts, however, could retard a program or service, if there are negative implications (Palumbo, 1987, p. 22).

Another barrier is that evaluation of a program, service, or operation is often a one-time effort or at least occurs on an irregular basis. Librarians therefore might make decisions based on outdated, incomplete, or erroneous data. Existing data might only reflect part of the program, service, or operation, yet librarians might mistakenly treat the data as being up-to-date and comprehensive.

Furthermore, evaluators must recognize power and personality relationships among the stakeholders affected by the evaluation. Clearly, some stakeholders may have greater power than others, and some may be more willing to use that power to enhance or detract from the evaluation. In addition, individual personalties may greatly affect the evaluation process and its ultimate impact.

Evaluators should be aware of the environment in which the study will be conducted and how that environment might impact on the study—its planning, data collection, data interpretation, and conclusions and recommendations. Evaluators must be sensitive to the political climate and political implications for the completion of the study, and for providing study findings that meet the needs of decision makers. Evaluators need to offer recommendations that are realistic for the organization to consider, while decision makers need to select those most feasible to implement.

Feasibility may refer to factors such as having the fewest political consequences or as requiring minimal organization change or reallocation of resources. Clearly, evaluators must understand the politics of the organization and be sensitive to the political climate when they set up the study, execute data collection, process the data, and write the results. At the same time, decision makers must be forewarned that they will have to "live with" the findings, regardless of what they turn out to be.

Evaluation should not be confrontational. When it is, the value of the findings and recommendations to decision makers may be limited. Evaluators should work with decision makers and keep them informed of the study's progress. The purpose is to ensure that decision makers know how the study is proceeding, the problems encountered, and the general nature of the findings. In this way, potentially *startling* findings do not come as a total surprise.

Although evaluators prefer to be neutral and objective, they must realize that study results may have political uses. Many evaluators may feel uncomfortable operating in a political context. Muscatello (1989, p. 17) offers an excellent summary of the role of the evaluator and this person's relationship to the manager:

> the good evaluator will develop hard objective data and upon these data will build analyses and recommendations. The good manager, together with the evaluator, will ensure that the conclusions and recommendations reached during the study are overlaid first with relevant policy considerations and then with the realities of organizational politics, organizational environment, and future business strategies.

However, as already noted, the evaluator cannot ignore the organizational climate and politics in developing a set of recommendations.

The purpose of this chapter is to expand coverage of the political context provided in Chapter 1 and to provide a general overview of the political dimension of evaluation. The chapter also illustrates that evaluators and library staff can serve as change agents who link evaluation to planning and challenge the organization to improve—more effectively and efficiently meet its mission and the information needs of library clientele. Chapter 14 expands upon the concept of change and change agents.

EVALUATORS

Evaluators do not plan a study in isolation of political realities and organizational constraints. The purpose of a study is to provide the library with findings that are realistic, as well as useful, relevant, and *acceptable* to decision makers. Library decision makers must be willing to accept study findings and recommendations and to convert them into organizational change. Clearly, the relationship between evaluators and decision makers must be symbiotic, not hostile.

It would be impractical for evaluators, for example, to recommend the hiring of additional staff, if the organization has a no growth budget and is finding it difficult to keep up with inflation. Evaluators must adjust to the financial, staffing, and other realities under which an organization operates. Unless this is done, the evaluation report will not contain information useful for decision making and change. Evaluators want their report to lead to action and not merely be filed on the shelf.

As Muscatello (1989, p. 17) observes,

> there will, of course, be instances when no matter what focus an . . . [evaluator] gives to implementation, the politics of the organization will shut down recom-

Figure 13-1. Potential Dysfunctions*

EYE WASH:	An attempt to justify a weak or bad program by deliberately selecting for evaluation only those aspects that "look good" on the surface: Appearance replaces reality.
WHITE WASH:	An attempt to cover up program failure or errors by avoiding any objective appraisal: Vindication replaces verification.
SUBMARINE:	An attempt to "torpedo" or destroy a program regardless of its effectiveness: Politics replaces research.
POSTURE:	An attempt to use evaluation as a "gesture" of objectivity or professionalism: Ritual replaces research.
POSTPONEMENT:	An attempt to delay needed action by pretending to seek "facts" and the program continues indefinitely: Research replaces effective services.
DUCKING RESPONSIBILITY:	Administrators may look to evaluation as a means to get them "off the hook" and make someone else responsible: Delegation replaces administration.
SCARE TACTICS:	An attempt to "shock" or "scare" staff by showing them just "how bad it really is" and tie-in the testing to formal personnel evaluation, etc.: Blame replaces improvement.

* Based, in part, on Edward A. Suchman, "Action for What? A Critique of Evaluation Research," in *Evaluating Action Programs*, edited by Carol H. Weiss (Boston, MA: Allyn and Bacon, Inc., 1972).

mended options. Nevertheless, he or she must continually work to ensure that the findings and recommendations that issue from evaluations have a high survival rate.

Of course, this may be easier to accomplish if the evaluator is a member of the organization and not an outsider hired to study a particular problem. The danger for an inside evaluator, however, is that he or she might be perceived as having a vested interest in the recommended change.

Evaluators should realize that a number of potential dysfunctions can result from the evaluation. Figure 13-1 summarizes these dysfunctions. Indeed, some of them may occur by happenstance, or the evaluator may be pressured to "encourage" one or more of these dysfunctions to occur. Either way, the evaluator should be aware of "hidden agendas" that may be used to influence the evaluation into accomplishing some of the dysfunctions identified in Figure 13-1.

HIDDEN AGENDAS

Conceivably, administrators may not want an objective evaluation to be conducted, or else they might prefer one that can be manipulated in support of existing or planned policy. As a first step, evaluators want to assess the organization and try to discover any hidden agenda(s). A hidden agenda, however, may not be initially apparent. The dilemma is most troublesome when a study has received substantial funding and the evaluators have finalized the reflective inquiry and procedures before they discover the hidden agenda (see Chapter 4). Even in such situations, it is hoped that the evaluators can maneuver around a hidden agenda and obtain some latitude in investigating the problem.

An example of a hidden agenda would be where decision makers prefer the completion of a marketing study aimed at "selling" a particular program or service to library clientele or an oversight body (e.g., board of trustees). The study is not really intended to consist of research or evaluation, but, rather, to demonstrate widespread support for a particular action. A public library, for instance, might conduct a community analysis to demonstrate community support for a new library building—regardless of the "facts." Such information might be used to further persuade city officials to agree to a new building.

In most cases, evaluators of library programs or services do not encounter an extreme situation: either conform to the expectations of administrators or discontinue the study. Rather, evaluators must make adjustments and be aware of the hidden agenda and reasons for staff cooperation or nonsupport. Such knowledge becomes important as evaluators set up and carry out the study. Evaluators do not want to place themselves in a situation, whereby, upon completion of the study, administrators can easily dismiss the report or successfully challenge the reflective inquiry and study procedures. Conceivably, the challenge could damage the reputation and credibility of the evaluator.

FALSIFIED DATA

Sources, such as *The Chronicle of Higher Education*, have reported instances in which researchers, some using government funds, apparently falsified experiments and documentation. Presumably, such practices only occasionally occur with evaluation studies.

The purpose for falsification would be to ensure that the outcome conformed with the expectations of either the evaluators or library management. Such practices, needless to say, should be discouraged. When utilized, they reflect adversely on the library and the evaluator's reputation. The assumption is that such unethical practices cannot remain hidden. Evaluators have too much to lose if their honesty and trustworthiness are injured. They could be disgraced and, it is hoped, would not have continued opportunities to conduct studies.

Evaluators should be motivated by the challenge of studying a problem of importance to a library, providing decision makers with useful information, and encouraging the organization to become more effective overall. Of course, evaluators can also be motivated by more tangible rewards such as being hired to conduct studies. Successful and ethical work usually leads to further opportunities; conversely, shoddy and unethical work typically will not lead to new opportunities to conduct evaluation studies.

Evaluators often present their reports in both written form and orally. The more opportunities that there are to learn (question and challenge the evaluators), the more difficult it probably is to hide or disguise unethical conduct. Those listening to a presentation should, first, want to discuss a study's reflective inquiry, procedures, reliability, and validity. They should also clearly understand the assumptions and limitations under which the study was completed. Once reassured on these points, they can discuss the interpretation of study findings and the recommendations.

Two central questions emerging from a completed study are: "Who owns the dataset," and "Who should have direct access to it?" Neither question is a simple one to answer. If the data resulted from a study receiving financial support from a funding organization or institution, the completed data collection instruments and the resulting machine-readable dataset may not be the exclusive property of the evaluator. If the library at which the evaluator conducted the study provided the person with release time, is the dataset still the property of the organization? Such issues should be resolved before the evaluation is initiated.

Another issue to consider in access to the datasets relates to privacy and confidentiality of data. Evaluators may have to promise participants that their responses would be held in confidence. Furthermore, it certainly may be unethical to release datasets in which specific organizations or individuals can be identified by their responses. Finally, in some instances where funding for the evaluation came from government agencies, specific guidelines and requirements might have to be followed to determine the releasability of the dataset and determine who may access those data.

Having direct access to the dataset may offer an opportunity to check on the veracity of the evaluator. The lack of access to a dataset may not, however, signify that the evaluator committed unethical practices and is trying to hide something. Why should evaluators provide access to a dataset generated from their own resources? If others asked evaluators to make additional computer runs, but the evaluators would have to pay for these runs out of their own finances, refusal cannot be equated with unethical practices. The issues are complex and may involve copyright as well as other factors. An evaluator has made an investment in the completion of a study. Others wanting access to the data should recognize this investment.

STRATEGIES FOR EVALUATORS TO USE IN UNDERSTANDING AND ADDRESSING THE POLITICAL CLIMATE

This section discusses some "common-sense" approaches for library evaluators to use in recognizing hidden agendas and politically sensitive issues. Before drawing conclusions about these agendas and issues, evaluators should collect as much information as possible and keep an open mind while they shift through information, form impressions, test these impressions, and draw conclusions. The key phrase is "open mind." Evaluators should not make prejudgments; but if they do, they should also be willing to make readjustments. After all, initial or hastily formed impressions may be inaccurate or misleading, and provide an erroneous foundation for a problem statement or a research study.

Initial Steps

Evaluators need a clear and accurate understanding of the organization and the constraints under which it operates. They should identify the major stakeholders that might be interested in the study and its findings. Identification of these groups will emerge from discussions with library staff and analysis of the problem statement's significance. The evaluator must ask: "To whom is the study important, and what uses might these groups make of the study's findings?" The evaluator must also assess why the study is being conducted and the type of cooperation that different groups might provide.

After identification of the stakeholders, the evaluator should meet with each and gain their perspectives on the study, its conduct, and utility for decision making. At times, stakeholders might reveal their feelings about other stakeholders. Evaluators must handle such discussions carefully. They do not want to be identified as biased toward one stakeholder or viewpoint. In addition, careless talk might get back to other stakeholders and produce adverse consequences. Besides, there might not be simple truths to complex issues.

The evaluator should also examine the library's annual report as well as other key documentation that convey the organization's mission, goals, and objectives. The evaluator will also examine current and historical documentation pertinent to the problem under investigation.

Advisory Board

Evaluators, together with the library administration, might establish an Advisory Board (sometimes called an evaluation task force) consisting of members representing varied groups and constituencies that have an interest or stake in study findings and their utilization. The Board should be carefully selected, in part, to address political factors. At times, evaluators and the administration might believe it necessary to co-opt certain individuals. In addition, they might select individuals with specific knowledge and research skills. Board members should be people who believe that the evaluation project is worth doing, who are willing to publicly support the project, can assist the evaluators in completing the study, and who have authority or influence to act on study findings. Board members should be willing to devote the time necessary for the completion of the study.

The purpose of the Board is to review the conceptualization of the study, data collection instruments, and tentative findings and recommendations. It may also offer suggestions for data collection sites and participants. Board members can also explain the project to those constituencies they represent. In this regard, different stakeholders have a means of ensuring that the study addresses their concerns and that appropriate, relevant, and useful results emerge. At the same time, these stakeholders have an investment in the study and its outcome.

Patton (1987) identifies another advantage of forming such a Board. He observes that the Board (p. 122):

allows the evaluator to share responsibility for decision making and utilization by providing a forum for the political and practical perspectives that best come from those stakeholders who will ultimately be involved in using evaluation results.

Patton (Ibid., pp. 122–123) summarizes the advantages of involving a group in evaluation as being:

- An environment of openness can be established to reduce suspicions and fears about what is going on in the evaluation. The key stakeholders who participate in the process know how decisions are made and who was involved in making them. This can reduce political paranoia
- Participants in the group process become sensitized to the multiple perspectives that exist around any program. They are exposed to divergent views, multiple possibilities, and competing values. Their view is broadened, and they are exposed to the varying agendas of people with different stakes in the evaluation. This increases the possibility of conducting an evaluation that is responsive to different needs, interests, and values
- New ideas often emerge out of the dynamics of group interaction
- A sense of shared responsibility for the evaluation can be engendered that is often greater than the responsibility that would be felt by isolated individuals. Commitments made in groups, in front of others, are typically more lasting and serious than promises made to an evaluator in private
- An open forum composed of various stakeholders makes it difficult to suppress touchy questions or negative findings. Issues get raised and findings get publicized that otherwise might never see the light of day
- The evaluator has the opportunity to observe firsthand the interactions among various stakeholders and to assess their interpersonal relationships. This information can be very helpful in developing utilization strategies

- A certain momentum can often be established through group processes that helps reduce delays or roadblocks resulting from the attitudes or actions of one person
- The evaluator(s) and stakeholders in a group process will often jell into a kind of support group. It's not the evaluator against the world. The other participants in the group can lend support, help, and understanding
- The group will often continue to function after the evaluation is completed, Participants can develop a shared commitment to follow through on utilization of evaluation findings and recommendations.

A Board composed of "a group of competent, politically sensitive, and creative people" is "greater than the sum of its parts" (Ibid., p. 123).

OBTAINING POLITICAL SKILLS

Unfortunately there is no quick means for acquiring the necessary political skills. Few formal or continuing education courses focus on the development of political skills. As a consequence, aspiring evaluators might seek out those individuals known to possess such skills and either work with them on projects in a mentoring relationship or see if these people will enlighten them as to the issues and skills related to political awareness.

Aspiring evaluators might also establish small scale projects and learn through a trial and error process. They should encourage critical assessment of their performance—as both researchers and individuals able to read the political climate.

Of course, aspiring evaluators can also read the literature and be familiar with those writings on the politics of evaluation. They might also attend national conferences dealing with evaluation and meet different leaders, including those presenting papers.

Another way to gain experience would be to run for local office (such as the board of trustees for the local library or the school committee). Such experience can provide insights into political processes and dealing with different constituencies. Indeed, working effectively with a broad range of constituency groups, and recognizing the political perspectives of these groups, are essential characteristics for a successful evaluator.

DISCUSSION ITEMS

---

1. Assume that the state library has commissioned you to prepare the public libraries in the state to collect performance measures on a monthly basis.

How would the decision concerning which measures to gather be made? In addition, how might the libraries collect meaningful data—useful for planning and decision making?

2.   Read Charles R. McClure's "A View from the Trenches: Costing and Performance Measures for Academic Library Public Services" [*College & Research Libraries*, 47 (July 1986): 323–336]. How would you negotiate the differing perspectives (those between library directors and middle managers) to gather performance measures that are truly useful for planning and decision making?

3.   Identify examples of hidden agendas and suggest how you might maneuver around them.

4.   Do you believe that falsification of data presents a serious problem for library and information science? What are possible impacts for both the evaluators and the evaluation study as a result of falsifying data?

5.   Suggest specific strategies for identifying and addressing the political climate?

6.   Suggest strategies, in addition to those highlighted in this chapter, for obtaining political skills?

7.   What specific steps can you take to understand and be aware of political realities when conducting an evaluations study?

Chapter Fourteen
Organizational Change

As Swisher and McClure (1984, p. 1) note,

> Librarians today are faced with a broad range of challenges and opportunities to improve the effectiveness of their libraries, to respond better to the information needs of their clientele, and to provide leadership to make the library an important component in the information environment. . . . The prerequisite skills to address such challenges and opportunities are in areas of producing and understanding action research, making decisions as how best to allocate scarce resources, and planning for increased organizational effectiveness—that is, accomplishment of goals and objectives.

Evaluation, which comprises a type of action research, is a self-diagnostic activity that encourages examination of the quality of library activities and services. Ongoing evaluation is integral to the maintenance of a dynamic, effective, and efficient organization.

Evaluation should incorporate planning, research, and change. Wanting to make changes is a necessary prerequisite for professional development, the meeting of organizational goals and objectives, and satisfying the information needs of current and potential clientele in a timely and comprehensive manner. Change, as used in this chapter, is any planned or unplanned alteration in the status quo that affects an organization's structure, services, programs, or allocation of resources. Furthermore, it is assumed that:

- Change is a normal pattern of growth and development for individuals as well as organizations
- Change is neither inherently "good" nor "bad"
- Certain types of management styles and interpersonal techniques best facilitate change.

Thus, librarians must develop specific strategies to encourage change if they are to successfully resolve the information needs of their clientele for access to information located either internal or external to the library.

Librarians interested in encouraging the change process must be knowledgeable about that process. They must be able to identify and to close significant performance gaps in the organization. They must be able to cope with factors that affect organizational performance. These factors might be condensed into five groups that interact with each other (Hage and Finsterbusch, 1987, p. 49):*

- Environmental context (setting limits on resources)
- Strategy group (e.g., values and leadership style)
- Process group (e.g., behavioral processes)
- Structural group (e.g., organizational and job design)
- Resource group (e.g., the attitudes and abilities of people).

The environmental context (Ibid., p. 48):

> limits the outputs and performances, determines what strategies are appropriate and sets limits on resources. . . . Next strategy affects processes and resources affect structures. Next, structures affect processes. Finally, strategy, processes, structures, and resources affect performances and outputs.

Dealing with environmental contexts requires the library to have established priorities.

Coping with change, performances, and outputs necessitates that librarians have clearly defined objectives that guide which changes might be accomplished and how to implement these changes. The staff must also have adequate time to accomplish change. Successful change, especially at an organizational level, takes time, a receptive managerial climate, and an ability to manage resistance to change (Baker, 1989). Change also requires access to information that can make a difference—information on the effectiveness and efficiency of library programs, services, and activities. That information typically comes from a broad range of evaluation activities.

In brief, change agents must avoid "inept management strategies," provide "adequate information about change," and be "sensitive to employee fears about change." They must also demonstrate that real reasons for change exist. At the same time, managers must be willing to comment on the necessary resources, assist in easing employee concerns during the transition process, and link change to improved service (Baker, 1989, p. 61).

THE CHANGE PROCESS

Decision making is a process closely related to planning and the research process. Decision making aims to influence value judgments held by other individu-

---

* Hage and Finsterbusch, *Organizational Change as a Development Strategy.* Copyright © 1987 by Lynne Rienner Publishing Co., Boulder, CO. Reprinted with permission.

als. But if one defines decision making as that process whereby information is converted into action, decision making is largely concerned with the process of acquiring, analyzing, and reporting information to accomplish an objective (McClure, 1980). Because librarians make decisions on a regular basis, they must be able to convert a broad range of information sources and research findings into a coherent plan of action. This chapter therefore discusses change as a planned activity that leads to the *better* accomplishment of stated departmental and organizational objectives.

According to Hage and Finsterbusch (1987, p. 50),*

> Most organizational changes result from the perception of performance or output gaps by organizational decision makers. Then the strategy of change must identify what component of the organizational system is to be changed and how the change is to be implemented. The strategy must select the intervention level, tactics, data-collection methods, and the resources required in implementing the change.

In other words, having articulated a problem statement, the decision maker marshals the resources necessary to investigate the problem and to produce insights useful for decision making.

Change may also be examined in a systems context. A system is a set of two or more interrelated elements that are coordinated for the accomplishment of certain goals. The properties of each element affect each other and the behavior of the system as a whole; the manner in which they affect the whole depends on the behavior of at least one other component of the system, and the system is more than the sum of its parts. In short, interaction among the various elements in the system combines to produce an attribute of the system that is not achievable by the individual parts alone.

Evaluation research is conducted for a purpose. It investigates either an actual problem or one that decision makers suspect might exist and impede on organizational effectiveness (see Chapter 4 and the discussion of a problem statement). Evaluation research therefore should be relevant to (and impact on) decision making—either lead to change or show that, contrary to popular belief, the problem was, in fact, insignificant.

A key question relating to organizational change is: "Who will receive the information generated from an evaluation study, and what will these individuals do with that information?" By undertaking evaluation research, decision makers have decided that they need information and can tolerate whatever the study discloses. For example, the results of a study might disclose that the reference staff of a university library only answer correctly half of the factual and bibliographic questions posed. Clearly, the library would have to live with the conse-

---

* Hage and Finsterbusch, *Organizational Change as a Development Strategy*. Copyright © 1987 by Lynne Rienner Publishing Co., Boulder, CO. Reprinted with permission.

quences of the university administration knowing the rate of accuracy. This is not to say that libraries should avoid potentially political evaluation. Rather, the library should assess all possible consequences prior to supporting the conduct of evaluation research.

Change necessitates that decision makers receive the kind of information they can use. Many comprehensive evaluation reports are lengthy, are never read by anyone outside the evaluation team, and are not used in decision making. Many community analyses conducted by local libraries fit into this category. They are conducted presumably to assist the library in planning its services and programs. However, upon completion of the study, the report goes unused and is merely filed as evidence that the library had conducted such a study.

To be useful for decision making and change, evaluation research must provide relevant and timely information that has utility. This information might be supplied to decision makers when needed. In some instances, they might receive tentative findings while the study is in progress. Such findings, it should be emphasized, are incomplete. Still, decision makers might be forewarned of potentially surprising findings. Clearly, evaluators must understand and adapt to the cognitive styles of decision makers.

In addition, the results of an evaluation study should be plausible. Weiss and Bucuvalas (1980) found that evaluation research should be relevant and of high quality, conform to prior knowledge and expectations, and offer feasible recommendations that can lead to action. They referred to these attributes as a "truth test" and a "utility test" (Ibid., p. 302). The former test asks (Ibid., p. 311):

- Is the research trustworthy?
- Can I rely on it?
- Will it hold up under attack?

The latter test questions:

- Does the research provide direction?
- Does it yield guidance—either for immediate action or for considering alternative approaches to problems?

INTERNAL CHANGE IN THE ORGANIZATION

Evaluation studies assist library managers in making internal change (e.g., modifying the actions, services, and assumptions under which the library operates) or external change (e.g., attempting to modify the environment and the characteristics of the environment that impact on the provision of library services). For librarians to initiate successful change in the library, they must be politically knowledgeable about the management of the library, interact extensively with other staff members, and assume a leadership role.

When the evaluation study has been completed, library staff serving as change agents (those people who adapt the organization's structure to a changing environment, control the speed and direction of organizational change, and manage conflict [Stueart and Moran, 1987, p. 224]) must link the findings and recommendations to action—planning, change, and decision making. Obtaining staff acceptance of change and the unknown may necessitate use of the following five strategies, which are intended primarily for use within the organization: demonstration, re-education, power, persuasion, and facilitative (Zaltman and Duncan, 1977).

Demonstration

Demonstration is the process by which the target individual or group observes, first-hand, the actual innovation or change that is desired. This strategy assumes that people can better understand the nature of the change if they actually witness how change works or is accomplished. The assumption is that the change, in fact, can be demonstrated. For this strategy to be effective, the demonstration must be carefully planned in advance, the equipment (if any) must be examined to make certain that it works properly, and the demonstrator must be competent.

Re-education

Re-education is the unbiased presentation of facts, in a rational and logical manner, to justify change. Two assumptions underlying this strategy are that (1) the target individuals are rational and capable of discerning facts and adjusting their behavior based on these facts, and (2) adequate time is available for the target individuals to "learn" or perhaps "unlearn" previous beliefs.

Re-education as a change strategy is best used in conjunction with other strategies suggested in this section. It is especially feasible when there is little direct control over those who are to be changed. Re-education is essential when change requires target individuals to use new skills or competencies. Re-education is best used, all things being equal, when change does not have to be immediate. Furthermore, it is most effective when dealing with educated and knowledgeable individuals.

Power

Power is the use of coercion, direct threats, withholding of rewards, or other actions to obtain the compliance of individuals involved in the change process. For this strategy to be successful, however, there must be an obligatory relationship between the change agent and the target individuals. An assumption is that the change agent offers acceptable rewards and punishment as a result of the target individuals' action.

The use of power, as a strategy to encourage change, is likely to be dysfunctional at a later date. Although power strategies may be desirable when commitment from target individuals is low, these strategies are unlikely to increase commitment, even though behavior, in fact, is modified. Furthermore, the less desirable it is to have the change strategy modified, or to alter the outcomes desired by the change, the more likely that a strategy based on power is necessary. And, finally, power strategies may be useful when change must be immediate.

Persuasion

Change might be encouraged by presenting information to target individuals through bias and careful structuring of the message. Typically, the change agent attempts to create change by reasoning, urging, and inducement. Such strategies can be based on a rational or emotional appeal, or on unsupported arguments.

The greater the time constraints and the lower the ability to use power, the more necessary it may be to use persuasive strategies. Such strategies often are necessary when the change agent does not exercise direct control over the resources or values of others involved in the change. Finally, persuasive strategies tend to be more effective when change agents have already established an atmosphere of trust between themselves and the target individuals.

Facilitative

These change strategies make it easier to implement change among target individuals, to accommodate the accomplishment of objectives and value preferences, and to supply resources that reinforce intended change. Target individuals, however, must recognize that change is necessary, concur that change is desirable, and be willing to receive assistance and guidance.

The larger the magnitude of the intended change, the more important it is to utilize facilitative strategies. The purpose of a facilitative strategy is to make change easy and to compensate low motivation with appropriate resources. For example, target individuals may receive a personal microcomputer when staff use of microcomputers to increase productivity is the desired change.

Although the five, general strategies are presented in isolation, they are most likely to be used in combination. For example, to be successful, a change objective that advocates the physical renovation of the technical services department may require aspects of each strategy. In addition, there must be a common understanding of the problems posed by that change, agreement and participation in the change process, and establishment of a supportive administrative climate (Samuels, 1982). Furthermore, many of these strategies are also appropriate when attempting to affect change external to the library.

AFFECTING EXTERNAL CHANGE

Affecting change within the library usually requires careful planning, the utilization of specific resources, staff development, and a significant amount of time. Affecting change outside the organization (especially in the policy environment) requires even greater skills on the part of the change agent. The reasons for this increased difficulty include: (1) the change agent usually has minimal direct control or authority over external environmental factors, (2) a number of competing views or other individuals attempt to make changes related to that specific concern, and (3) greater quantities of resources are necessary.

Environmental change calls for change agents to have an extremely good understanding of the change situation, its impact on the environment, and the factors that tend to support versus discourage change to occur. For change agents to have such information requires empirical evidence to support their position and excellent knowledge about the relationships affecting and affected by the proposed change. Because environmental change typically results in large impacts, those responsible for such change will want detailed, reliable, and valid data supporting the proposed changes.

In short, librarians must be able to convince decision makers that a proposed change has merit. The ability to define a specific problem, obtain or collect data related to that problem, analyze the data, and produce results and conclusions based on that data is essential. Indeed, the research process and the ability to rely on accurate and timely data in support of a specific position are essential for the strategies of re-education, persuasion, and facilitating. Librarians attempting to change broader environmental factors must be able to conduct evaluation research, write succinct and clear summaries of that research, and disseminate those findings to appropriate individuals.

SKILLS FOR CHANGE AGENTS

This section offers some practical suggestions for librarians wanting to increase their skills as change agents. First, change agents should learn how to analyze the change situation. Figure 14-1 summarizes the factors related to the situation. Each of the items in the figure requires careful attention before library staff develop an overall and effective strategy for change. That strategy should overcome any resistance and obtain the necessary resources and time for implementation.

Second, change agents should have certain interpersonal skills and address planning considerations. Figure 14-2 summarizes some of these skills and characteristics. Recognition of these factors, and planning to guarantee that these characteristics are indeed met during a change process, will greatly assist librarians in better accomplishing the intended changes.

Figure 14-1.   Analyzing the Change Situation

A. Awareness of the change target
　　1. Identify specific people/situations to be changed
　　2. Describe desirable behaviors/results for change to be "successful"
B. What is the degree of commitment among target individuals for accepting this change?
C. What is the magnitude of the proposed change?
　　1. Possible effects on involved individuals
　　2. Possible effects on the organization
　　3. Possible effects on the environment
D. How much time is available to accomplish the change?
E. What are the motives and justification for the change?
　　1. Individual
　　2. Organizational
　　3. Environmental
F. Anticipated types of resistance to the change
　　1. Ignorance
　　2. Suspended judgment
　　3. Situational
　　4. Personal
　　5. Experimental
G. Resources available to the change agent
　　1. Personal
　　2. Money
　　3. Equipment
H. Amount of technology needed to accomplish change?
I. Capacity of the target individuals to accept and sustain change once it has been accomplished?
J. Relationship between change agent and target individual(s)
　　1. Formal: Superior-Peer-Subordinate-None
　　2. Information: Friendly-Acquaintance-None
　　3. Value Compatibility: High-Low

In short, personal skills in areas of learning how to analyze the change situation, and developing characteristics that facilitate change, are likely to increase the probability that the desired change, in fact, will occur (Zaltman and Duncan, 1977). Still, change agents must evaluate the change and its impact on library services and activities. The purpose is to ensure that the change has the intended affect and that future action is not necessary.

Change agents must possess some knowledge of research, statistics, politics, and decision making. Even if change agents do not conduct the evaluation

Figure 14-2.   Characteristics of an Effective Change Agent

1. The change agent should strive to create as broad a power base (legitimate, expertise, and friendship) as possible
2. The change agent should work through opinion leaders when initiating the change strategy
3. The change agent should have the self-confidence and positive self-image to accept setbacks with poise, and not project anger or frustration to the target individuals
4. The change agent should strive to maximize his or her credibility in the eyes of the target individuals in terms of motives, competence, and truthfulness
5. The change agent should take care that target individuals are accurately informed about the entire change process
6. The change agent should build capabilities within the new system so that a vacuum is not created when the change agent leaves the system
7. The change agent should strive to involve the target individuals as much as possible in the change process
8. The change agent should strive to be sensitive to the needs and perspectives of the target individuals when designing change strategies
9. The change agent must be knowledgeable and competent regarding
   a. Interpersonal skills
   b. The nature of the change itself
   c. Administrative skills
10. The change agent always seeks the simplest solution when designing a change strategy
11. To maximize cooperation between the change agent and the target individual(s), specific benefits for the individuals are clarified and explained.

themselves, they should be able to question the evaluator intelligently and to convey the knowledge gained to high-level administrators. A central question becomes "Where does one gain the necessary skills and competencies? Continuing education is one option.

CONTINUING EDUCATION

Enough cannot be said about the importance of staying abreast of current developments, increasing the level and quality of one's skills and competencies, and adopting an attitude of commitment to ongoing self-improvement. One might speculate that the current rate of obsolescence for graduates in library/information science is three to four years. By this it is meant that, within that time period, half of the knowledge gained for the master's degree has changed, been replaced, or become outdated. Thus, the burden for librarians to stay current is indeed a heavy one.

Furthermore, simply being a "good" cataloger or reference librarian is no longer adequate for a professional position. The successful librarian must be able to demonstrate skills in systems analysis, computer science, administration, interpersonal relations, research and evaluation, and a host of other areas. But perhaps most importantly, the successful librarian must know how to learn—that is, how to teach oneself and how to think critically. There are always skills and competencies that librarians can learn or improve upon.

Evaluation skills might be obtained through a trial-and-error process, reading and applying the literature, or participation in a continuing education program. Such a program might be developed by individual libraries, several libraries jointly, professional associations, publishing houses or special consulting companies, or library schools or other graduate schools. These programs might consist of a course, workshop, or seminar.

A number of library schools, such as the ones at Simmons College, Syracuse University, the University of California-Berkeley, and the University of Wisconsin-Madison, offer courses related to planning and evaluation. For example, one school offers a four-credit course on "Evaluation of Library/Information Services." The catalog description of the course is:

> Evaluation, a critical component of the planning process, assesses the effectiveness and efficiency of library services in the context of stated goals and objectives, In a seminar environment, students develop evaluation skills and apply these to practical problems confronting libraries and information centers.

Designed for students regardless of the specific type of library or information center interesting them, this course focuses on the planning process and the role of evaluation in advancing that process. Evaluation encourages libraries to improve their programs, services, and operations. Course objectives include:

- To introduce students to the relationship between planning and evaluation, and the components of evaluation research
- To develop evaluation techniques/skills in the student
- To develop and implement an actual plan for assessing library effectiveness or efficiency
- To foster an attitude that recognizes the importance of planning and evaluation for the development of programs/services.

Figure 14-3, which reprints the main topics addressed in such a course, underscores the importance of evaluation skills in the larger context of research methods and management.

Figure 14-3. Syllabus for an Evaluation Course

A. Introduction to the Course
B. The Planning Process
C. Systems Analysis, Resource Integration, and Allocation
D. Environment for Planning/Evaluation - Mission Statement, Philosophy/Assumptions, Goals and Objectives
E. Evaluation—Definition; Types of Studies (Research versus the Collection of Management Data); the Need, Importance, and Value to Library Management; the Relationship of Evaluation to the Planning Process and Environment; and the Role of Needs Assessment
F. Role of a Planning/Evaluation Document
G. Standards and Performance Measures
H. Evaluation Types, Planning Data, Effectiveness and Efficiency
I. Action Research—Determining the "Evaluability" of Services and Study Constraints, Steps in Doing Evaluation, Evaluation Designs, Sample Size, Reliability and Validity, Case Studies, Evaluation Methodologies
J. Microcomputers and Decision Support Systems
K. Data Collection and Analysis (Statistics and Microcomputer Statistical Analysis Software)
L. The Effective Presentation of Study Findings
M. Uses/Abuses of Planning/Evaluation, Utilization of Planning and Evaluation Results, Evaluating the Planners/Evaluators, and Future Prospects for Planning and Evaluation of Library/ Information Services
N. Conclusion (Change Agents)

Courses such as this encourage educational change and provide a bridge between library educators and practicing librarians, especially when students conduct an evaluation study for a library. It is important to maintain a continual dialogue between library educators and practicing librarians and to see that library education impacts on those who have already completed formal course work and degree programs.

Individual Commitment and Dedication

Continuing education programs, as well as planning and evaluation, assume that libraries are dedicated to the provision of high-quality services that meet the immediate and long-term needs of library clientele. Constraints hinder an individual's ability to accomplish specific objectives. But one's ability to rise above those constraints, to develop strategies that circumvent the problems and result in improved services and collections, is based primarily on an individual's commitment and dedication. Individuals who become librarians realize that the profession will never make them wealthy; the primary component of the profession is one of service.

Dedication to service goals implies a commitment to providing the best possible services, to keeping oneself current and knowledgeable about new developments, and to persevering when coping with the various constraints encountered. Frequently, enthusiasm and commitment contribute to obtaining the necessary resources.

BRIDGING THE GAP

The gap between library managers' need for management data to help them make informed decisions and improve the overall effectiveness of libraries, and the researcher-evaluators' ability to meet this need must be bridged. Currently, a number of library managers:

- Have limited understanding of the importance and usefulness of evaluation data as a means of assessing and improving library services
- Provide limited support and assistance to those individuals within a library who are interested in conducting formal evaluations of library services and activities
- Are satisfied with the status quo and do not evaluate alternative programs or services
- Frequently prefer "intuitive" or "seat-of-the-pants" decision making rather than taking the time to obtain evaluative data on a particular issue or decision problem.

However, in an age of growing accountability and a need to better justify library services and program, managers will have to rely increasingly on empirical evidence.

For their part, evaluators and researchers exacerbate the existing problem by:

- Ignoring basic steps in the evaluation process (as outlined and discussed in Chapter 2)
- Conducting sloppy and cursory evaluations that are obviously error-ridden; fail to collect reliable, valid, and useful data; or are otherwise based on inappropriate (or unidentified) assumptions
- Writing final reports that fail to offer specific recommendations and/or providing no suggestions for improving the situation
- Failing to take into consideration the political environment and other constraints that may affect the evaluation.

But evaluators are dependent on the managers to implement their findings—

thus, it is to their advantage to improve both the quality of their evaluations and to better demonstrate why such evaluations are essential to the overall health of the library. However, drawing "battle lines" between the two groups will not help in the process of assessing library services and being able to demonstrate accountability for such services.

Part of the problem also lies with a philosophical conflict on the part of evaluators. While they have been trained to take a distant and objective view of a particular problem, management requires them to "get involved" and offer specific suggestions and recommendations for how the problem can be addressed and resolved. Thus, an effective evaluator must be not only objective in the conducting of the evaluation, but also realistic and political in the suggestion of possible strategies to resolve the problem. However, such strategies cannot be seen as "self- serving" or the evaluator can lose credibility.

A number of strategies have been offered in this book for bridging this gap. Probably the most important is for those interested in conducting evaluations to be better skilled and more knowledgeable about the evaluation process. Second, evaluation teams that include managers, evaluators, and other library staff interested in a particular problem or issue should learn to work together in a team context. Third, all library staff have to avoid the "reactive" mentality of responding to daily crises and problems and set aside time for careful consideration of what areas of the library require assessment and how best to conduct that assessment.

Library staff who become interested in evaluation must set themselves up to succeed. In other words, they should target areas for evaluation where there are straightforward problems. They should attack those areas for which there is wide agreement that evaluation is needed, and they should use evaluation methodologies that are not complicated. Perhaps most importantly, they should make certain that library management supports the evaluation, that the findings are presented in an understandable format, and that the problem is "actionable" before they start on the evaluation. In short, the evaluators should select their evaluation targets carefully.

A recent study on the status of research in library and information science concludes that there is "guarded optimism" about the development of a research base in the field (McClure and Bishop, 1989). However, the development of a research base is increasingly being used in library and information science as a means for making decisions, conducting in-house evaluations of library services and activities, or otherwise encouraging the decision-making process to be based more on empirical evidence than intuition.

The thrust of this book has been to encourage evaluation of library and information services largely in terms of:

• Producing relevant management data that can actually be used for improved library decision making

- Affecting the day-to-day process or activities by which decision making occurs in a specific library
- Changing attitudes toward basing decisions on empricial evidence rather than making "informed guesses" as to which particular strategy might have the best result.

Indeed, the thrust of this book is that a regular, ongoing process of evaluation of library services is a critical component for operating effective libraries. But that regular, ongoing process succeeds best when there is a partnership relationship between evaluators and library managers. Evaluators should nurture such partnerships.

THE FUTURE

What broad trends can be expected in the future? Some years ago, Naisbitt (1982) suggested that the following "mega-trends" will change everyone's life and business:

- Restructuring of America from an industrial society to one based on information and knowledge
- Unprecedented diversity among people, groups, and institutions; an incredibly market-segmented, decentralized society
- Return to old-fashioned self-reliance
- Greater direct involvement of employees in organizational decision making
- Home computers will be a liberator; they can provide quick access to information previously available only to other companies and individuals
- Increased demand for personal contacts and expanding human interrelationships, as people are exposed to more high technology
- Decentralization of all our institutions—business, governmental, social, and political—largely due to the proliferation of home computers and information systems.

Since his forecast, some of these trends appear to have materialized.

More recently, Wurman in his book *Information Anxiety* (1989, p. 334) states that information anxiety is

produced by the ever-widening gap between what we understand and what we think we should understand. It is the black hole between data and knowledge, and it happens when information doesn't tell us what we want or need to know.

He argues that information professionals in the future must do a better job of translating, synthesizing, and "making sense" out of the mountains of information available. Indeed, for librarians, his message is clear: providing information will not be enough in the future—a broad range of value-added services and products will be necessary if libraries are to compete effectively in the information age.

Librarians and other information access professionals should think of these or other posssible trends that may increase the gulf between the information haves and have nots. If forecasts from the various futurists are even partially correct about these trends, significant and prompt changes in library collections, services, and philosophies are needed.

THE NEED FOR RESEARCH/EVALUATION

Without research to identify, compare, and select change alternatives, to evaluate the success of a decision, or to determine the impact of the decision on the environment, the decision making process is sabotaged and ineffective decisions are likely (Janis and Mann, 1977). Indeed, a typical (and usually ineffective) approach to decision making in some library settings is simply to define the situation in which a decision is necessary, and then implement the decision. This "two-step" process of decision making helps to explain why some libraries cannot flourish in today's (let alone tomorrow's) information environment, and thus are beginning to atrophy or die.

In conclusion, the complexity of operating effective and efficient libraries requires greater knowledge about the evaluation process and how that process impacts library decision making and planning. Having this knowledge can only increase in importance as greater opportunities and challenges, and decreased flexibility for library funding, become apparent. In order for libraries to maintain or increase their share of information-related markets, librarians will have to be both producers and consumers of evaluation information. More than likely, that type of research will result from an evaluation study that collects information useful for local decision making.

Evaluation research is crucial for improved decision making and services. However, that research should not ignore either the theory base of library and information science or research that has applied that theory to practice. The logical structure component of the reflective inquiry (see Chapter 4) identifies relevant theory and cautions against the violation of theory. Nonetheless, librarians can approach data collection from two points of view: a research perspective and a management perspective. Regardless of which approach is taken, the question becomes, "How much error am I willing to accept and what are the consequences of making such error?"

The essence of planning, action research, and evaluation "is constantly to question, study and improve the effectiveness of library information services and operations" (Swisher and McClure, 1984, p. 193). Evaluation embraces change and encourages libraries to treat change as a positive force. By engaging in planning and research, librarians have a better idea of the future and they can meet that future with relevant, effective, and efficient services and activities. Furthermore, they can meet new challenges and innovations, and libraries will continue to play an important and positive role in the information society.

DISCUSSION ITEMS

1. Provide an example for each change strategy: demonstration, re-education, power, persuasion, and facilitative.
2. Identify some environmental factors that could inhibit the change process.
3. Identify some structural factors that could inhibit the change process.
4. Assess the "truth test" and "utility test" from the perspective of management and research data.
5. What skills do you believe are most essential for a change agent to possess?
6. How could a person aspiring to be a change agent obtain each of the skills identified in answering the previous question?
7. Assess the continuing education opportunities for a librarian seeking to develop research skills.
8. Identify and analyze a change situation (see Figure 14-1).
9. Why do some library managers support the conduct of action research and evaluation studies, and others do not?
10. Does change, in fact, improve library effectiveness? Discuss.

BIBLIOGRAPHY

An Action Plan for a Federal-State Cooperative System for Public Library Data. Washington, D.C.: National Commission on Libraries and Information Science, 1989.

Allen, Gillian. "Patron Response to Bibliographic Databases on CD-ROM," *RQ*, 28 (Fall 1989): 103–109.

Alzonton, Sammy R. and Noella Van Pulis. "Patterns of Searching and Success Rates in an Online Public Access Catalog," *College & Research Libraries*, 44 (March 1984): 110–115.

Anderson, Scarvia and Samuel Ball. *The Profession and Practice of Program Evaluation.* San Francisco, CA: Jossey-Bass, 1978.

Anthony, William P. *Practical Strategic Planning.* Westport, CT: Quorum Books, 1985.

Ary, Donald, L.C. Jacobs, and A. Razavieh. *Introduction to Research in Education.* 3rd edition. New York: Holt, Rinehart and Winston, 1985.

Baker, Sharon L. "Managing Resistance to Change," *Library Trends*, 38 (1989): 53–61.

Ballard, Thomas H. "Planning and Output Measures," *Public Libraries*, 28 (September/October 1989): 292–295.

Baughman, James C. "Toward a Structural Approach to Collection Development," *College & Research Libraries*, 38 (May 1977): 241–248.

Benham, Frances and Ronald R. Powell. *Success in Answering Reference Questions: Two Studies.* Metuchen, NJ: Scarecrow, 1987.

Blalock, Hubert M., Jr. *Conceptualization and Measurement in the Social Sciences.* Beverly Hills, CA: Sage, 1982.

———. *Social Statistics.* New York: McGraw-Hill, 1972.

Boland, Richard J. "Tutorial on Management Systems," in *Library Automation as a Source of Management Information*, edited by F. W. Lancaster. Champaign, IL: University of Illinois, Graduate School of Library and Information Science, 1983, pp. 10–26.

Bommer, Michael R. W. and Ronald W. Chorba. *Decision Making for Library Management.* White Plains, NY: Knowledge Industry Publications, Inc., 1982.

Borg, Walter R. and Meredith D. Gall. *Educational Research.* New York: Longman, 1983.

Borgman, Christine L. *End User Behavior on the Ohio State University Libraries' Online Catalog: A Computer Monitoring Study.* Dublin, OH: OCLC, 1983.

Boucher, Virginia P. *Interlibrary Loan Practices Handbook.* Chicago, IL: American Library Association, 1984.

Bourne, C. P. "Some User Requirements Stated Quantitatively in Terms of the 90% Library," in *Electronic Information Handling*, edited by Allen Kent and Orrin E. Taulbee. Washington, D.C.: Spartan Books, 1965, pp. 93–110.

Boynton, Andrew C. and Robert W. Zmud. "An Assessment of Critical Success Factors," *Sloan Management Review*, 25 (Summer 1984): 17–27.

Bradley, Jana and Larry Bradley. *Improving Written Communication in Libraries*. Chicago, IL: American Library Association, 1988.

Buckland, Michael K. *Library Services in Theory and Context*. New York: Pergamon Press, 1983.

Bundy, Mary Lee and Amy Bridgman, "A Community Based Approach to Evaluation of Public Library Reference Service," *The Reference Librarian*, 11 (Fall/Winter 1984): 159–174.

Bunge, Charles. *Professional Education and Reference Efficiency*. Springfield, IL: Illinois State Library, 1967.

Burckel, Nicholas C. "Participatory Management in Academic Libraries: A Review," *College & Research Libraries*, 45 (January 1984): 25–34.

Busha, Charles H. and Stephen P. Harter. *Research Methods in Librarianship*. New York: Academic Press, 1980.

Bybee, C. R. "Fitting Information Presentation Formats to Decision Making: A Study in Strategies to Facilitate Decision Making," *Communication Research*, 8 (1981): 343–370.

Campbell, Donald T. and Julian C. Stanley. *Experimental and Quasi-Experimental Designs for Research*. Skokie, IL: Rand McNally, 1966.

―――― and Julian C. Stanley. "Experimental and Quasi-Experimental Designs for Research on Teaching," in *Handbook of Research on Teaching*, edited by N.L. Gage. Washington, D.C.: American Educational Research Association, 1963.

CD-ROM in Print, 1988–1989. Westport, CT: Meckler, 1988.

Char, Lin Kim. "The Problem of the Non-user," *Singapore Libraries*, 17 (1987): 25–31.

Chen, Ching-chih and Peter Hernon. *Information Seeking*. New York: Neal-Schuman, 1982.

Childers, Thomas and Nancy A. Van House. "Dimensions of Public Library Effectiveness," *Library & Information Science Research*, 11 (1989a): 273–301.

―――― and Nancy A. Van House. "The Grail of Goodness: The Effective Public Library," *Library Journal*, 114 (October 1, 1989b): 44–49.

Christensen, John O., Larry D. Benson, H. Julene Butler, Blaine H. Hall, and Don H. Howard. "An Evaluation of Reference Desk Service," *College & Research Libraries*, 50 (July 1989): 468–483.

Clark, Philip M. "Developing a Decision Support System: The Software and Hardware Tools," *Library Administration & Management*, 3 (Fall 1989): 184–191.

――――. "Sample Size Determination: A Comparison of Attribute, Continuous Variable and Cell Size Methods," *Library & Information Science Research*, 6 (October-December 1984): 407–424.

Conroy, Barbara. *Library Staff Development and Continuing Education: Principles and Practices*. Littleton, CO: Libraries Unlimited, 1978.

Cooper, Michael D. "Usage Patterns of an Online Search System," *Journal of the American Society for Information Science*, 34 (1983): 343–349.

Cooper, Randolph B. "Review of Management Information Systems Research: A Management Support Emphasis," *Information Processing & Management*, 24 (1988): 73–102.

Cronback, L.J. "Test Validation," in *Educational Measurement*, edited by R.L. Thorndike. Washington, D.C.: American Council on Education, 1971, pp. 443–507.

Cronin, Mary J. *Performance Measurement for Public Services in Academic and Re-*

search Libraries. Occasional Paper 9. Washington, D.C.: Association of Research Libraries, Office of Management Studies, 1985.

Cummings, Martin M. "Cost Analysis: Methods and Realities," *Library Administration & Management*, 3 (Fall 1989): 181–183.

Curran, Charles and Philip M. Clark. "Implications of Tying State Aid to Performance Measures," *Public Libraries*, 28 (November/December 1989): 348–354.

D'Elia, George. "Materials Availability Fill Rates—Useful Measures of Library Performance," *Public Libraries*, 24 (Fall 1985): 106–110.

————. "A Response to Van House," *Public Libraries*, 27 (Spring 1988): 28–31.

DeProspo, Ernest R. "Potential Limits and Abuses of Evaluation," *School Media Quarterly*, 3 (Summer 1975): 302–306.

Dillon, Martin, Dave Stephens, Kevin Flash, and Mark Crook. "Design Issues for a Microcomputer-Based Collection Analysis System," *Microcomputers for Information Management*, 5 (1988): 263–273.

Drott, M. Carl. "Random Sampling: A Tool for Library Research," *College & Research Libraries*, 30 (March 1969): 119–125.

———— and B. C. Griffith. "Interlibrary Loan Analysis in Collection Development," *Library Resources & Technical Services*, 20 (Winter 1976): 98–100.

DuMont, Rosemary Ruhig and Paul F. DuMont. "Measuring Library Effectiveness: A Review and an Assessment," in *Advances in Librarianship*, vol. 9, edited by Wesley Simonton. New York: Academic Press, 1979, pp. 103–140.

Fitzgibbons, Shirley A. "The Concept of Service Orientation: An Exploratory Study in the Concept in Relationship to the Library and Information Services Field." Ph.D. dissertation, Rutgers University, 1976.

Frost, Carolyn O. "The Literature of Online Public Access Catalogs, 1980–85: An Analysis of Citation Patterns," *Library Resources & Technical Services*, 33 (October 1989): 344–357.

Getz, Malcolm and Doug Phelps. "Labor Costs in the Technical Operation of Three Research Libraries," *Journal of Academic Librarianship*, 10 (1984): 209–219.

General Accounting Office. Program Evaluation and Methodology Division. *Designing Evaluations*. Transfer Paper 4. Washington, D.C.: U.S. Government Printing Office, 1984.

————. *Using Statistical Sampling*. Transfer Paper 6. Washington, D.C.: U.S. Government Printing Office, April 1986.

Gherman, Paul M. and Lynn S. Cochrane. "Developing and Using Unit Costs: The Virginia Tech Experience," *Library Administration & Management*, 3 (Spring 1989): 93–96.

Goldhor, Herbert. "Book Review: Output Measures for Public Libraries," *Library Quarterly*, 53 (April 1983): 180–181.

Gouke, Mary N. and Sue Pease. "Title Searches in an Online Catalog and a Card Catalog," *Journal of Academic Librarianship*, 8 (July 1982): 137–143.

Graziano, E. E. "Interlibrary Loan Analysis: Diagnostic for Scientific Serials Backfile Acquisitions," *Special Libraries*, 53 (May-June 1962): 251–257.

Guba, Egon G. and Yvonna S. Lincoln. *Effective Evaluation*. San Francisco, CA: Jossey-Bass, 1981.

"Guidelines for Speakers." Washington, D.C.: American Association for the Advancement of Science, AAAS Meeting Office, n.d.

Hage, Jerald and Kurt Finsterbusch. *Organizational Change As a Development Strategy.* Boulder, CO: Lynne Rienner Publishers, 1987.

Halperin, Michael. "Waiting Lines," *RQ*, 16 (Summer 1977): 297–299.

Hardesty, Larry and John Wright. "Student Library Skills and Attitudes and Their Change: Relationships to Other Selected Variables," *Journal of Academic Librarianship*, 8 (September 1982): 216–220.

Hawks, Carol Pitts. "Management Information Gleaned from Automated Library Systems," *Information Technology & Libraries*, 7 (June 1988): 131–138.

Heim, K. M. "Organizational Considerations Relating to the Implementation and Use of Management Information Systems," in *Library Automation as a Source of Management Information*, edited by F. W. Lancaster. Champaign, IL: University of Illinois, Graduate School of Library and Information Science, 1983, pp. 59–71.

Heindel, Alan J. and H. Albert Napier. "Decision Support Systems in Libraries," *Special Libraries* 72 (1981): 319–327.

Hernon, Peter. "Information Needs and Gathering Patterns of Academic Social Scientists, with Special Emphasis Given to Historians and Their Use of U.S. Government Publications," *Government Information Quarterly*, 1 (1984): 401–429.

_____. *Use of Government Publications by Social Scientists.* Norwood, NJ: Ablex Pub. Corp., 1979.

_____, Pat K. Bryant, Maya De, Barbara D. Farah, Andrew J. Golub, Hae-young Reih Hwang, and Li-ling Kuo. *Statistics for Library Decision Making.* Norwood, NJ: Ablex Pub. Corp., 1989.

_____ and Charles R. McClure. "Quality of Data Issues in Unobtrusive Testing of Library Reference Service: Recommendations and Strategies," *Library & Information Science Research*, 9 (April-June 1987a): 77–93.

_____ and Charles R. McClure. *Unobtrusive Testing and Library Reference Service.* Norwood, NJ: Ablex Pub. Corp., 1987b.

_____, Charles R. McClure, and Gary R. Purcell. *GPO's Depository Library Program: A Descriptive Analysis.* Norwood, NJ: Ablex Pub. Corp., 1985.

_____ and Maureen Pastine. "Student Perceptions of Academic Librarians," *College & Research Libraries*, 38 (March 1977): 129–139.

_____ and John V. Richardson. *Microcomputer Software for Performing Statistical Analysis: A Handbook Supporting Library Decision Making.* Norwood, NJ: Ablex Publishing Corp., 1988.

Hirschheim, R. A. "User Experience with and Assessment of Participative Systems Design," *MIS Quarterly*, 9 (1985): 295–303.

Holsti, Ole R. *Content Analysis for the Social Sciences and Humanities.* Reading, MA: Addison-Wesley Pub. Co., 1969.

Homer, Garth. "Management Information Systems Can Help Senior Library Managers," *Canadian Library Journal*, 43 (1986): 141–145.

Huck, Schuyler W., William H. Cormier, and William G. Bounds, Jr. *Reading Statistics and Research.* New York: Harper and Row, 1974.

Intner, Sheila S. "Responsibilities of Technical Service Librarians to the Process of Collection Evaluation," *Library Trends*, 33 (Winter 1985): 417–436.

Ives, Blake and Olson, Margrethe H. "User Involvement and MIS Success: A Review of Research," *Management Science* 30 (1984): 586–603.

James E. Rush Associates. *Library Systems Evaluation Guide*. 8 vols. Powell, OH: James E. Rush Associates, 1983–1984.

Janis, Irving L. and L. Mann. *Decision Making*. New York: The Free Press, 1977.

Jick, Todd D. "Mixing Qualitative and Quantitative Methods: Triangulation in Action," in *Qualitative Methodology*, edited by John Van Maanen. Beverly Hills, CA: Sage, 1983, pp. 135–147.

Johnson, Edward R. "A Realistic Objectives Management Program," in *Austerity Management in Academic Libraries*, edited by John F. Harvey and Peter Spyers-Duran. Metuchen, NJ: Scarecrow Press, 1984, pp. 161–175.

———— and Stuart H. Mann. *Organizational Development for Academic Libraries*. Westport, CT: Greenwood Press, 1980.

Jorgensen, Danny L. *Participant Observation*. Newbury Park, CA: Sage, 1989.

Kantor, Paul B. "Analyzing the Avaliability of Reference Services," in *Library Effectiveness: A State of the Art*. Chicago, IL: American Library Association, 1980, pp. 131–149.

————. "Quantitative Evaluation of the Reference Process," *RQ*, 21 (Fall 1981): 43–52.

————. *Objective Performance Measures for Academic and Research Libraries*. Washington, D.C.: Association of Research Libraries, 1984.

Kaplan, Abraham. *The Conduct of Inquiry*. Scranton, PA: Chandler Publishing, 1964.

Kaser, David. "Library School Libraries," *Journal of Education for Librarianship*, 5 (Summer 1964): 17–19.

Kast, Fremont E. and James E. Rosenzweig. *Organization and Management: A Systems and Contingency Approach*. New York: McGraw-Hill, 1985.

Katzer, Jeffrey. "ALA and the Status of Research in Library/Information Science," *Library & Information Science Research*, 11 (April-June 1989): 83–87.

————, Kenneth H. Cook, and Wayne W. Crouch. *Evaluating Information: A Guide for Users of Social Science Research*. 2nd edition. Reading, MA: Addison-Wesley, 1982, 1990.

Kenney, L. "The Implications of the Needs of Users for the Design of a Catalogue: A Survey at the International Labor Office," *Journal of Documentation*, 22 (1966): 195–202.

Kerlinger, Fred N. *Foundations of Behavioral Research*. New York: Holt, Rinehart and Winston, 1973, 1986.

Kiewitt, Eva L. "Reference Collections of Accredited Library School Programs," *Journal of Education for Librarianship*, 19 (Summer 1978): 55–59.

Kirk, Roger E. *Experimental Design*. Belmont, CA: Brooks/Cole Pub. Co., 1968.

Krathwohl, David R. *Social and Behavioral Science Research*. San Francisco, CA: Jossey-Bass, 1985.

Krueger, Richard A. *Focus Groups*. Newbury Park, CA: Sage, 1988.

Lake, Matt and William Rodarmor. "38 Tools for Great Writing," *PC World*, 7 (July 1989): 178–183.

Lancaster, F.W. *If You Want to Evaluate Your Library* . . . . Champaign, IL: University of Illinois, Graduate School of Library and Information Science, 1988.

————. *The Measurement and Evaluation of Library Services*. Washington, D.C.: Information Resources Press, 1977.

Lantz, Brian. "Evaluation of Technical Services Functions: Towards a Management Information System," *Journal of Librarianship*, 18 (1986): 257–279.

LeCompte, M.D. and J.P. Goetz. "Problems of Reliability and Validity in Ethnographic Research," *Review of Educational Research*, 52 (1982): 31–60.

Lee, Alec. *Applied Queuing Theory*. New York: St. Martin's Press, 1966.

Lee, Clarence. "An Application and Analysis of Six Output Measures Correlated with User Satisfaction in the Branch Libraries of the Carnegie Library of Pittsburgh System." Ph.D. dissertation, University of Pittsburgh, 1987.

Library Data Collection Handbook. Chicago, IL: American Library Association, 1981.

Lin, Nan. *Foundations of Social Research*. New York: McGraw-Hill, 1976.

Lincoln, Yvonna S. and Egon G. Guba. *Naturalistic Inquiry*. Beverly Hills, CA: Sage, 1985.

_____ and Egon G. Guba. "Research, Evaluation, and Policy Analysis: Heuristics for Disciplined Inquiry," *Policy Studies Review*, 5 (February 1986): 546–565.

Line, Maurice B. "Student Attitudes to the University Library: A Survey at Southampton University," *Journal of Documentation*, 19 (September 1963): 100–117.

Lynch Beverly P. "The Future Library Market for Scholarly Books," *Scholarly Publishing*, 19 (January 1988): 86–90.

Lynch, Mary Jo. "Information Technology, Library Management, and OCLC," *Information Technology* 4 (1985): 122–129.

_____. "Measurement of Public Library Activity: The Search for Practical Methods," *Wilson Library Bulletin*, 57 (January 1983): 388–393.

Mark, Melvin M. and Thomas D. Cook. "Design of Randomized Experiments and Quasi-Experiments," in *Evaluation Research Methods: A Basic Guide*, edited by Leonard Rutman. Beverly Hills, CA: Sage Publications, 1984, pp. 65–120.

Marshall, Catherine and Gretchen B. Rossman. *Designing Qualitative Research*. Newbury Park, CA: Sage, 1989.

McCart, Anne. "The Application of Social Judgment Analysis to Library Faculty Tenure Decisions," *College and Research Libraries*, 44 (September 1983): 345–357.

McClure, Charles R. *Information for Academic Library Decision Making: The Case for Organizational Information Management*. Westport, CT: Greenwood Press, 1980.

_____. "Management Information for Library Decision Making," in *Advances in Librarianship*, vol. 13, edited by Wesley Simonton. New York: Academic Press, 1984a, pp. 1–47.

_____. "Measurement, Planning and Decision Support Systems," in *Library Performance, Accountability and Responsiveness: Essays in Honor of Ernest R. DeProspo*, edited by Charles C. Curran. Norwood, NJ: Ablex Pub. Corp. 1990, pp. 17–32.

_____. "Output Measures, Unobtrusive Testing, and Assessing the Quality of Reference Services," *The Reference Librarian*, 11 (Fall/Winter 1984b): 215–233.

_____. "The Planning Process: Strategies for Action," *College & Research Libraries*, 39 (November 1978): 456–466.

_____. "Preparing the Library Organization for Microcomputer-Based Decision Making," in *Microcomputers for Library Decision Making*, edited by Peter Hernon and Charles R. McClure. Norwood, NJ: Ablex Pub. Corp., 1986a, pp. 39–60.

_____. "A View from the Trenches: Costing and Performance Measures for Academic Library Public Services," *College & Research Libraries*, 47 (July 1986b): 323–336.

_____ and Ann Bishop. "The Status of Research in Library/Information Science:

Guarded Optimism," *College & Research Libraries*, 50 (March 1989): 127–143.

———— and Betsy Reifsnyder. "Performance Measures for Corporate Information Centers," *Special Libraries*, 75 (July 1984): 193–204.

———— and Peter Hernon. *Improving the Quality of Reference Service for Government Publications*. Chicago, IL: American Library Association, 1983.

————, Peter Hernon, and Gary R. Purcell. *Linking the U.S. National Technical Information Service with Academic and Public Libraries*. Norwood, NJ: Ablex Publishing Corp., 1986.

————, Douglas L. Zweizig, Nancy A. Van House, and Mary Jo Lynch. "Output Measures: Myths, Realities and Prospects," *Public Libraries*, 25 (Summer 1986): 49–52.

————, Amy Owen, Douglas L. Zweizig, Mary Jo Lynch, and Nancy A. Van House. *A Planning and Role Setting for Public Libraries: A Manual of Options and Procedures*. Chicago, IL: American Library Association, 1987.

————, Liz Hagerty-Roach, Lindsay Ruth, and Pat England. "Design of a Public Library Management Information System: A Status Report," *Library Administration & Management*, 3 (1989a): 192–198.

————. *Design of a Management Information System for DeKalb County Public Library: Final Report for Phase I*. Manlius, NY: Information Management Consultant Services, Inc., 1989b.

Metz, Paul. *The Landscape of Literatures*. Chicago, IL: American Library Association, 1983.

Mitchell, Barbara Jo, Norman E. Tanis, and Jack Jaffee. *Cost Analysis of Library Functions*. Greenwich, CT: JAI Press, 1978.

Morgan, David L. *Focus Groups*. Newbury Park, CA: Sage, 1988.

Morris, Lynn Lyons, Carol Taylor Fitz-Gibbon, and Marie E. Freeman. *How to Communicate Evaluation Findings*. Beverly Hills, CA: Sage, 1987.

Munro, M.C. "Determining the Manager's Information Needs," *Journal of Systems Management*, 29 (1978): 34–39.

Murfin, Marjorie E. and Gary M. Gugelchuk. "Development and Testing of a Reference Transaction Assessment Instrument," *College & Research Libraries*, 48 (July 1987): 314–338.

Muscatello, Daniel B. "Evaluation and the Management Process," *Evaluation Practice*, 10 (August 1989): 12–17.

Myers, Marcia J. and Jassim M. Jirjees. *The Accuracy of Telephone Reference Information Services in Academic Libraries*. Metuchen, NJ: Scarecrow, 1983.

Naisbitt, John. *Megatrends: Ten New Directions Transforming Our Lives*. New York: Warner Books, 1982.

National and Model Interlibrary Loan Codes. Chicago, IL: American Library Association, 1980.

Naumann, Justus D. and A. Milton Jenkins. "Prototyping: The New Paradigm for Systems Development," *MIS Quarterly*, 6 (September 1982): 29–44.

New, Doris E. and Retha Z. Ott. "Interlibrary Loan Analysis as a Collection Development Tool," *Library Resources & Technical Services*, 18 (Summer 1974): 275–283.

Olsgaard, John N. "Characteristics of Managerial Resistance to Library Management Information Systems," in *Library Automation as a Source of Management Information*, edited by F. W. Lancaster. Champaign, IL: University of Illinois, Graduate School of Library and Information Science, 1983, pp. 92–110.

Olson, Linda M. "Reference Service Evaluation in Medium-Sized Academic Libraries: A Model," *Journal of Academic Librarianship*, 9 (January 1984): 322–329.

Orr, R. H. "Measuring the Goodness of Library Services: A General Framework for Considering Quantitative Measures," *Journal of Documentation*, 29 (September 1973): 315–332.

Paisley, William J. *Behavioral Studies on Scientific Information Flow: An Appendix on Method*. New London, NH: Gordon Research Conference on Scientific Method, 1969 (mimeographed material).

Palumbo, Dennis J. "Politics and Evaluation," in *The Politics of Program Evaluation*, edited by Dennis J. Palumbo. Newbury Park, CA: Sage, 1987, pp. 12–46.

Patton, Michael Quinn. "Evaluation's Political Inherency: Practical Implications for Design and Use," in *The Politics of Program Evaluation*, edited by Dennis J. Palumbo. Newbury Park, CA: Sage, 1987, pp. 100–145.

Perkins, D., ed. *Guidelines for Collection Development*. Chicago, IL: American Library Association, 1979.

Pings, Vern M. "Use or Value of Goals and Objectives Statements," *Journal of Library Administration*, 1 (Fall 1980): 55–62.

Pizer, I.H. and A.M. Cain. "Objective Tests of Library Performance," *Special Libraries*, 59 (1968): 704–711.

PLDS Statistical Report '88. Chicago, IL: American Library Association, 1988.

Powell, Ronald R. *Basic Research Methods for Librarians*. Norwood, NJ: Ablex Pub. Corp., 1985, 1990.

——. "Reference Effectiveness: A Review of Research," *Library & Information Science Research*, 6 (January-March 1984): 3–19.

——. *The Relationship of Library User Studies to Performance Measures: A Review of the Literature*. Occasional Paper 181. Champaign, IL: University of Illinois, Graduate School of Library and Information Science, 1988.

Pritchard, S. J. "Purchase and Use of Monographs Originally Requested on Interlibrary Loan in a Medical School Library," *Library Acquisitions: Practice and Theory*, 4 (1980): 135–139.

Quigley, H. "An Investigation of the Possible Relationship of Interbranch Loan to Cataloging," *Library Quarterly*, 14 (1944): 333–338.

Reeves, Edward B., Benita J. Howell, and John Van Willigen. "Before the Looking-Glass: A Method to Obtain Self-Evaluation of Roles in a Library Reference Service," *RQ*, 17 (Fall 1987): 25–32.

Rethinking the Library in the Information Age. 3 vols. Washington, D.C.: U.S. Department of Education, 1988.

Robbins, Jane and Douglas Zweizig. *Are We There Yet? Evaluating Library Collections, Reference Services, Programs, and Personnel*. Madison, WI: University of Wisconsin, School of Library and Information Studies, 1988.

Roberts, Michael and K. J. Cameron. "Barometer of Unmet Demand: Interlibrary Loan Analysis and Monographic Acquisitions," *Library Acquisitions: Practice and Theory*, 8 (1984): 31–42.

Rockart, John F. "Chief Executives Define Their Own Data Needs," *Harvard Business Review*, 57 (1979): 81–93.

Rossi, Peter H. and Howard E. Freeman. *Evaluation: A Systematic Approach*. Beverly Hills, CA: Sage Publications, 1982 and 1985; Newbury Park, CA: Sage, 1989.

————, Howard E. Freeman, and Sonia R. Wright. *Evaluation: A Systematic Approach.* Beverly Hills, CA: Sage Publications, 1979.

Runyon, Robert S. "Towards the Development of a Library Management Information System," *College & Research Libraries*, 42 (1981): 539–548.

Rutman, Leonard. *Evaluability Assessment.* Beverly Hills, CA: Sage, 1980.

Samuels, Alan R. "Organizational Climate and Library Change," in *Strategies for Library Administration*, edited by Charles R. McClure and Alan R. Samuels. Littleton, CO: Libraries Unlimited, 1982, pp. 421–431.

Schauer, Bruce P. *The Economics of Managing Library Service.* Chicago, IL: American Library Association, 1986.

Shank, Russell. "Management, Information and the Organization: Homily Form the Experience of the Data Rich But Information Poor," in *Library Automation as a Source of Management Information*, edited by F. W. Lancaster. Champaign, IL: University of Illinois, Graduate School of Library and Information Science, 1983, pp. 2–9.

Slonim, Morris J. *Sampling in a Nutshell.* New York: Simon and Schuster, 1960.

Spector, Paul E. *Research Designs.* Beverly Hills, CA: Sage Publications, 1981.

Stone, S. *Inter-library Loans: A Study of Antecedents and Outcomes of Inter-library Loan Requests.* Sheffield, England: University of Sheffield, Centre for Research on User Studies, 1983.

Stueart, Robert D. and Barbara B. Moran. *Library Management.* 3rd edition. Littleton, CO: Libraries Unlimited, 1987.

Suchman, Edward A. "Action for What? A Critique of Evaluation Research," in *Evalauting Action Programs*, edited by Carol H. Weiss. Boston, MA: Allyn and Bacon, 1972, pp. 52–84.

Swisher, Robert and Charles R. McClure. *Research for Decision Making: Methods for Librarians.* Chicago, IL: American Library Association, 1984.

Thomas, H. A. and C. A. Waghorn. *Management Information Systems for Public Libraries.* London, England: British Library Research and Development Department, 1986.

Tjoumas, Renee and Esther E. Horne. "Collection Evaluation: Practices and Methods in Libraries of ALA Accredited Graduate Library Education Programs," *Advances in Library Administration and Organization*, 5 (1986): 109–138.

Toifel, Ronald C. and Wesley D. Davis. "Investigating Library Study Skills of Children in the Public Schools," *Journal of Academic Librarianship*, 9 (September 1983): 211–215.

Tolle, John E. *Current Utilization of Online Catalogs: Transaction Log Analysis.* Dublin, OH: OCLC, 1983.

Tuckman, Bruce W. *Conducting Educational Research*, 2nd edition. New York: Harcourt Brace Jovanovich, 1978.

Urquhart, J.A. and J.L. Schofield. "Measuring Readers' Failure at the Shelf in Three University Libraries," *Journal of Documentation*, 28 (1972): 233–241.

Van House, Nancy A. "In Defense of Fill Rates," *Public Libraries*, 27 (Spring 1988): 25–27

————. "Output Measures: Some Lessons from Baltimore County Public Library," *Public Libraries*, 24 (Fall 1985): 102–105.

————. "Public Library Effectiveness: Theory, Measures, and Determinants," *Library & Information Science Research*, 8 (1986): 261–283.

_____, Beth Weil, and Charles R. McClure. *Measuring Academic Library Performance: A Practical Approach*. Prepared for the Association of College and Research Libraries, Committee on Performance Measures, Ad Hoc. Chicago, IL: American Library Association, 1990.

_____, Mary Jo Lynch, Charles R. McClure, Douglas L. Zweizig, and Eleanor Jo Rodger. *Output Measures for Public Libraries: A Manual of Standardized Procedures*. Chicago, IL: American Library Association, 1987.

Van Maanen, John. "The Process of Program Evaluation," *The Grantsmanship Center News*, 27 (January/February 1979): 29–74.

Waldhart, Thomas J. "The Growth of Interlibrary Loan among ARL University Libraries," *Journal of Academic Librarianship*, 10 (1984): 204–208.

Watstein, Sarah B. "Book Mutilation: An Unwelcome By-product of Electronic Security Systems," *Library and Archival Security*, 5 (1983): 11–26.

Weber, Robert P. *Basic Content Analysis*. Beverly Hills, CA: Sage, 1985.

Weech, Terry L. and Herbert Goldhor. "Obtrusive versus Unobtrusive Evaluation of Reference Service in Five Illinois Public Libraries," *Library Quarterly*, 52 (October 1982): 305–324.

Weiss, Carol H. *Evaluation Research*. Englewood Cliffs, NJ: Prentice-Hall, 1972.

_____ and Michael J. Bucuvalas. "Truth Tests and Utility Tests: Decision-Makers' Frames of Reference for Social Science Research," *American Sociological Review*, 45 (April 1980): 302–313.

Wender, R. W. "Analysis of Loans in the Behavioral Sciences," *Special Libraries*, 60 (October 1969): 510–513.

Westbrook, Lynn. *Qualitative Evaluation Methods for Reference Services: An Introductory Manual*. Washington, D.C.: Association of Research Libraries, Office of Management Services, 1989.

Williams, Robert V. "Productivity Measures in Special Libraries: Prospects and Problems for Use in Performance Evaluation," *Special Libraries*, 79 (Spring 1988): 101–114.

Williams, Saundra and Eric Wedig. "Improving Government Information and Documents Reference Skills through a Staff Development Program," *RQ*, 24 (Winter 1984): 143–145.

Wilson, Pauline. *Stereotype and Status: Librarians in the United States*. Westport, CT: Greenwood Press, 1982.

Wilson, T. D. "Follow-up on Interlibrary Loan Analysis," *Special Libraries*, 53 (October 1962): 493–495.

Worthen, Blaine R. and James R. Sanders. *Educational Evaluation: Theory and Practice*. Belmont, CA: Wadsworth Pub. Co., 1973.

Wurman, Richard S. *Information Anxiety*. New York: Doubleday, 1989.

Yin, Robert K. *Case Study Research: Design and Methods*. Beverly Hills, CA: Sage, 1984, 1989.

Zaltman, Gerald and Robert Duncan. *Strategies for Planned Change*. New York: Wiley, 1977.

Author Index

Subject Index